VISUAL QUICKSTART GUIDE

NETSCAPE 2

FOR WINDOWS

Elizabeth Castro

Visual QuickStart Guide
Netscape 2 for Windows
Elizabeth Castro

Peachpit Press
2414 Sixth Avenue
Berkeley, CA 94710
(510) 548-4393
(510) 548-5991 (fax)

Find us on the World Wide Web at: http://www.peachpit.com

Peachpit Press is a division of Addison Wesley Longman

Copyright © 1996 by Elizabeth Castro

Cover design: The Visual Group

Notice of rights
All rights reserved. No part of this book may be reproduced or transmitted in any form or by any means, electronic, mechanical, photocopying, recording, or otherwise, without prior written permission of the publisher. For more information on getting permission for reprints and excerpts, contact Trish Booth at Peachpit Press.

Notice of liability
The information in this book is distributed on an "As is" basis, without warranty. While every precaution has been taken in the preparation of this book, neither the author nor Peachpit Press shall have any liability to any person or entity with respect to any loss or damage caused or alleged to be caused directly or indirectly by the instructions contained in this book or by the computer software and hardware products described herein.

ISBN: 0-201-88615-4

0 9 8 7 6 5 4 3 2 1

♻ Printed on recycled paper

For Becky and Jenny who taught me my multiplication tables,
my Uncle Myron Pollyea who taught me exponential powers,
and Stephen Ucich, my first (and only) computer teacher.

Special thanks to:

Kaethin Prizer, **Kate Reber,** and **Nolan Hester** at Peachpit Press for their great suggestions and corrections, and for their calm replies to frantic, last minute questions.

The folks who frequent the **netscape.navigator** newsgroup and who seem to know all the answers.

Andreu, for everything else.

Table of Contents

Introduction ix
What is the Web, really? ix • What is a Web page? x • Netscape Navigator 2 x

Part I: Netscape Navigator 11

Chapter 1: The Web Browser 13
Opening or closing a browser 13 • Choosing a home page 14 • Controlling a browser's appearance 15 • Choosing fonts for the browser 16

Chapter 2: Surfing the Web 17
Basic surfing 17 • What is a Web page? 18 • Sites, home pages, and servers 19 • Following links 20 • Changing the appearance of links 21 • Jumping to a known page 22 • Going back and forward 23 • Going further back or further ahead 24 • Using the History window 25 • Going to your home page 26 • Reloading and refreshing a page 27 • Stopping a page from loading 28 • Viewing images on the Web 29 • Helper applications 30 • Setting up helper apps 31 • When no helper app is available 32

Chapter 3: Frames 33
Frames and framesets 33 • Following a link in a frame 34 • Opening a frame in a new window 35 • Resizing and scrolling around a frame 36 • Going backward or forward in a frame 37

Chapter 4: Transferring Files 39
Transferring files 39 • Accessing an FTP site 40 • Accessing a Gopher site 41 • Downloading files 42 • Uploading a file with FTP 43 • Uploading multiple files 44

Chapter 5: Saving and Printing 45
Saving and printing Web pages 45 • Saving a Web page 46 • Saving a page without jumping to it 47 • Saving an image 48 • Copying and pasting parts of a page 49 • Reading a saved page offline 50 • Printing a page 51 • Setting up printing options 52

Table of Contents

Chapter 6: Finding Stuff on the Web 53

Tips for using search services 53 • Finding Web pages by subject 54 • Searching for Web pages by keyword 56 • Searching for people and organizations 58 • Finding an article in a newsgroup 60 • Finding shareware through the Web 61 • Finding information in an open page 62 • Checking out Netscape's pages 63 • Finding Netscape documentation 64 • Finding technical support 65 • Finding info about your Netscape software 66

Chapter 7: Bookmarks 67

What is a bookmark? 67 • Using bookmarks to navigate the Web 68 • Checking what's new 69 • Setting the New Bookmarks Folder 70 • Setting the Bookmarks Menu Folder 71 • Adding a bookmark from a Web site 72 • Adding a bookmark by hand 73 • Creating aliases of bookmarks 74 • Creating a bookmark folder 75 • Editing a bookmark or folder 76 • Adding a separator 77 • Sorting your bookmarks file 78 • Saving a bookmarks file 79 • Opening a different bookmarks file 80 • Opening a bookmarks file as a Web page 81 • Importing bookmarks 82

Chapter 8: The Mail Window 83

The parts of the Mail window 83 • Opening the Mail window 84 • Saving your mail password 84 • The Mail window's four default folders 85 • Creating new folders 86 • Importing messages from another folder 87 • Selecting messages 88 • Moving and copying messages 90 • Deleting messages and folders 91 • Conserving disk space 92 • Putting your messages in order 93 • Flagging messages 94 • Marking mail as read or unread 95 • Threading messages 96 • Changing the size of the panes 97 • Changing the columns 98 • Changing your messages' appearance 99

Chapter 9: Reading and Sending Mail 101

Getting new mail 101 • Having Netscape check for mail periodically 102 • Reading mail 103 • Navigating through your messages 104 • Composing a new message 105 • Viewing or hiding the parts of a message 106 • Replying to a message you've received 107 • Composing messages offline 108 • Sending the messages in the Outbox 109 • Editing messages in the Outbox 110 • Quoting every message 111 • Quoting individual messages 112 • Custom quoting 113 • Forwarding a message 114 • Forwarding a message as a quote 115 • Attaching files to a message 116 • Attaching a URL to a message 117 • Mailing a document 118 • Creating a signature file 119 • Using a signature file 120

Chapter 10: The Address Book 121

The Address Book window 121 • Adding an address 122 • Adding an address from an incoming message 123 • Creating a mailing list 124 • Using an address or list 125 • Changing or deleting an address or list 126 • Finding an address 127 • Saving an address book 128 • Importing an address book 129 • Opening an address book as a Web page 130

Chapter 11: The News Window 131

The parts of the News window 131 • Using the News window 132 • Where newsgroup names come from 133 • Opening a news host 134 • Getting a list of all newsgroups 135 • Getting a list of new newsgroups 136 • Viewing a newsgroup by name 137 • Viewing a newsgroup from other windows 138 • Subscribing to a newsgroup 139 • Showing only subscribed newsgroups 140 • Marking messages as read 141 • Marking an entire newsgroup as read 142 • Hiding read messages 143 • Getting more messages 144

Chapter 12: Reading and Posting News 145

Reading the postings in a newsgroup 145 • Posting a message to a newsgroup 146 • Replying to a newsgroup post 148 • Composing postings offline 149 • Sending mail from the News window 150

Part II: Netscape Navigator Gold 151

Chapter 13: The Editor Window 153

Opening a blank Editor window 153 • Opening a new page with a template 154 • Opening a new page with the Page Wizard 156 • Editing an existing page 158 • Editing a saved file 159 • Adding a title and keywords 160 • Saving your Web page 161 • The Editor window's toolbars 162 • Repositioning the toolbars 163 • Hiding or showing the toolbars 164

Chapter 14: Formatting a Web Page 165

Adding basic character formatting 166 • Changing the size of text 167 • Changing the color of text 168 • Applying many character styles at once 169 • Clearing character styles 170 • Using paragraph styles 171 • Applying paragraph styles 172 • Creating lists 173 • Indenting a paragraph 175 • Aligning text 176 • Creating a block quote 177 • Applying many paragraph features at once 178

Chapter 15: Adding Images to a Page 179

Image Formats 179 • Inserting an image 180 • Using alternative text 181 • Using low resolution images to speed viewing 182 • Image size 183 • Why the resolution is not so important 183 • Why the number of colors is so important 183 • Wrapping text around images 184 • Stopping text wrap 185 • Adding space around an image 186 • Changing the display size of an image 187 • Creating a border around an image 188 • Aligning images 189 • Adding a horizontal line 190 • Changing a horizontal line 191 • Choosing colors and/or a background image 192

Table of Contents

Chapter 16: Creating Links in a Page 193
Links and URLs 193 • Copying a link from another source 194 • Creating a link manually 196 • Creating a target 198 • Creating a link to a target on the same page 199 • Linking to a target on a different page 200 • Creating a link to an image 201 • Changing or removing a link 202

Chapter 17: Advanced Page Design 203
Standard HTML 204 • Adding nonbreaking spaces 205 • Adding HTML tags manually 206 • Editing HTML tags manually 208 • Specifying a program for editing HTML tags 209 • Adding JavaScript to your page 210

Chapter 18: Publishing a Page 211
Testing your page 212 • Publishing your page 214 • Setting up a default publishing location 216 • Viewing your published page 217 • Advertising your site 218

Part III: Preferences 219

Chapter 19: General Preferences 221
Appearance 222 • Fonts 223 • Colors 224 • Images 225 • Apps 226 • Helpers 227 • Language 228

Chapter 20: Editor Preferences 229
General 230 • Appearance 231 • Publish 232

Chapter 21: Mail and News Preferences 233
Appearance 234 • Composition 235 • Servers 236 • Identity 237 • Organization 238

Chapter 22: Network Preferences 239
Cache 240 • Connections 241 • Proxies 242

Chapter 23: Security Preferences 243
General 244 • Site Certificates 245

Index 247

Introduction

The beauty—and the peril—of the World Wide Web is that everyone can publish their own information quickly and easily. As such, the Web is the fastest growing area in the computer world today. Each month thousands of new pages are added, by huge companies and private citizens alike.

Some pages are serious collections of commercial information. Others are personal accounts of travels, history, and life itself. Still others attempt to fill the void that the paper publishing industry is unable to answer. Perhaps the nicest thing about the Web is that there are pages about everything, from cancer research to bowling, from solar panel design to hot new bands.

What is the Web, really?

The Internet is a huge collection of computers that are connected to each other. Some computers are connected to the Internet through a telephone and modem (and are thus only *on* the Internet when they are connected). Other computers are permanently connected (generally, universities and large companies fall into this category).

There are different ways of communicating over the Internet, called *protocols*. E-mail is the most common protocol, but you may have heard of FTP, Gopher, Usenet, and HTTP, as well. This last protocol, HTTP, is the method computers use to connect to each other and view Web pages.

Introduction

What is a Web page?

A Web page is nothing more than a text document with special tags. These tags add formatting, images, and hypertext links to the page. But because a Web page is a text document, in ASCII format, it can be opened on virtually any platform, from Macintosh to Windows, and including everything in between.

Although you could open a Web page with a text editor, the special tags are not interpreted unless you open the page with a browser. There are many different kinds of browsers, with different versions of each for each kind of computer platform.

Netscape Navigator 2

Netscape Navigator 2 is the most popular browser, used by some 70% of the Web public. Commonly known as Netscape (but *not* Navigator), the new version of the software combines a first-class browser with news and mail capabilities.

A special edition of the software, called Netscape Navigator Gold (or Netscape Gold, for short), also gives you the ability to create your own Web pages without having to know much about HTML.

This book is divided into four principal sections: browsing (for viewing the Web), mail (for e-mail), news (for reading newsgroups), and editing (for creating Web pages with Netscape Gold).

The illustrations in the first three sections of this book were taken with Netscape. Only the editing section shows Netscape Gold. However, you can use Netscape Gold to do everything the "plain" version does, and more.

Part I:
Netscape Navigator
Web surfing, mail, and news

The Web Browser

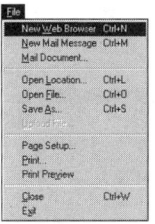

Figure 1.1 *Choose New Web Browser in the File menu to open a new browser.*

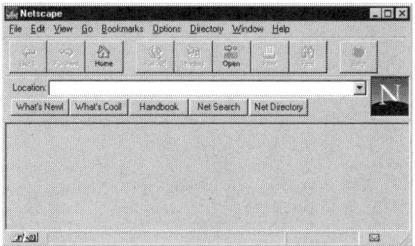

Figure 1.2 *A fresh browser opens.*

Netscape has three types of principal windows: the Mail window, the News window, and Web browsers (sometimes called *browser windows*). You use browsers to view the pages available on the World Wide Web. Although you may only open one Mail or News window, you may open as many browsers as your computer's memory will permit. In this way, you can display several different pages at once. This is often useful if you want to follow a link on one page without losing track of the original source page.

Apart from viewing Web pages, browsers are also used to access FTP and Gopher sites.

Opening or closing a browser

Each time you launch Netscape, the program opens a new browser and connects to the specified home page. You can open a new browser at any time, in order to see new Web pages, without replacing the one in the current browser.

To open a browser:

Choose New Web Browser in the File menu **(Figure 1.1)**.

To close a browser:

Choose Close in the File menu or click the browser's close box.

Chapter 1

Choosing a home page

The first time you open a browser, Netscape jumps to the Web page that you have specified in the General Preferences dialog box. Although Netscape calls this your *home page,* don't confuse it with a Web site's home page. Instead, it is simply any page on the World Wide Web that you wish to jump to automatically upon opening Netscape. You may also set Netscape to open any HTML file on your hard disk.

To choose a home page:

1. Choose General Preferences in the Options menu **(Figure 1.3)**. The General Preferences dialog box appears.

2. Click the Appearance tab. The Appearance preferences appear **(Figure 1.4)**.

3. In the middle section, titled Startup, click Home Page Location.

4. Type the URL of the home page in the field directly below the Home Page Location option.

✔ Tips

- Choose Blank Page next to Start With to have Netscape open new browsers with a blank page.

- You may save your bookmarks file or address book as an HTML file and then choose that file as your home page. For a home page that resides on your hard disk, type **file:///path/filename** in the Home Page Location field, where *path* is the location of the file on your hard disk and *filename* is its complete name, including its extension.

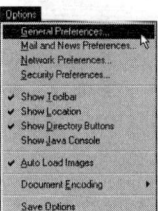

Figure 1.3 *Choose General Preferences in the Options menu.*

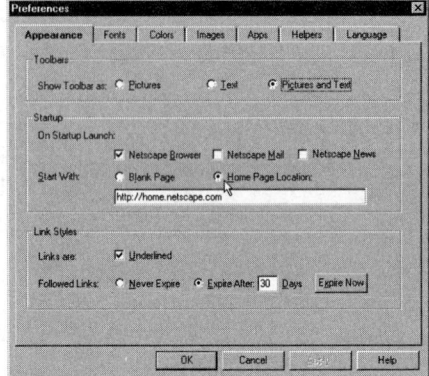

Figure 1.4 *Click Home Page Location under Startup and then type the URL of the desired page.*

14

The Web Browser

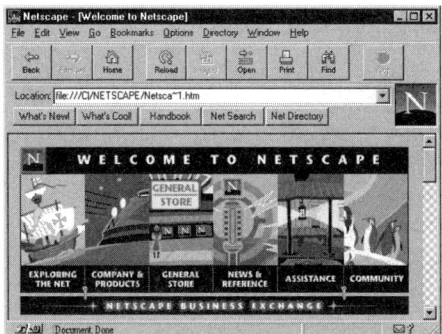

Figure 1.5 *The toolbar, location field, and directory buttons are showing, by default.*

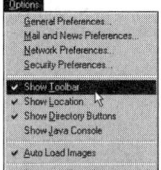

Figure 1.6 *Choose the appropriate command from the Options menu to hide (or reveal) the corresponding feature.*

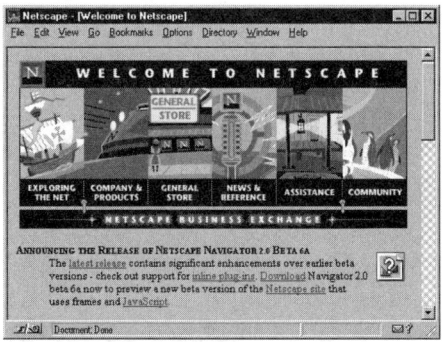

Figure 1.7 *Once you hide the extra window items, you see more of the actual page.*

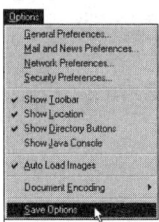

Figure 1.8 *Choose Save Options in the Options menu so that the next time you open Netscape the same features are hidden (or revealed).*

Controlling a browser's appearance

Each browser can contain a toolbar full of buttons, a Location field, Directory buttons, and a status area **(Figure 1.5)**. You can choose to hide everything but the status area to save room on your screen and see more of your Web pages. You can also resize the window as necessary.

The toolbar contains a series of navigation and utility buttons. The Location field shows the URL address of the current Web page and can also be used to jump to different Web pages. The Directory buttons take you to particular pages on Netscape's Web site, or to other sites that Netscape has chosen for you.

To hide (or reveal) the toolbar, Location field, or Directory buttons:

Choose Show Toolbar, Show Location, or Show Directory Buttons in the Options menu to remove (or restore) the checkmark that is next to the command **(Fig. 1.6)**. The corresponding feature will disappear (or appear).

To save the browser's appearance:

Choose Save Options in the Options menu **(Figure 1.8)**. The next time you open Netscape, the browser will retain the size and features you have chosen.

15

Chapter 1

Choosing fonts for the browser

In an attempt to keep Web pages as universal as possible, text only appears in one of two fonts, a proportional font like Times in which individual letters have different sizes or a fixed width font like Courier in which all the characters are the same size.

You can choose which font (and size) you wish to use for displaying proportional text and which font (and size) should be used for displaying fixed width text.

To choose fonts for the browser:

1. Choose General Preferences in the Options menu **(Fig. 1.9)**. The General Preferences dialog box appears.

2. Click the Fonts tab. The Fonts preferences are displayed **(Figure 1.10)**.

3. Click the Choose Font button next to the font you wish to specify.

4. In the Choose Base Font dialog box that appears choose the font that you wish to use **(Figure 1.11)**.

5. Choose a base size for the font.

6. Click OK to return to the Fonts preferences dialog box **(Figure 1.12)**.

7. If desired, repeat steps 3–6 to choose a font for the other style.

8. Click OK to close the main dialog box.

✓ Tip

- Most text viewed on a Web page is displayed in the proportional font. Block quotes, computer commands, and form fields are all displayed in the secondary, fixed width font.

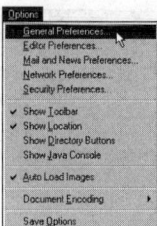

Figure 1.9 *Choose General Preferences in the Options menu.*

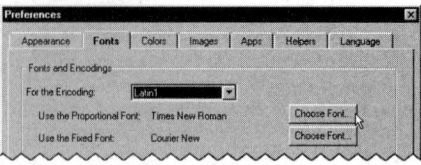

Figure 1.10 *In the Fonts tab of the General Preferences dialog box, click Choose Font next to the type of font you wish to choose.*

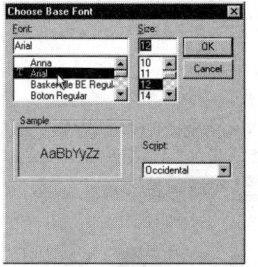

Figure 1.11 *Select the font and size that you wish to use. Then click OK.*

Figure 1.12 *Once you've chosen a new font, it is displayed in the Fonts tab.*

Figure 1.13 *Here's a new look at Netscape's home page, with Arial 12 as a base font. Notice that the title is also in Arial, but several sizes larger.*

16

Surfing the Web

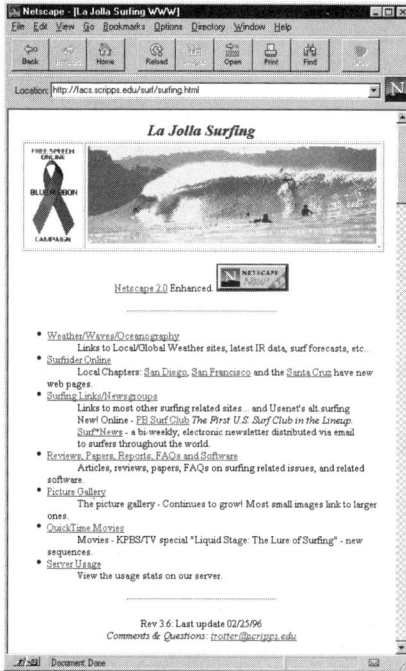

Figure 2.1 *There are over four million Web pages that you can surf to, each one different from the next.*

This is what you've been waiting for: actually getting to surf the World Wide Web. Although *surf* seems like a strange way to describe your activities as you sit in front of a computer, probably some distance from the beach, it does capture the idea of jumping from one Web page to another, perhaps reading and exploring as you go along, perhaps just enjoying the spray of information.

From its navigation buttons and keyboard shortcuts for getting from one place to another, to its clever new frames and history menu for remembering where you've been, Netscape makes surfing the Web as easy as it's ever been.

There are over four million Web sites (at press time), and several thousand more are added daily. You could spend your whole life wandering from page to page and never get to the end (although you might circle around to where you started). It's something like reading an encyclopedia: you'd learn a lot, but it would take you a long time.

In this section, we'll talk about how to get around on the Web with Netscape, assuming you already know where you want to go, or, on the other hand, that you don't really care where you end up. For more information on finding specific topics or pages, see Chapter 6, *Finding Stuff on the Web*.

Chapter 2

What is a Web page?

So what are these things that you surf to? Actually, a Web page is nothing more than a text file written with special tags that format the contents, point to other pages, and insert images and sounds **(Fig. 2.2)**. The tags are called *HyperText Markup Language*, or HTML, and are quite easy to learn **(Figure 2.3)**. For more information about writing Web pages, consult on page 151.

With four million Web pages in existence, there is an incredible variety of designs and approaches, and of the kinds of information presented. It is probably safe to say that you can find a Web page about any topic you might choose to research—from Contra dancing to the Ethernet, from a subway map of major cities of the world to a database of every language spoken on the train.

Some Web pages are personal, designed by a single individual with information about themselves, their family and friends, perhaps their dog or cat, and their hobbies—as well as links to their favorite pages at other sites. Personal does not mean sloppy. As you'll find out, many of the best pages are created by people with no economic interest in the Web.

Other pages are strictly—or more subtly—commercial, created by (or for) a company in order to offer promotional information, technical support, upgrades, special tips, and other benefits to the public. Often, a commercial page's mission is simply to impress—with dazzling graphics, sounds or videos.

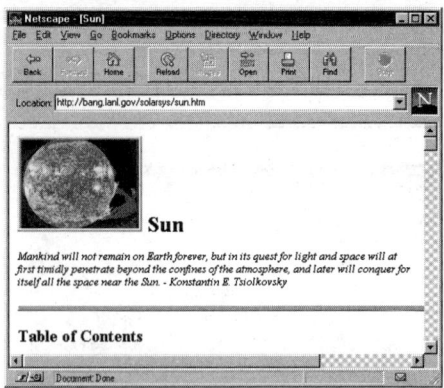

Figure 2.2 *This is a typical Web page. It was written by Calvin Hamilton, a private citizen like you or me, with the sole intention of sharing information and resources across the Internet.*

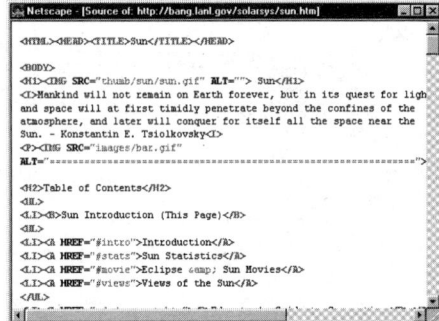

Figure 2.3 *This is the actual text file that creates the page shown in Figure 2.2. The HTML codes are those that are found within the less than and greater than signs "<>".*

Surfing the Web

Sites, home pages, and servers

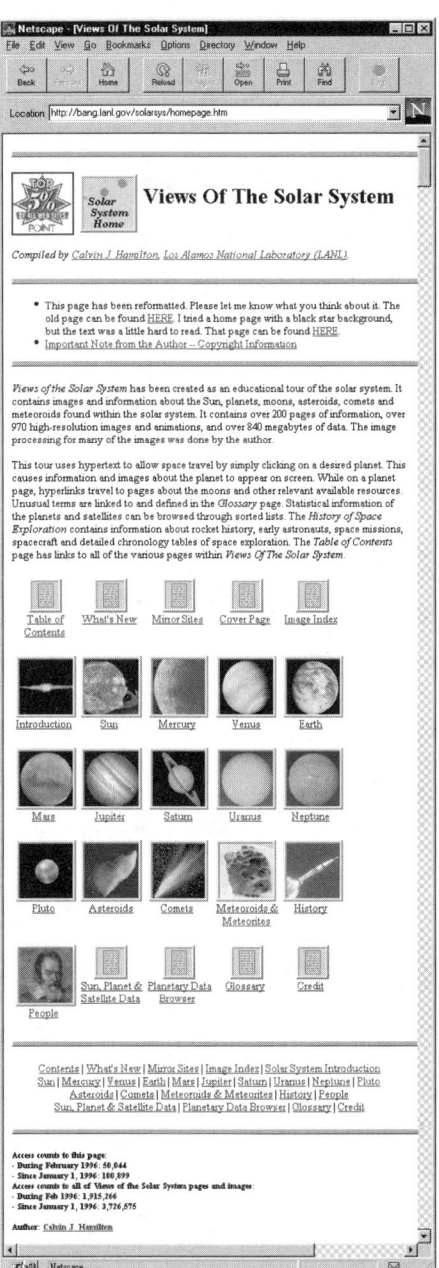

Figure 2.4 *This is the home page for the Solar System site. It contains an introduction, links to the other pages at the site, and links to related sites.*

A Web *page* is a single text file written in HTML. A Web *site* is a collection of Web pages that belong to a single individual or company. Most Web sites have a special page, called a *home page,* that serves as a door to the rest of the site **(Figure 2.4)**. A home page generally has a banner explaining what the site contains—commercial sites usually include their company logo on the home page—as well as links to the other pages available at the site.

Beware: Although Netscape Communications knows exactly what a home page is, they've chosen to use the same term to denote the page that you jump to automatically upon launching the program *(see page 14)*. The page you choose may or may not be a *real* home page.

Web pages, including any graphics, sounds, videos or other external files, are stored on *servers*, dedicated computers that are connected to the Internet 24 hours a day—so that anyone, in any part of the world, can reach the Web page at any time.

Although you might think a server looks like something out of a movie—a huge hulking thing with those reel-to-reel tapes—any kind of computer can be a server, including Macs, PCs running Windows, and most often, Unix machines. The most important criterion for a server is not size or speed, but rather that it have a high-speed connection to the Internet so that it can handle the incoming requests for the Web sites it contains.

In addition to Web sites, servers can also contain FTP and Gopher sites, and manage e-mail and Usenet newsgroups.

19

Chapter 2

Following links

A Web page's most distinguishing characteristic, and certainly the feature that has made Web surfing so popular and exciting, is its *links*. By clicking a link, you jump to another page, either at the same site or at a different site—which can be on the same server or, just as easily, at a site halfway around the world. You may also use links to jump to FTP and Gopher sites and to write e-mail.

Generally, new links—that is, the ones you have not yet visited—appear underlined and in blue (or in gray on monochrome monitors). Once you have followed a link to its destination, it will appear in purple so you can quickly distinguish new links from those you've already visited.

To follow a link:

1. In the current Web page, decide which link you wish to follow. Point to the link with the mouse. The link's URL appears in the status area at the bottom of the window **(Figure 2.5)**.

2. Click the link. Netscape takes you to the link's destination **(Figure 2.6)**.

✔ Tips

- Open the link in a new window by right clicking the link and choosing Open Link in New Window from the pop-up menu that appears.

- You can always tell if a link is really a link by pointing at it with the mouse. If it is a link, the pointer will change into a pointing finger, and the link's destination will appear in the status area at the bottom of the browser.

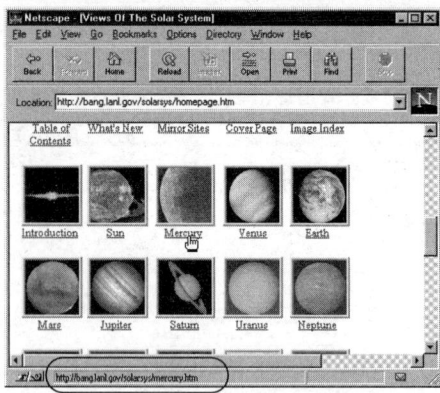

Figure 2.5 *When you place the pointer over a link (which is usually blue and underlined), the URL for the destination page appears in the status area at the bottom left corner of the browser.*

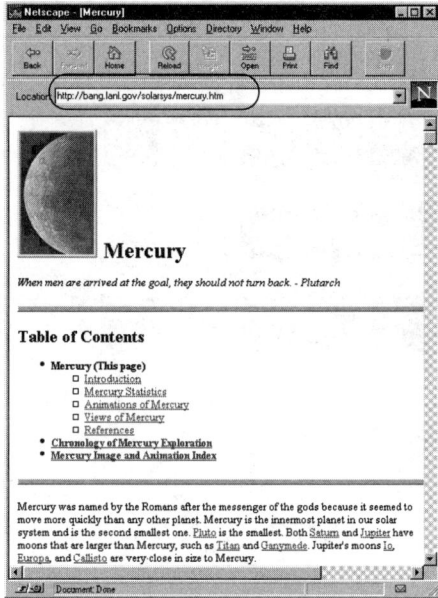

Figure 2.6 *When you click a link, Netscape loads the corresponding page. Notice how the URL in the Location field above matches the URL in the status area at the bottom left corner of Figure 2.5.*

Surfing the Web

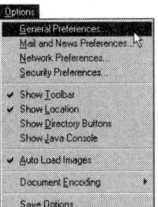

Figure 2.7 *Choose General Preferences in the Options menu.*

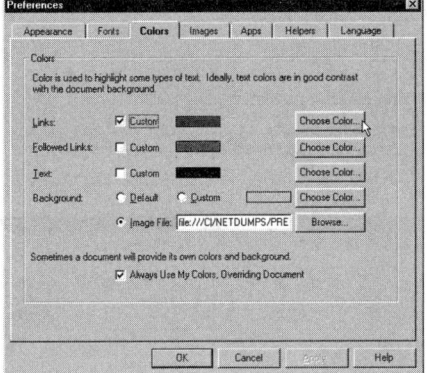

Figure 2.8 *Click the Colors tab, click Custom next to Links or Followed links, and then click Choose Color.*

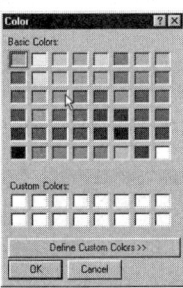

Figure 2.9 *Choose the desired color and click OK.*

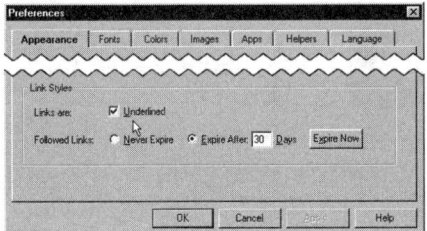

Figure 2.10 *Click on the Appearance tab and then click Underlined next to Links in the bottom section.*

Changing the appearance of links

Most pages show new links in blue and visited links in purple. However, a Web page designer can present her links in any colors she chooses—which can sometimes be confusing. Netscape also gives *you* the ability to view links in the colors that you prefer, and to show them underlined, or not.

To change the appearance of links:

1. Choose General Preferences in the Options menu **(Figure 2.7)**. The General Preferences box appears.

2. Click the Colors tab to show the preferences for Colors **(Figure 2.8)**.

3. Click the Custom box next to the type of links that you wish to change.

4. Click the corresponding Choose Color button. The Color dialog box appears.

5. Click on a new color in the Color dialog box and then click OK to save the changes. The new color appears to the right of the Custom box **(Fig. 2.9)**.

6. Repeat steps 3–5 for each kind of link.

7. To ensure that the links are always displayed with the colors you have chosen, click Always Use My Colors, Overriding Document.

8. Click the Appearance tab at the top of the General Preferences dialog box.

9. In the Link Styles section, check the Underlined box to display links with an underline; uncheck the box to remove underlining **(Figure 2.10)**.

10. Click OK to save the changes.

21

Jumping to a known page

If you already know the URL of the Web that you want to visit, the easiest way to get to the page is to be direct: tell Netscape.

To jump to a known page:

1. Choose Open Location in the File menu **(Fig. 2.11)** or click the Open button on the toolbar. The Open Location box appears **(Figure 2.12)**.

2. Type the desired URL in the text box, paying special attention to upper and lower case letters and punctuation.

3. Click Open to jump to the corresponding destination **(Figure 2.13)**.

✓ Tips

- If a URL begins with *www (ftp, gopher)*, you don't need to type the protocol (**http://**, **ftp://**, or **gopher://**) at the beginning. Further, if a Web page address is in the form of *www.site.com*, you only need to type **site**.

- You can also type a URL in the Location field just under the toolbar to jump to the corresponding page. As soon as you begin to type, the label changes to *Go to* **(Figure 2.14)**.

- Choose New Web Browser in the File menu before going to a new page to open the page in a new browser.

- You may jump to FTP and Gopher sites using these same techniques.

- The last ten locations that you type into the Location field are stored in a pop-up menu to the field's right. You may jump to any of these stored locations by using the pop-up menu.

Figure 2.11 *Choose Open Location in the File menu.*

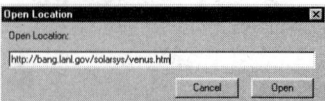

Figure 2.12 *In the Open Location dialog box that appears, type the URL of the page that you wish to jump to.*

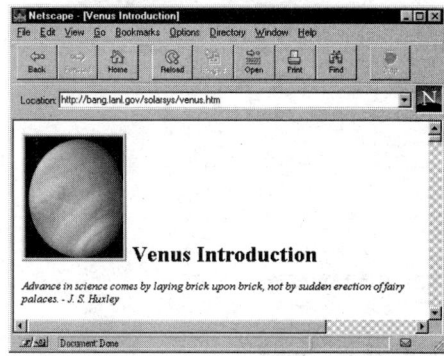

Figure 2.13 *Netscape loads the specified page.*

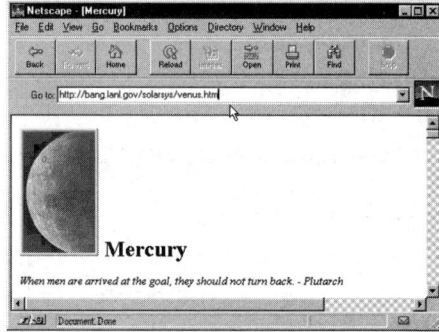

Figure 2.14 *In the Location field between the toolbar and the content area, type the URL of the desired page. As soon as you begin to type, the word* Location *changes to* Go to.

Surfing the Web

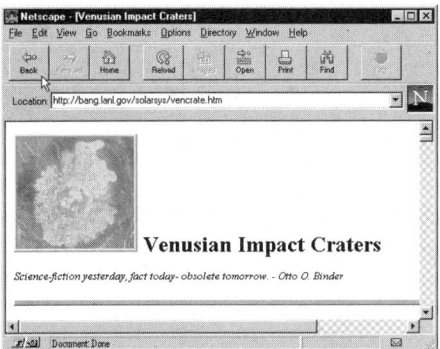

Figure 2.15 *Click the Back button to return to the last page you were browsing.*

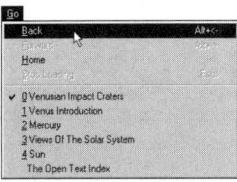

Figure 2.16 *You can choose Back from the Go menu to get the same result.*

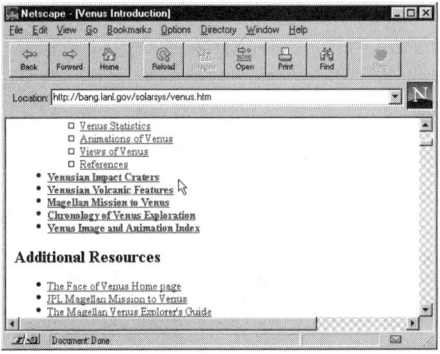

Figure 2.17 *In this example, Netscape goes back to the Venus Introduction page, which, as you can see in Figure 2.16 is after the current page (Venusian Impact Craters) in the Go menu.*

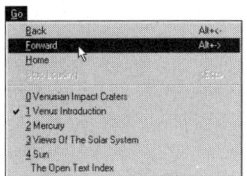

Figure 2.18 *You can also choose Forward in the Go menu to load the page above the checked (currently displayed) item in the Go menu.*

Going back and forward

Perhaps one of the most difficult problems you'll have on the Web is to how to follow all of the links that interest you. Typically, you will find one Web page with several links that you want to follow. It's important to know how to get *back* to the page with the important links, once you've explored one or more of them.

To go back to the previous page:

Click the Back button in the toolbar **(Figure 2.15)** or choose Back in the Go menu **(Figure 2.16)**. Netscape will load the page that you visited immediately before jumping to the present page **(Figure 2.17)**.

Going back means returning to the pages that brought you to the present page. *Going forward*, then, is turning around once again and following the same path that you did before. It's something like going back to where you came back from.

There are two conditions to going forward. First, you have to have gone back before you can go forward. Second, you must not have chosen a new link on an earlier page that brings you in a new direction. Since Netscape only remembers one path at a time, if you switch paths, all the most forward pages are forgotten.

To go forward:

Click the Forward button or choose Forward in the Go menu **(Figure 2.18)**. Netscape brings you to the corresponding page **(Figure 2.15)**.

23

Chapter 2

Going further back or further ahead

As you wander around the Web, Netscape records the title and URL of each page that you visit and stores it in the Go menu. You can go back and revisit a page by choosing its title in the menu.

To go further back or further ahead:

Select the desired page from the Go menu **(Figure 2.19)**. Netscape jumps to the corresponding page **(Figure 2.20)**.

✔ Tips

- Unfortunately, the Go menu only keeps track of the path of pages that has brought you to the current page. So, if you backtrack (with the Back command or the Go menu) and then choose a link that leads you in a different direction, the references to the *later* pages will be lost **(Fig. 2.21)**.

- One way to make sure the Go menu keeps track of *every* page you visit is to avoid using the Back and Forward commands and even the Go menu itself. If you need to go back to a page you have already visited, use the Open Location command instead.

- To record a page's URL permanently, create a bookmark for it. For more details, see Chapter 7, *Bookmarks*.

- Although the History window contains the same information as the Go menu, you may prefer to use it since it floats quietly on your screen—always at your fingertips. For more information, consult *Using the History window* on page 25.

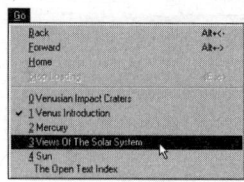

Figure 2.19 *You can choose any page in the Go menu to jump to that page.*

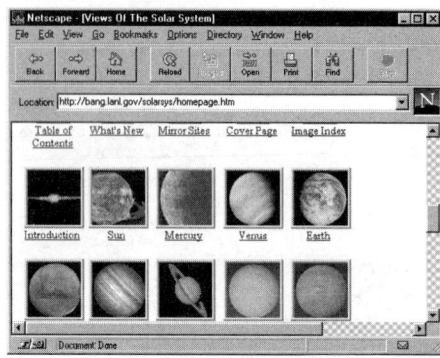

Figure 2.20 *A page that is loaded from the Go menu often appears faster than a brand new page since Netscape has already saved a copy of the page in its memory cache. In addition, when using the Go menu or Back and Forward commands you always return to the area of the page that you last visited.*

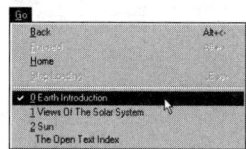

Figure 2.21 *If you backtrack and then set off in a new direction (as in this case, going back from Venus to the home page and from there, on to Earth) and then view the Go menu, the old path (that led to the Venus page) will no longer be shown.*

Surfing the Web

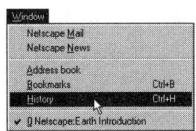

Figure 2.22 *Choose History in the Window menu to show the History window.*

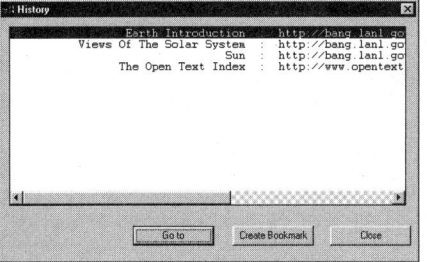

Figure 2.23 *The History window lets you see the pages that you have visited in the current session. You can jump to any page in the current session by double clicking it and add a bookmark by choosing the Create Bookmark button.*

Using the History window

Netscape's History window keeps track of your travels on the Web. Each time you jump to a new page, the page's URL and title are added to the History window. However, the History window, like the Go menu, only keeps track of one path of pages at a time. That is, if you backtrack and then follow a new link in a new direction, all the pages after that page will be erased from the History window.

The principal advantage of the History window over the Go menu is that the History window can stay open on your screen while the Go menu cannot.

To use the History window:

1. Choose History in the Window menu **(Figure 2.22)** to view the History window **(Figure 2.23)**.

2. Double click on a page to jump to that page. You can also click once and then click the Go to button.

3. Click on a page and then click Create Bookmark to add a bookmark for that page to your Bookmarks window. For more information on bookmarks, see Chapter 7, *Bookmarks*.

4. To close the History window, simply click the Close button.

✔ Tip

■ If you have the History window open as you begin to backtrack, an arrow appears next to the current page in the History window, while the pages further ahead on the path remain visible.

25

Chapter 2

Going to *your* home page

You can return to the home page that you specified in the General Preferences dialog box at any time with a simple click. For information on how to set your home page, consult *Choosing a home page* on page 14.

To go to your home page:

Click the Home button in the tool bar **(Figure 2.24)** or choose Home in the Go menu **(Figure 2.25)**. Netscape loads the home page specified in the Appearance tab of the General Preferences dialog box **(Figure 2.26)**.

✓ Tips

- Remember, the Home button and Home menu commands bring you to *your* specified home page, not to the home page of the site that contains the page you are currently viewing (which would be much more useful, if you ask me).

- Further, even if you have specified that Netscape *start* with a blank page, the program will still jump to the page specified in the General Preferences box when you use the Home button or command.

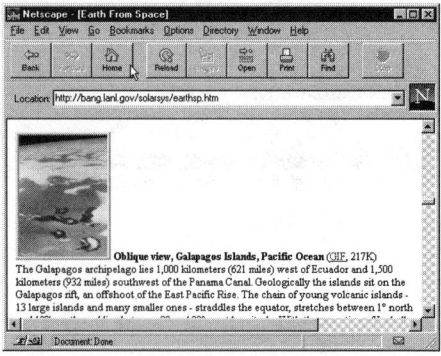

Figure 2.24 *Click the Home button to load the page specified in the General Preferences dialog box (not the site's home page).*

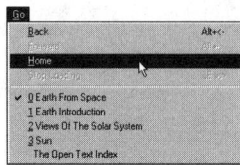

Figure 2.25 *You can also choose Home in the Go menu to load your home page.*

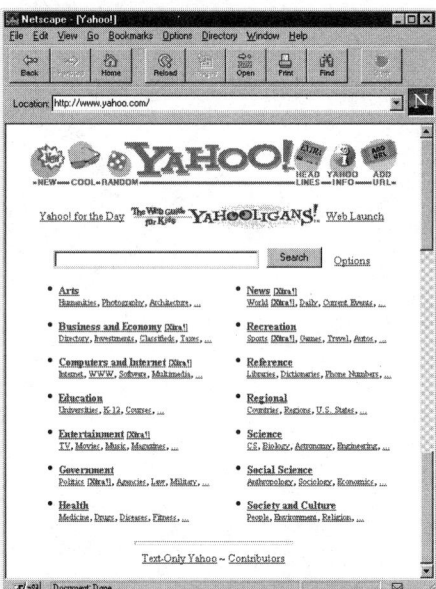

Figure 2.26 *This is my home page. A home page should either be a page that you consult often, or a page with a lot of links to other pages.*

Surfing the Web

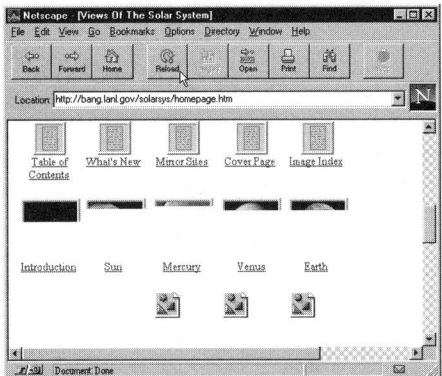

Figure 2.27 *Click the Reload button to have Netscape consult the server for any changes and to update the page accordingly. The Reload button also comes in handy if you've stopped the page from loading in mid-transfer, as shown.*

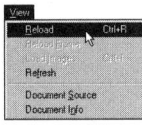 **Figure 2.28** *You can also choose Reload in the View menu to have Netscape update the page.*

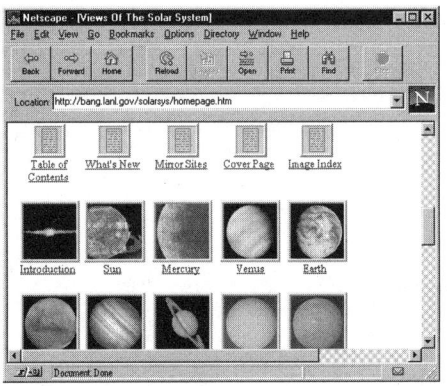

Figure 2.29 *Once the page is reloaded, the images and text appear in full.*

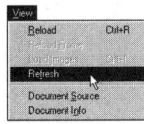 **Figure 2.30** *Choose Refresh to get rid of any screen redraw related deformations.*

Reloading and refreshing a page

When you jump to a page, Netscape automatically loads a copy of the page into its memory cache. The next time you jump to the page, instead of asking the server for the information (which might be rather slow, depending on the type of connection you have and the type of server that contains the page), it loads the page from memory.

However, if you suspect (or know) that the contents of the page have changed, if the page has not loaded completely, or if it has not loaded properly, you will want Netscape to load the page from the server and not from memory.

To reload a page:

Click the Reload button **(Figure 2.27)** or choose Reload in the View menu **(Figure 2.28)**. If the page's contents have changed, Netscape will get the new information from the server and will update the page accordingly. If the page has not changed, Netscape will reload it from memory **(Figure 2.29)**.

Sometimes, Netscape fails to view a page correctly, perhaps not aligning or displaying the text properly. In this case, even if you don't think the page's contents have changed, you may wish to refresh the page to view it properly.

To refresh a page:

Choose Refresh in the View menu **(Figure 2.30)**. Netscape refreshes the page and redraws the screen.

27

Chapter 2

Stopping a page from loading

As you get used to working with Netscape you'll get a feel for how fast it takes to get from one page to another and how long it takes average pages to load. There are three principal reasons why you might want to abort a jump to a page. First, you may simply have changed your mind, or made an errant click. Second, the page may be taking so long that you decide to go somewhere else. Finally, you may notice, as you watch the status bar, that Netscape takes an unusually long time to connect to the host. This is a good clue that either the server is busy or that the page is no longer located where you thought it was. Just abort the jump and move on.

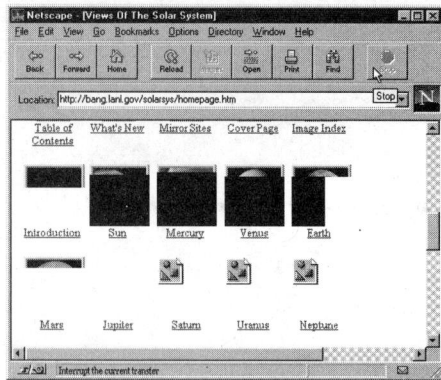

Figure 2.31 *You can stop a page from loading completely by clicking the Stop button.*

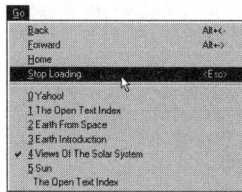

Figure 2.32 *You can also choose Stop Loading in the Go menu to break the communication between Netscape and the page's server.*

To stop a page from loading:

1. Click the Stop button in the toolbar **(Figure 2.31)** or choose Stop Loading in the Go menu **(Figure 2.32)**. Netscape immediately stops trying to load the page and shows you what it's come up with so far, if anything. The word "Done" should appear in the status bar at the bottom left area of the window and the Netscape icon should stop shooting comets.

2. If part of the page has already loaded, and if you decide you really do want to continue loading the page, click the Reload button, or choose Reload in the View menu, to load the entire page.

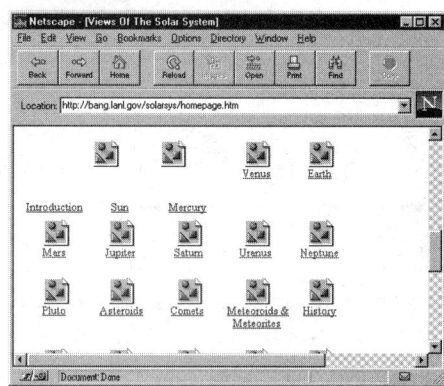

Figure 2.33 *When you stop a page from loading completely, the images may appear as icons.*

✔ Tip

■ You can also press Esc to stop loading a page.

28

Surfing the Web

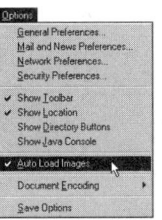

Figure 2.34 *Choose Auto Load Images in the Options menu. A checkmark means the option is active. When the checkmark is absent, the images will not be loaded automatically.*

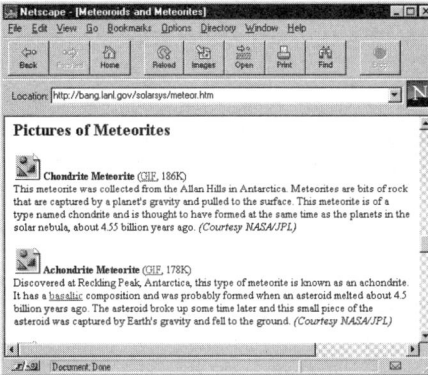

Figure 2.35 *With the Auto Load Images option off, the images are replaced with icons.*

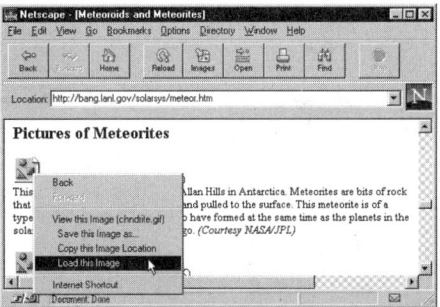

Figure 2.36 *Load an individual image by right clicking it and choosing Load this Image.*

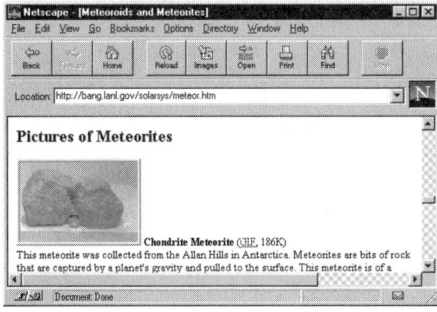

Figure 2.37 *The selected image is loaded.*

Viewing images on the Web

The two most common kinds of images that you'll find on the Web are GIF and JPEG images. Netscape can open both of these kinds of images automatically. However, since images tend to be large (and are always larger than text), they can take a long time to download and view. By default, Netscape automatically downloads all the JPEG and GIF images on the pages that you jump to. If you have a particularly slow connection, you may want to view only the text.

Deactivating automatic image download:

Choose Auto Load Images in the Options menu to remove the checkmark from the command **(Figure 2.34)**. The next time you jump to a page, the images will be displayed with placeholders **(Fig. 2.35)**.

When you have the Auto Load Images command deactivated, you can choose to load all the images in a particular page, or to load one or more individual images.

To load all the images on a page:

Choose Load Images in the View menu. The placeholders are replaced by the corresponding images. You can also click the Load Images button in the toolbar.

To load a particular image:

Right click the desired image and choose Load this Image in the pop-up menu **(Figure 2.36)**. Netscape displays the corresponding image **(Figure 2.37)**.

29

Chapter 2

Helper applications

Currently, Netscape can't view all kinds of files internally. Although this will change as more features are added, right now you can count on Netscape only for text, and certain kinds of images, especially GIF and JPEG. For other kinds of files, like sounds or movies, it calls up another application—usually one that is small and fast and dedicated to opening and viewing one particular kind of file—to do the job.

The small, dedicated applications used for opening and viewing multimedia files on the web are called "helper applications" and can often be downloaded for free via FTP. There are helper apps (as they're affectionately known) for decompressing files, viewing PostScript files, viewing video and images, listening to sounds and more.

Common helper apps for Windows:

Type	Name
Graphics	LView Pro
	Paintshop Pro
Sound	Wham, Wplany
	RealAudio
Video	Media Player
	mpegplay
PostScript	ghostscript
	ghostview
PDF	Amber

You can find helper apps to download on many pages all over the Web. For more help, consult Chapter 6, *Finding Stuff on the Web*.

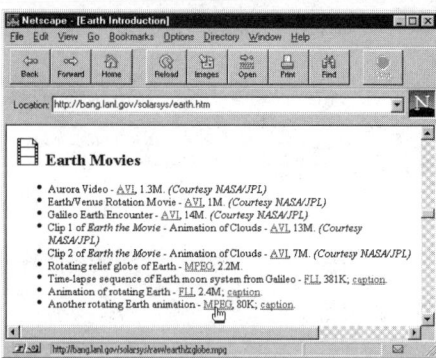

Figure 2.38 *If you click a link to a multimedia file that Netscape can't open on its own, it will launch a helper application to deal with the file.*

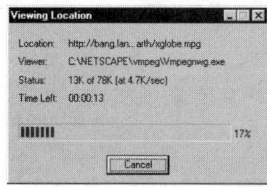

Figure 2.39 *Netscape automatically downloads the files that it can't read on its own.*

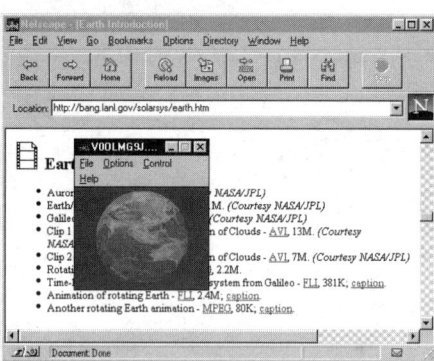

Figure 2.40 *Once the file has finished downloading, Netscape launches the helper application which opens the file and displays it. This is a movie of the Earth rotating.*

30

Surfing the Web

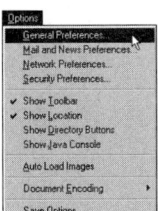

Figure 2.41 *Choose General Preferences in the Options menu.*

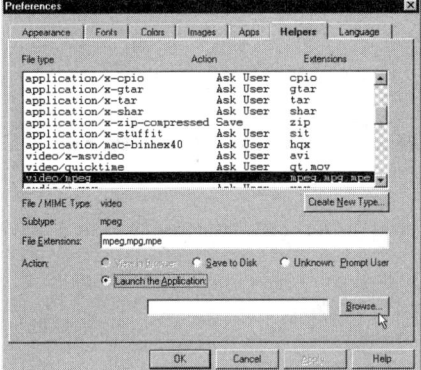

Figure 2.42 *Choose the desired file type in the list, click Launch Application and then click Browse.*

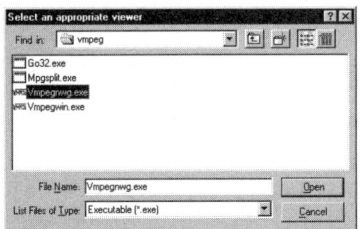

Figure 2.43 *Find the helper application on your hard disk and click OK.*

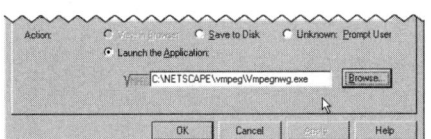

Figure 2.44 *The helper application's name and logo are shown in the General Preferences dialog box.*

Setting up helper apps

Once you've downloaded the helper applications on your hard disk, you must tell Netscape where they can be found and which ones should be used with which files.

To set up helper apps:

1. Choose General Preferences in the Options menu **(Figure 2.41)**. The General Preferences box appears.

2. Click the Helpers tab to view the Helpers apps preferences.

3. Select the file type that you wish to associate with a particular helper application **(Figure 2.42)**.

4. Next to Action, choose Launch the Application.

5. Click Browse. A dialog box appears in which you can indicate the name and location of the helper application.

6. Locate the helper app and click OK **(Figure 2.43)**. The program's icon, if it has one, appears next to its path and file name in the Helpers tab **(Figure 2.44)**.

7. Repeat steps 3–6 for each helper app you wish to assign to a particular kind of file.

✓ Tip

■ Some installers complete this step for you. Check the helper app's documentation to be sure.

31

Chapter 2

When no helper app is available

There may be many kinds of files that you never—or rarely—encounter and don't have the corresponding helper application to open them. In this case, you can have Netscape either save the file to disk or ask you what program to use to open the file.

To set options when no helper app is available:

1. Choose General Preferences in the Options menu **(Figure 2.45)**.

2. Click the Helpers tab to view the Helpers apps preferences.

3. Select the file type that you want to set options for **(Figure 2.46)**.

4. Choose Save to Disk if you want Netscape to automatically save the file in your hard disk. Choose Unknown: Prompt User to have Netscape alert you each time it encounters a file it doesn't know what to do with.

5. Click OK to save the changes.

✓ Tips

- One reason you might want to use the Save to Disk option is for files from another platform that you don't want to open on the present computer.

- Netscape automatically views text files in the browser. To automatically save text files, select the *text/plain* file type and then choose Save to Disk. Don't choose Save to Disk for *text/html* files, or you won't be able to view Web pages.

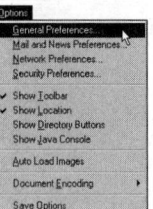

Figure 2.45 *Choose General Preferences in the Options menu.*

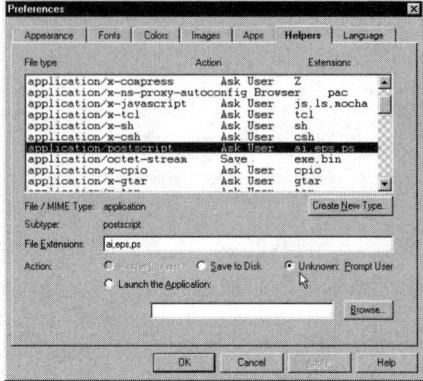

Figure 2.46 *Select the desired file type and then either Save to Disk or Unknown: Prompt User in the Action section.*

Frames

With version 2, Netscape introduced frames, an ingenious feature that divides each window into individual panes that each hold their own URL. Frames make it easy to hold on to one page (say, that contains a series of links, like a table of contents) while viewing a whole series of others (where the links lead). Navigating such sites can be confusing; this chapter should make it easier to get around.

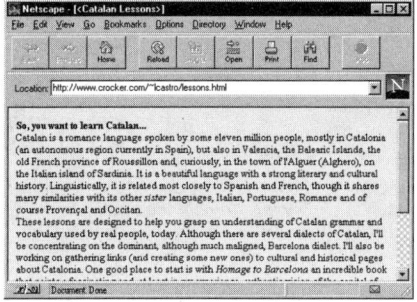

Figure 3.1 *A frame is a regular page with its own URL (like the one above) that is fit into a frameset like the one in Figure 3.2.*

Frames and framesets

A *frame* is nothing more than a regular Web page that has been shoe-horned into a smaller area within another Web page, called a *frameset*. The frameset contains information about the size of the frames within it, including their sizes, names, scrolling qualities, and URLs **(Figure 3.2)**.

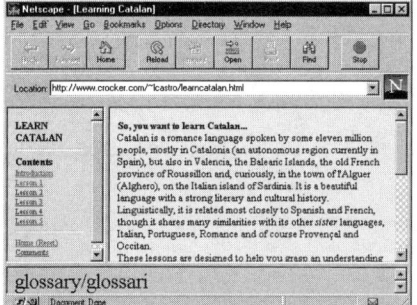

Figure 3.2 *A frameset is a page that is divided into individual frames, each of which displays the information from its own URL.*

When you click on a link inside a frame, one of two things can happen. If the link is to a page at the same site, it will usually appear inside the currently open frameset, replacing the contents of one of the existing frames. The other frames remain unchanged so that you can still see the information that they contain **(Fig. 3.3)**.

If the link is to a page at a different site, the page will usually open up in a new window. If it doesn't and you want it to, consult *Opening a frame in a new window* on page 35 for more details.

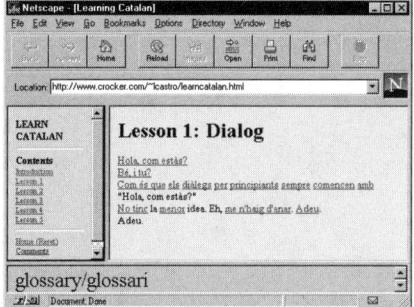

Figure 3.3 *Oftentimes when you click a link in one frame, the corresponding URL is shown in one of the other frames, while all the remaining frames remain constant.*

Perhaps the most important thing to remember is that you, the Web surfer, cannot create or add frames to an existing page. You can only navigate the frames that are already there.

Chapter 3

Following a link in a frame

Following a link on a page with frames is practically identical to following links on regular pages *(see page 20)*: simply click and go. The difference is where the result will be displayed. When you click on a link in a frameset, the link is usually opened in one of the frames, while the other frames remain unchanged.

To follow a link in a frame:

1. Place the pointer over the link that you wish to jump to **(Figure 3.4)**. You may have to scroll around in the frame to make the link visible.

2. Click the link. Netscape brings you to the link's destination **(Figure 3.5)**. Many times, the page will be displayed inside one of the frames in the current frameset.

✔ Tips

- You can't open a link in a specific frame unless the designer has allowed for it, but you can open the link in a new window *(see page 35)*.

- Usually, a frameset contains a narrow frame with links, a central frame where those links are displayed and sometimes a static frame that contains a logo or toolbar.

- You can often resize frames to better suit your needs. For more information, consult *Resizing and scrolling around a frame* on page 36.

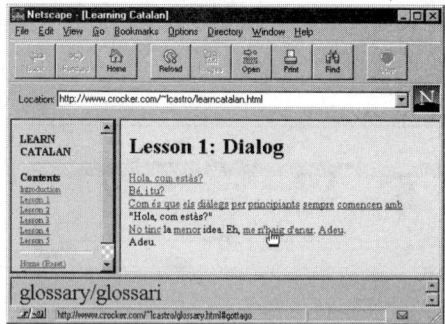

Figure 3.4 *Follow a link in one of the frames in the usual way, by positioning the cursor over the link until it turns into a hand and clicking the mouse.*

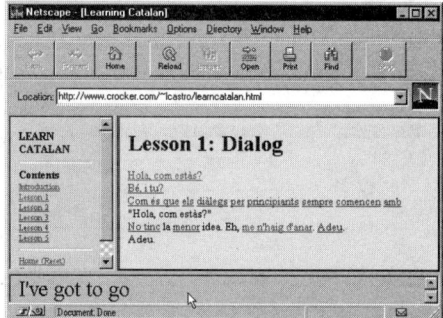

Figure 3.5 *In this example, the corresponding page is displayed in the bottom frame.*

Frames

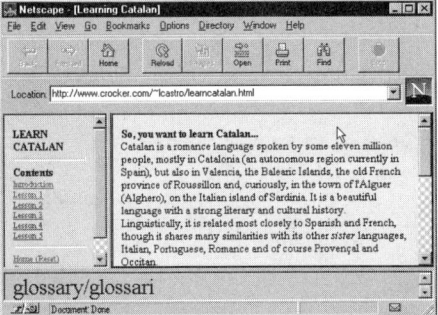

Figure 3.6 *Click in the frame (not on a link) to select it. Note the black border around the frame.*

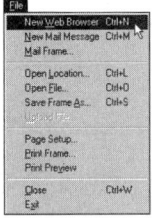

Figure 3.7 *Choose New Web Browser in the File menu.*

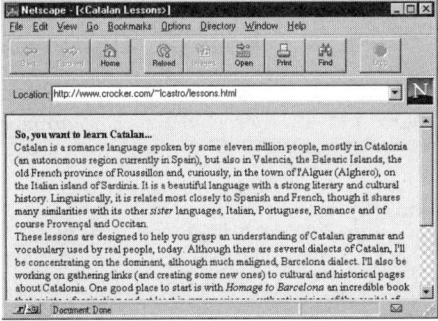

Figure 3.8 *The selected frame is displayed in the new browser.*

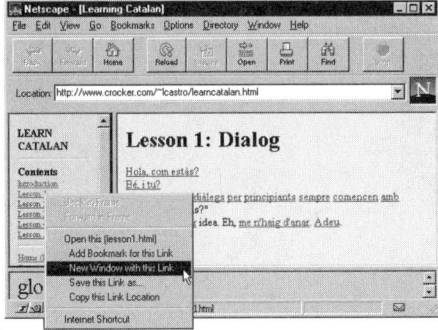

Figure 3.9 *Right click a link to the frame and choose New Window with this Link.*

Opening a frame in a new window

Often, links are *targeted* to particular frames. That means that when you click the link, the corresponding URL appears within a specific frame. If the frame is too small or too unwieldy, you may wish to open the link in a separate, independent window.

To open a frame in a new window:

1. Click in the desired frame (anywhere except over a link) to select it. A black border appears around the frame to show it is selected **(Figure 3.6)**.

2. Choose New Web Browser in the File menu **(Figure 3.7)**. Netscape opens a new browser and fills it with the selected frame **(Figure 3.8)**.

✓ Tips

- If there is a link to the frame that you want to open in a new window, you can right click the link and then choose New Window with this Link in the pop-up menu that appears **(Figure 3.9)**.

- Sloppy Web page designers sometimes make links to external sites appear inside a frame. If the external site happens to have its own frames, the whole frameset will be stuffed into the frame on the original page. The best thing to do is go back *(see page 37)* and then open the link in a new window.

35

Chapter 3

Resizing and scrolling around a frame

Depending on how the Web page designer has written the HTML for the frameset, a frame can either have a fixed size (in pixels), a relative size (that depends on the size of the whole browser), or be adjustable by the user.

In my opinion, since there is no way to foresee what size browser a user will have, designers should always make frames adjustable. Unfortunately, not all Web page designers agree.

To resize a frame:

1. Place the pointer over one of the borders of the frame **(Figure 3.10)**. If it changes into a double pointed arrow, you can change the size of the frame.

2. Drag the border to the desired new position **(Figure 3.11)**.

Similarly, a designer can create a frameset so that a frame has scroll bars all the time, none of the time, or only when necessary.

To scroll around a frame:

1. If the scroll bars are visible, click on the up or down arrows to see more information at the top or bottom of the frame, respectively. Drag the scroll box to move more quickly. Click in the gray area to move one frame area at a time **(Figure 3.12)**.

2. Or, select the frame (by clicking in it) and use the arrow keys to move around the frame.

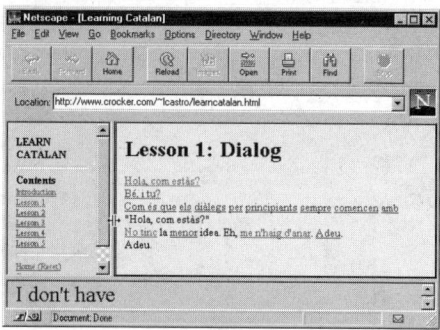

Figure 3.10 *Place the cursor between the frames. When it changes to a double-pointed arrow, drag it to resize the frames.*

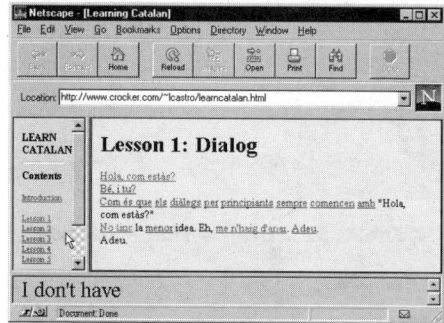

Figure 3.11 *The left column is slightly narrower now.*

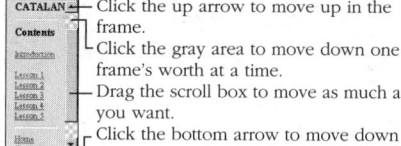

Figure 3.12 *The scroll bars (if they're visible) let you move around the frame to see additional information.*

36

Frames

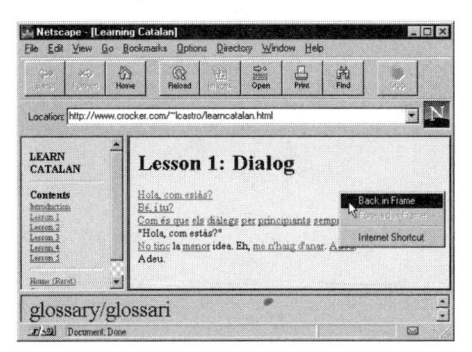

Figure 3.13 *Right click in the frame and choose Back in Frame (or Forward in Frame) from the pop-up menu.*

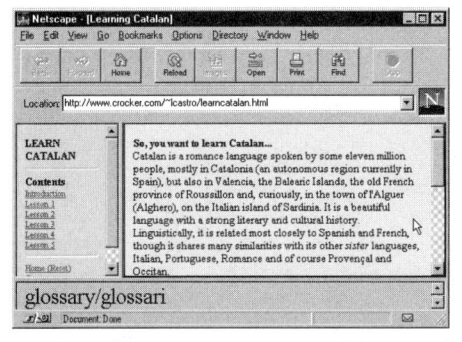

Figure 3.14 *The previous contents of the selected frame are shown. Notice that the other frames remain unchanged.*

Going backward or forward in a frame

The Back and Forward buttons in the toolbar refer to pages, not to frames. Remember that a set of frames is contained in a single page (called a *frameset*). If you click the Back or Forward button, you'll go back or forward *a whole page*, and in particular, to the page you were browsing before you jumped to the frameset page. If you want to go back or forward a frame, you have to use the pop-up menu.

To go backward or forward in a frame:

1. Place the pointer inside the frame that you want to go back or forward in, anywhere except over a link.

2. Press the right mouse button to display the pop-up menu **(Figure 3.13)**.

3. Choose Back in Frame or Forward in Frame in the pop-up menu. Netscape shows the appropriate information in the selected frame **(Figure 3.14)**.

✔ Tip

■ You can only go backward or forward in a frame if you've actually shown more than one URL in that frame. If not, the Back in Frame (or Forward in Frame) commands in the pop-up menu will be grayed out.

Transferring Files

In order to transfer files from one computer to another, like for example, from a server in New Jersey to your house, the two computers need to speak to each other the same way—with the same *protocol*. Before the Web, the most common protocols for downloading files were FTP (which stands for *file transfer protocol*) and Gopher. And even though today it's quite simple to download files from a Web page, most servers continue to offer files through the two older systems.

Netscape allows you to access FTP or Gopher servers in much the same way as you would regular Web servers by displaying their contents as a series of hierarchical folders.

FTP and Gopher servers do not have links to other sites, and generally they don't include explanatory text. They are dedicated to file transfer. Some sites are open to the public, while others are restricted to particular users.

To transfer files to another person or company via e-mail, consult *Attaching files to a message* on page 116.

Chapter 4

Accessing an FTP site

Many servers offer either anonymous or private FTP. Universities, Internet service providers, and computer manufacturers typically offer anonymous FTP access to their files, which may be doctoral dissertations, Web software or program updates, respectively, among many other possibilities. In addition, you may have access to a private FTP site at your own server.

To access an FTP site:

1. Choose Open Location in the File menu or click the Open button on the toolbar **(Figure 4.1)**. The Open Location dialog box appears.

2. For an anonymous FTP site, type **ftp.site** where *ftp.site* is the URL address of the desired FTP site **(Figure 4.2)**. To access a private FTP site, you'll have to type **ftp://user name:password@ftp.site**.

3. Click Open. Netscape contacts the FTP server and displays the contents of the FTP site **(Figure 4.3)**.

✔ Tips

- You can also type the FTP address in the Location text box under the toolbar, if it is showing *(see page 15)*.

- If the anonymous FTP address begins with the word *ftp*, you don't need to type the initial **ftp://**; Netscape will add it automatically **(Figure 4.4)**.

- Anonymous FTP sites often limit the number of people that can connect at a time. If you get an error message, try again later. According to Internet etiquette, you shouldn't access a university site during business hours.

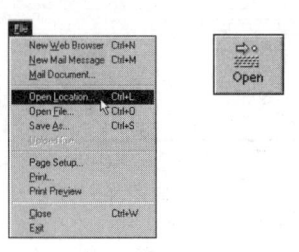

Figure 4.1 *Select Open Location in the File menu or click the Open button on the tool-*

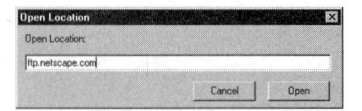

Figure 4.2 *Type the FTP address in the Open Location dialog box.*

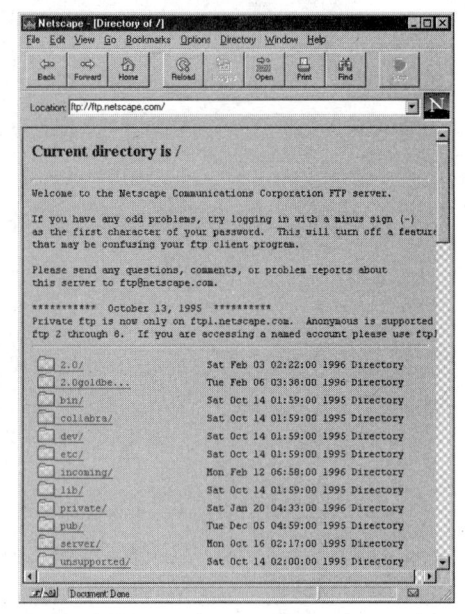

Figure 4.3 *The FTP site is displayed. For information on downloading files, see page 42.*

Figure 4.4 *You only have to begin the URL with ftp:// if the FTP address does not begin with the letters ftp.*

Transferring Files

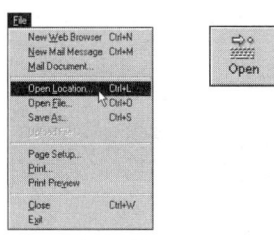

Figure 4.5 *Select Open Location in the File menu or click the Open button on the toolbar.*

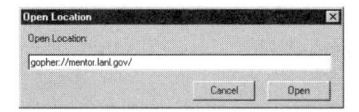

Figure 4.6 *Type the URL of the desired Gopher site in the Open Location dialog box.*

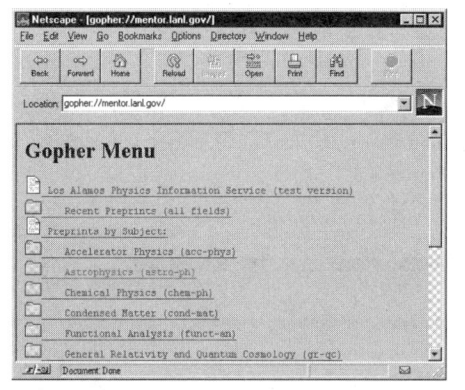

Figure 4.7 *The Gopher site is displayed. For information on downloading files, see page 42.*

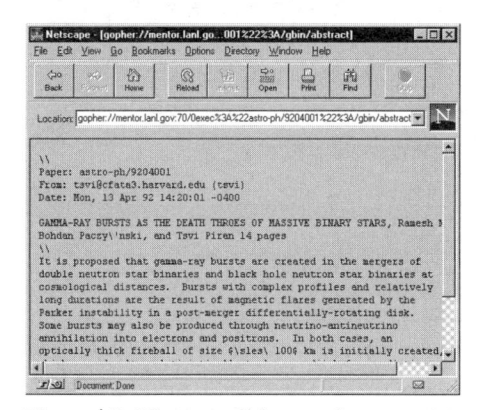

Figure 4.8 *When you click a text document, it is displayed in the browser.*

Accessing a Gopher site

The Gopher protocol, supported by many university sites, lets you search databases and retrieve files. Although there continues to be wide support for Gopher, it has been generally supplanted by the Web.

To access a Gopher site:

1. Choose Open Location in the File menu or click the Open button on the toolbar **(Figure 4.5)**. The Open Location dialog box appears.

2. Type **gopher.site** where *gopher.site* is the URL address of the desired Gopher site **(Figure 4.6)**.

3. Click Open. Netscape contacts the Gopher server and displays the available files on screen **(Figure 4.7)**.

4. Click on a folder to see its contents. Click on a text file to display it **(Figure 4.8)**.

✓ Tips

■ If the Gopher address begins with the word *gopher*, you don't need to type the initial **gopher://**; Netscape will add it automatically.

■ You can also type the Gopher address in the Location bar in the main Netscape window, if it is showing *(see page 15)*.

41

Chapter 4

Downloading files

Once you have accessed the desired FTP, Gopher or Web site, actually downloading a file is only a click away.

To download a file:

1. Access the desired site.

2. Click on the appropriate folders until you find the file you wish to download **(Figure 4.9)**.

3. Click the desired file. Netscape may ask you what to do with the file. Click Save File to save it to your hard disk **(Figure 4.10)**.

4. In the Save As dialog box that appears, choose the directory in which to save the file and click Save **(Figure 4.11)**.

5. Netscape initiates the transfer and shows the Saving Location dialog box which indicates the size of the file and how long it will take to download **(Figure 4.12)**.

6. If you change your mind about downloading the file, click the Cancel button in the Saving Location dialog box.

✓ Tips

- Netscape automatically displays text files in the browser instead of saving them. To save a text file, right click it and choose Save this Link as in the pop-up menu. For more information, consult *Saving a page without jumping to it* on page 47.

- You can set up Netscape so that it saves and/or uncompresses certain kinds of files automatically. For more information, consult *Setting up helper apps* on page 31.

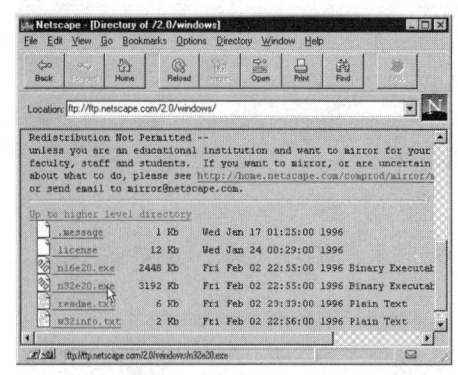

Figure 4.9 *Find the file that you wish to download from a site. You may have to wade through several layers of folders. Click the file to download it. Text files are automatically displayed in the browser.*

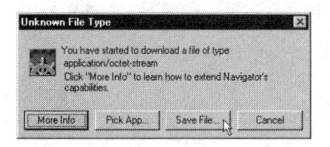

Figure 4.10 *Netscape may ask you want you want to do with the selected file. Click Save File to save it to your hard disk.*

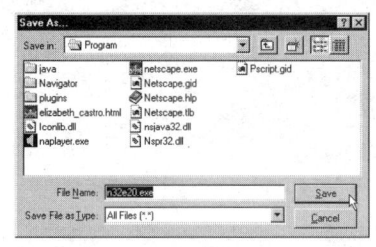

Figure 4.11 *Choose the directory on your hard disk in which you wish to save the file and click Save.*

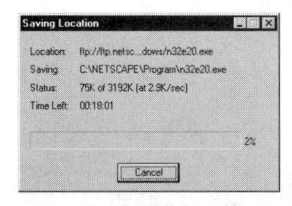

Figure 4.12 *The Saving Location dialog box tells you how large the file is, gives you an estimate of how long it will take to download (and how much has been downloaded so far), and lets you cancel the download if you change your mind.*

Transferring Files

Uploading a file with FTP

Although you can download a file from an FTP, Gopher or Web site, you can usually only upload a file to an FTP site. You might want to upload a Web page that you've created to your Internet service provider's server so that other users can have access to it. Or a software manufacturer might ask you to upload a file that lists your system extensions so that they can help you with a bombing program.

To upload a file with FTP:

1. Access the FTP site and navigate to the desired folder in which you wish to upload the file **(Figure 4.13 and Figure 4.14)**.

2. Choose Upload file in the File menu **(Figure 4.15)**.

3. In the dialog box that appears—that displays the contents of your hard disk—choose the desired file and click Open **(Figure 4.16)**. The file is transferred to the FTP site.

4. If you change your mind about uploading the file, click the Cancel button in the File Upload dialog box or the Stop button on the toolbar.

✓ Tips

■ You may continue using Netscape while you are uploading a file. Of course, it won't be as fast as if it were dedicated to the one task.

■ Be careful when you upload files. Once you've uploaded them, you can't change their location with Netscape. Of course, you can use a dedicated FTP client like Win_ftp to move files around on the FTP server.

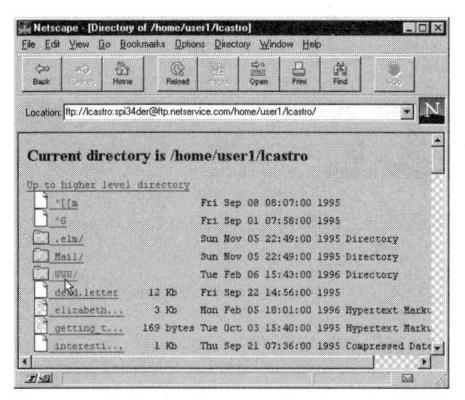

Figure 4.13 *Navigate to the FTP site where you want to upload the file.*

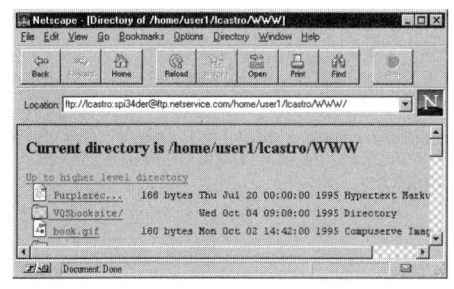

Figure 4.14 *Open the directory in which you wish to save the file (here, WWW).*

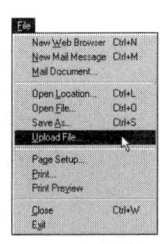

Figure 4.15 *Choose Upload File in the File menu.*

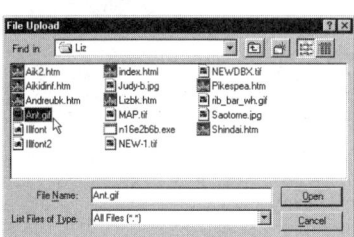

Figure 4.16 *Choose the file on your hard disk that you wish to upload. Click Open.*

43

Chapter 4

Uploading multiple files

If you use Netscape 2 with Windows 95, you can upload several files at once to an FTP site using drag and drop. You can drag files from the desktop, or from the Explorer, whichever is easier.

To upload multiple files:

1. Connect to your FTP site *(see page 40)* and navigate to the desired destination directory.

2. Select the desired files on the desktop or in the Explorer.

3. Drag the files to the Netscape browser showing the FTP site. When the pointer gains a plus sign, release the mouse button **(Figure 4.17)**.

4. Click the Netscape browser to make it active. An alert appears asking if you wish to upload the dragged files to the FTP site **(Figure 4.18)**.

5. Click OK in the alert. The files are uploaded.

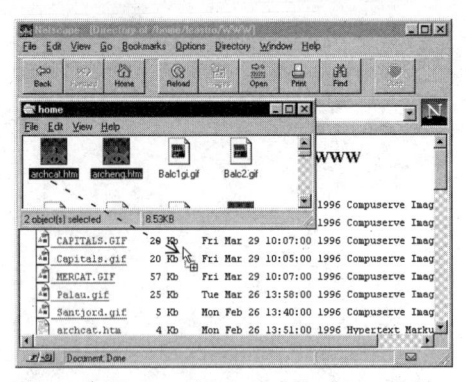

Figure 4.17 *Drag the desired files from a folder on the desktop to the open Netscape browser, showing the FTP site.*

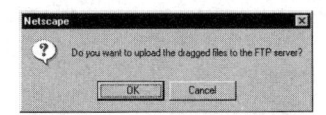

Figure 4.18 *Click on the Netscape browser and this alert appears. Click OK to complete the transfer.*

✓ Tip

- Although you *can* use the File Manager to drag files to the FTP site, you probably shouldn't. It will truncate file names to the 8.3 format—using .htm instead of .html— and convert them to all upper case. I've also had some problems dragging items from the Explorer that were created in a non-Windows 95 compliant program. Although the Explorer *shows* these files with upper and lower case letters, it drags them all upper case. The safest bet is to drag the files from a folder on the Desktop.

Saving and Printing

As you surf, you may find images and text that you would like to save. Although much of the material on the Web is copyrighted, you are allowed to save files for your own use—for example, to read a page or view an image after you have disconnected from your online service.

The images that you find on Web pages can only be saved in their original format. You will have to use a separate program like Paintshop Pro or Adobe Photoshop to convert them to other formats.

If you find a particularly interesting page and you want to keep a copy of it, or share it with someone who's (gasp) not on the Web, you can print out a copy.

Chapter 5

Saving a Web page

Netscape can save a Web page with or without its HTML tags. To open the file with a word processor and work with the data in some way, you should save the page *without* HTML tags—Netscape calls this "Plain Text" format.

To read the page with Netscape once you've disconnected from your online service, or to study other peoples' HTML, you should save the file *with* HTML tags—Netscape calls this "Source" format.

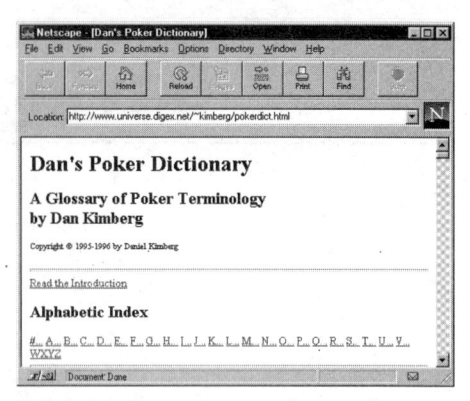

Figure 5.1 *First, navigate to the page that you want to save.*

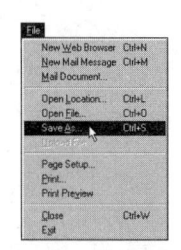

Figure 5.2 *Choose Save As in the File menu.*

To save a Web page:

1. Jump to the desired page **(Fig. 5.1)**.

2. Choose Save As in the File menu **(Fig. 5.2)**. The Save As box appears.

3. In the Save File as Type submenu at the bottom of the dialog box **(Fig. 5.3)**, choose Source to save the page with HTML tags, or Plain Text to save the page without HTML tags.

4. If you save the file with HTML tags, be sure to add the extension .htm to the file name so that all browsers on all platforms can recognize the file.

5. Give the file a name and click OK. A progress bar indicates how long it will take **(Figure 5.4)**.

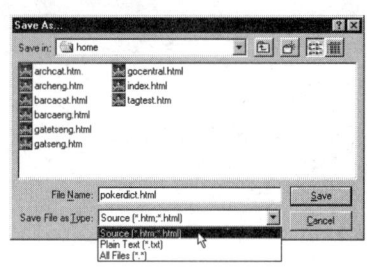

Figure 5.3 *Choose either Source or Plain Text in the Save File as Type pop-up menu, give the file a name (or use the existing one) and then click OK.*

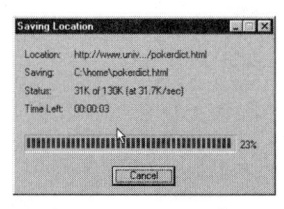

Figure 5.4 *The Saving Location dialog box indicates how long it will take to save the file to disk.*

✓ Tips

- Don't be confused by Netscape's use of *Text* and *Source*. All Web pages—even those saved with HTML tags in "Source" format—are text files.

- Images are not downloaded when you save a page unless you have Netscape Gold *(see page 158)*. To save images with "plain" Netscape, see page 48.

46

Saving a page without jumping to it

You can save a Web page without even navigating to it. This is convenient when you are on a page with several links to other interesting looking pages, since you can save each of the other pages without leaving the main page that has the links.

To save a page without jumping to it:

1. Jump to a page that contains a link to the page you wish to save.

2. Right click the link and choose Save this Link as in the pop-up menu **(Figure 5.5)**.

3. In the Save File as Type submenu at the bottom of the Save as box, choose Source to save the page with HTML tags, or Plain Text to save the page without HTML tags **(Figure 5.6)**.

4. If you save the file with HTML tags, be sure to add the extension .htm to the file name so that all browsers on all platforms can recognize the file.

5. Change the file name if desired and click OK.

✓ Tips

- Hold down the Shift key and right click a link to save the corresponding page.

- Use the original file names if you want the internal links between a set of related pages to work offline.

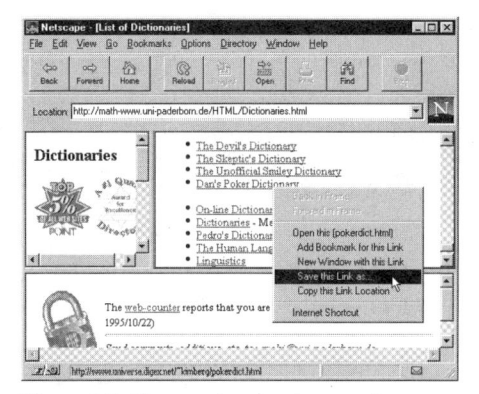

Figure 5.5 *First, navigate to the page that contains a link to the page you want to save. Right click the link and then choose Save this Link as in the pop-up menu.*

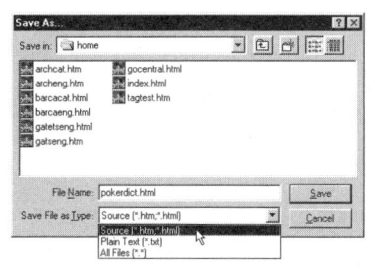

Figure 5.6 *Choose either Source or Plain Text in the Save File as Type pop-up menu, give the file a name (or use the existing one) and then click OK.*

Chapter 5

Saving an image

Inline images are not downloaded automatically when you save a Web page. Instead, you must save each image separately.

External images, on the other hand, are usually downloaded to your hard disk automatically when you view them. For more information, consult *Helper applications* on page 68.

To save an inline image:

1. Navigate to the page that contains the image.

2. Right click the image and choose Save this Image as in the pop-up menu **(Figure 5.7)**. The Save As dialog box appears **(Figure 5.8)**.

3. Click OK to save the image with the name and extension given. The Saving Location dialog box shows you how long the download will take to finish **(Figure 5.9)**.

✔ Tips

- Although you can change the extension of an image file when you save it, this will *not* magically change its format. To change an image's format, you need to use a program like Paintshop Pro or Photoshop.

- You can also save an image by holding down the Shift key and clicking the image with the right mouse button.

- If you save a page to edit with Netscape Gold, you *will* be allowed to save all the images it contains automatically *(see page 158)*.

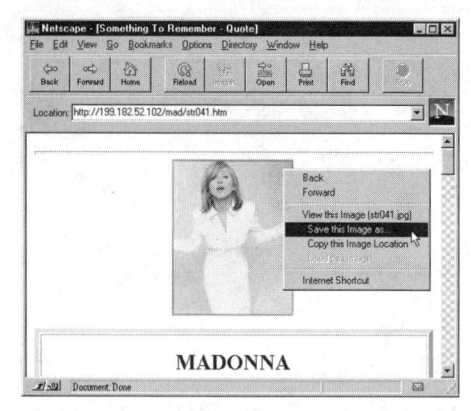

Figure 5.7 *To save an inline image, right click the image and choose Save this Image as in the pop-up menu.*

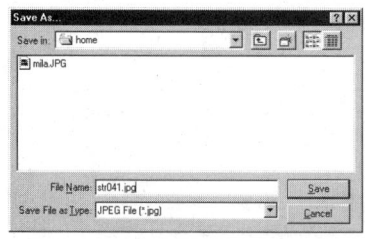

Figure 5.8 *In the Save As dialog box, choose a file name (or use the existing one) and click OK.*

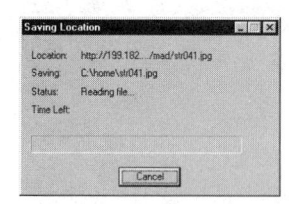

Figure 5.9 *The Saving Location dialog box shows how long it will take to download the image. You may continue browsing by clicking the main window.*

Saving and Printing

Copying and pasting parts of a page

There is no law that says you must save an entire page when you are only interested in one portion of it. In addition, copying the page as described below is a fast and easy way to transfer information to other files in other applications.

To copy and paste part of a page:

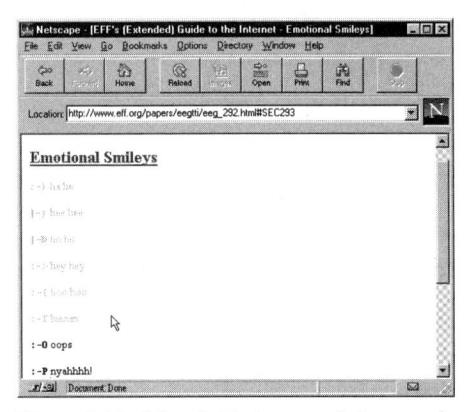

Figure 5.10 *Select (with the mouse) the part of the page that you wish to copy. Sometimes when you select, the text is shaded instead of highlighted (as shown here).*

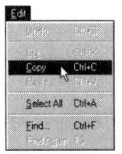

Figure 5.11 *Choose Copy in the Edit menu.*

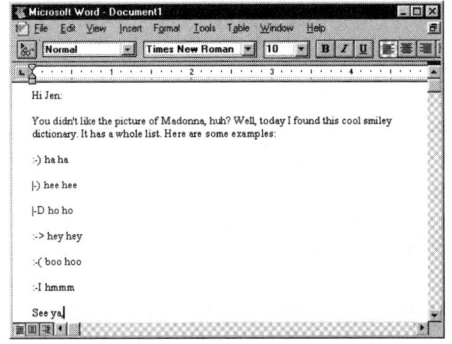

Figure 5.12 *Here I've pasted the copied material into a letter (in Word).*

1. With the mouse, select the part of the page that you wish to copy **(Figure 5.10)**.

2. Choose Copy in the Edit menu or press Ctrl+C **(Figure 5.11)**.

3. Place the cursor where you want to paste the material (perhaps in an e-mail note, in another application, or wherever).

4. Choose Paste in the Edit menu or press Ctrl+V. The text is pasted into the current window **(Figure 5.12)**.

✔ Tips

- HTML tags and images cannot be copied using this technique. To save a page with HTML tags, consult *Saving a Web page* on page 46. To copy images, consult *Saving an image* on page 48.

- You may not paste anything into an existing Web page in the Netscape browser. Of course, you may open a Web page (saved with HTML tags) with a word processor and then paste parts of other pages into it there.

49

Reading a saved page offline

If you've found an interesting, but long page that you would like to read without hearing the connect-time clock ticking anxiously at your back, you can save the page, disconnect from your online service, and then open the page to read.

To read a saved page offline:

1. Save the page *with HTML tags* using the techniques described on page 46 or page 47.

2. Without quitting Netscape, disconnect from your online service.

3. From Netscape's File menu, choose Open File **(Figure 5.13)**. The Open dialog box appears.

4. Choose the file you saved in step 1 and click OK **(Figure 5.14)**. The page will appear in the Netscape browser **(Figure 5.15)**.

5. Read at your leisure.

✔ Tips

- If you are saving several related pages for later reading, make sure to save them with their original names *(see page 47)*.

- You can also view saved GIF or JPEG images offline. Simply choose the image in step 4 above. You may have to type the extension (*.gif or *.jpg) in the List Files of Type box. The image appears by itself in the browser.

- If you saved the page in Plain Text format, it appears quite differently in the browser—without formatting, images or links **(Figure 5.16)**.

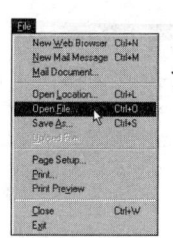

Figure 5.13 *To open a saved file, choose Open File in Netscape's File menu.*

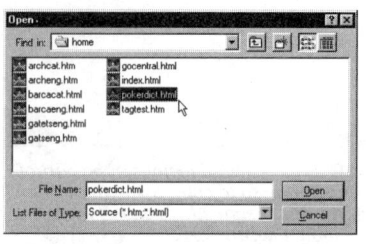

Figure 5.14 *In the Open dialog box, choose the desired file and click OK.*

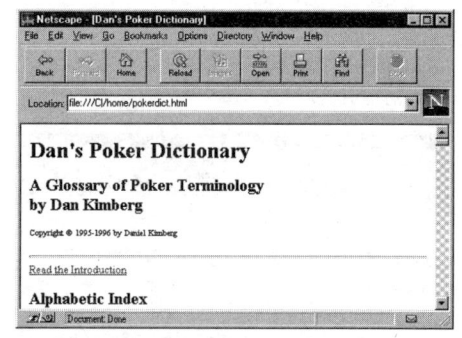

Figure 5.15 *The file (if saved as Source—with HTML tags) appears with the original formatting and links, but without images.*

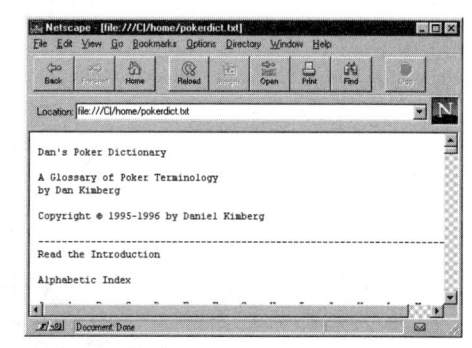

Figure 5.16 *If the file was saved as Plain Text (without HTML tags), it appears without formatting, links or images.*

Saving and Printing

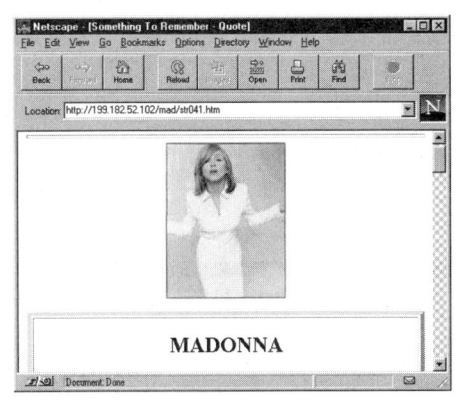

Figure 5.17 *Navigate to the page that you want to print.*

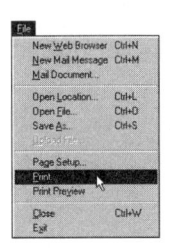

Figure 5.18 *Choose Print in the File menu or click Print on the toolbar.*

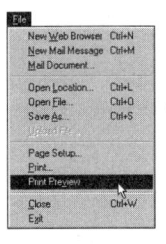

Figure 5.19 *Choose Print Preview in the File menu before printing to see how the page will appear.*

Printing a page

You may want to create a hard copy of one of the pages that you find on the Web for future reference. Netscape automatically resizes the information on the Web page to fit on the printed page.

To print a page:

1. Navigate to the page that you wish to print **(Figure 5.17)**.

2. Choose Print in the File menu or click the Print button on the toolbar **(Figure 5.18)**. The standard Print dialog box appears.

3. If desired, change the printing options.

4. Click OK. The page will be printed.

✔ Tips

- Printing an e-mail message, news posting or page that you are editing is practically identical. Simply view the desired item and choose Print from the File menu.

- Print an individual frame by clicking in the frame before choosing Print Frame in the File menu.

- For more printer options, consult *Setting up printing options* on page 52.

- Choose Print Preview in the File menu **(Figure 5.19)** before printing to get an idea of how the page will look.

Chapter 5

Setting up printing options

When you print a page, you can decide whether to include a header or footer, what margins to use, whether certain elements should appear in black or in color, and what order the pages should print in.

To set the printing options:

1. Choose Page Setup in the File menu **(Figure 5.20)**. The Page Setup dialog box appears **(Figure 5.21)**.

2. In the Page Options section, choose Beveled Lines to simplify beveled frames in tables and around images. Choose Black Text and Black lines to print horizontal lines without shading or color. Choose Last Page First to reverse the printing order.

3. In the Margins section, enter the amount of space for the margins.

4. In the Header section, check Document Title to print the page's title at the top of each page. Check Document Location (URL) to print the page's URL at the top of each page.

5. In the Footer section, check Page Number to add the page number to the bottom of each page. Check Page Total to print the total number of pages at the bottom of each page. Check Date Printed to print the current date at the bottom of each page.

6. Click OK to save the options.

✔ Tip

- The options in the Page Setup dialog box affect all the pages you print from that moment onwards, not just the current document.

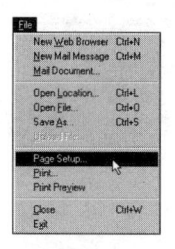

Figure 5.20 *Choose Page Setup in the File menu.*

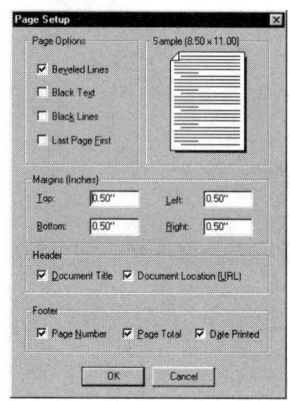

Figure 5.21 *In the Page Setup Options dialog box, adjust how graphic elements should print, the width of the margins, and the contents of the header and footer.*

Finding Stuff on the Web

With hundreds of thousands of Web pages, fourteen thousand newsgroups, and millions of e-mail users, it is sometimes a challenge to find the information that you're looking for. There are many companies who offer Internet search services in exchange for a glance at their advertisers' promotions.

There are services that search Web pages, services that search newsgroups, services that search for e-mail addresses and even services that catalog shareware. You simply jump to the service that is most likely to have the information you need.

Tips for using search services

First, when typing search or keywords, try to be as specific as possible without being too specific. That is, if you're looking for Web pages about Seiji Ozawa, instead of typing *conductors*, which is very general, you might try *Boston conductors* (since he is the conductor of the Boston Symphony). Or, instead of typing *Seiji Ozawa*, which is very specific, try just *Ozawa*.

Second—and this may sound obvious—be careful with spelling. If you don't spell the keywords right, the search service won't be able to find the desired page. If the word has an alternate spelling (which is often the case with words from other languages—Gorbachev or Gorbachov?) or if it is misspelled on the page itself, you can use the boolean operator OR to search for several spellings simultaneously.

Chapter 6

Finding Web pages by subject

One of the best known Web page search indexes is Yahoo!. Yahoo! sorts its Web index by topic, and creates a kind of Table of Contents for the Web. If you want to see several pages about the same or related general topics, or if you just want a place to start surfing, Yahoo! is a good place to begin.

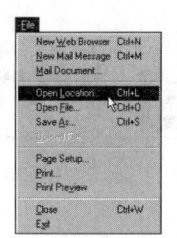

Figure 6.1 *Choose Open Location in the File menu (left) or click the Open button (right).*

Figure 6.2 *Type Yahoo's URL address in the dialog box and click Open.*

To use Yahoo! to find Web pages by topic:

1. Choose Open Location in the File menu or click the Open button on the toolbar **(Figure 6.1)**. The Open Location dialog box appears **(Figure 6.2)**.

2. Type **yahoo** in the text box and click Open. Netscape displays the Yahoo! home page **(Figure 6.3)**. Each main topic is divided into clickable subtopics.

3. Click any topic or subtopic of interest. Yahoo! displays a set of related links **(Figure 6.4)**. The links may be divided into indices (lists of related links), subtopics (which when clicked on reveal a list of links to pages about the subtopic) or Web pages (that fit the general topic but none of the subtopics listed).

4. Click the desired link **(Figure 6.5)**. The page is displayed.

✓ Tip

■ You can also search for keywords through Yahoo! by entering the words in the text box and clicking Search. However, there are other services that are better at straight word searches.

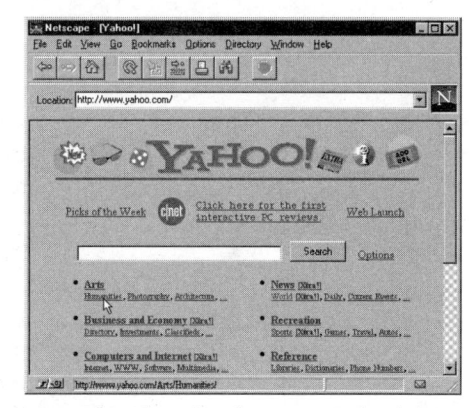

Figure 6.3 *The Yahoo! home page is divided into categories and subcategories, all of which are links to related articles.*

Finding Web pages by subject

54

Finding Stuff on the Web

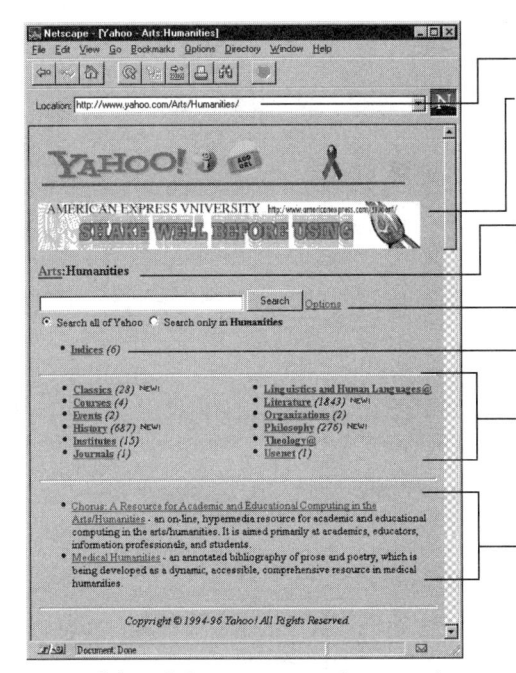

Figure 6.4 *A click on Humanities brings up this page of related links, divided into subcategories.*

- Yahoo's address is displayed in the Location text box.
- Advertisements are sprinkled liberally throughout the Yahoo! site. This is how Yahoo! makes money, but you don't have to pay attention.
- Yahoo! always lists the path that you have taken. You can click on the links to the earlier pages to go back (up) in the hierarchy of categories.
- You can also choose to search for a keyword, either in the entire Yahoo! index, or just in the pages that are in the currently selected category.
- The Indices are pages that contain a collection of links to the main topic (Humanities, in this case).
- Yahoo! divides all the articles into subcategories. The number after each category indicates how many articles it contains. An @ symbol means that the subcategory is further divided into smaller subcategories.
- The articles that are general enough to be related to the main category (Humanities) but that don't fit into any subcategories, are listed at the bottom of the page.

Figure 6.5 *A click on a link in Figure 6.4 brings you to the corresponding article out on the Web. You are no longer at the Yahoo! site.*

- The selected page is not part of the Yahoo! site; Yahoo! just helped you find it. This page is actually from New York University's Medical School.

Chapter 6

Searching for Web pages by keyword

There are two or three good search services that have indexed as much of the Web as they can find—by sending out automatic robots called *spiders* that go from server to server looking at all the Web pages and recording their addresses, titles and sometimes even their contents. Perhaps the best service I've found is Open Text, that claims to contain more than 8 billion words in its index.

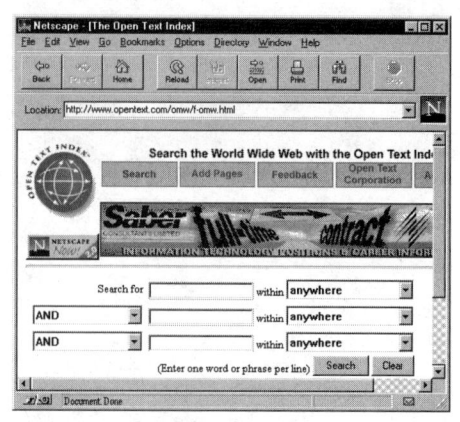

Figure 6.6 *Open Text's home page.*

To search for Web pages by keyword with Open Text:

1. Choose Open Location or click the Open button on the toolbar. The Open Location dialog box appears.

2. Type **www.opentext.com/omw/f-omw.html** (yes, even that dash) in the text box and click Open. Netscape displays the Open Text home page **(Figure 6.6)**.

3. Type a word or phrase in the first box **(Figure 6.7)**.

4. If desired, choose where you wish Open Text to search (anywhere, summary, title, first heading, web location) in the pop-up menu.

5. If desired, type more search words or phrases and a search location.

6. If you've entered more than one search string, choose a boolean operator in the submenu. Choose And to find pages that contain *both* search words or phrases. Choose Or to find pages with *either* one word or phrase *or the other*.

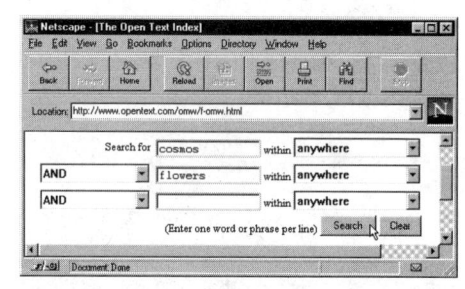

Figure 6.7 *Type the criteria (first,* cosmos, *and then,* flowers*). If desired, choose a boolean operator like AND or OR and a place. Then click Search. In this example we used AND to make sure that the pages found would be about Cosmos flowers and not the starry cosmos.*

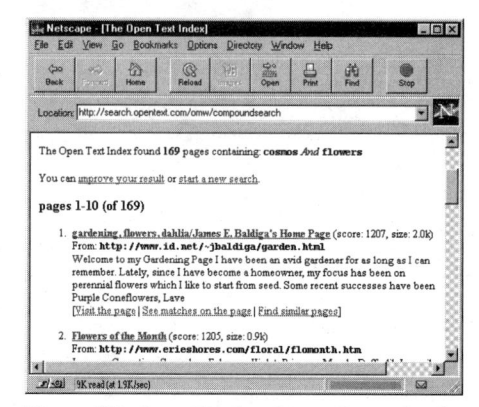

Figure 6.8 *Open Text lists the results, giving the name of the page, its size, its score (how well it satisfied the search criteria), and the page's address.*

Finding Stuff on the Web

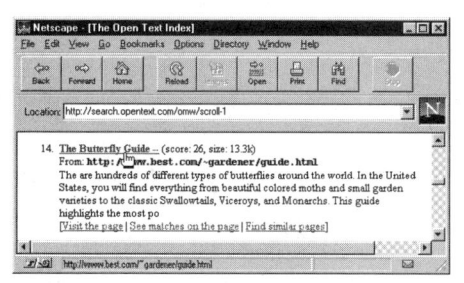

Figure 6.9 *Each found page gives several options: Visit this page, See matches on this page and Find similar pages. You can also click the page's title to jump to it.*

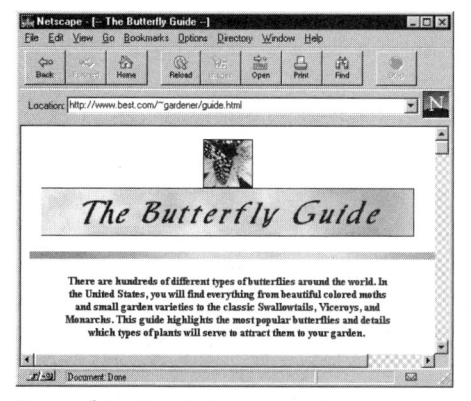

Figure 6.10 *The desired page is shown in the browser.*

7. Click Search to start the search. (Click Clear to start over from scratch.) Open Text shows the links to the pages that satisfied the search criteria **(Fig. 6.8)**.

8. Under each found page, you'll have three choices **(Figure 6.9)**. Click View page (or the title itself) to jump to that page **(Figure 6.10)**. Choose See Matches on this page to see where the search word(s) appear on the page without jumping to it. Choose Find similar pages to have Open Text analyze how the search criteria appear on the page and then find pages with a similar relationship.

✔ Tips

- Make sure you spell the keyword(s) correctly. If you type "Catchmear" when looking for lush, goat fiber, you are likely to be disappointed.

- Add word endings to make a search more complete. If you type "fiber" don't expect to find "fibers".

- Use a space to make searches more specific. Open Text finds all the pages that *begin* with the typed word. So if you type "straw" you'll also find "strawberry". But if you type "straw " with a space after the *w*, you'll only find "straw".

- Lycos *(http://www.lycos.com)*, Excite *(http://www.excite.com)*, and Altavista *(http://altavista.digital.com)* are three other word-based Web search services.

- To use Netscape's search services, choose Internet Directory, Internet Search and Internet White Pages in the Directory menu (or with the Directory buttons).

Searching for Web pages by keyword

57

Chapter 6

Searching for people and organizations

Remember Marcy from college? Haven't talked to her lately? Maybe you can find her. Although there's no centralized white pages (at least not for free), there are services that attempt to track down and index e-mail addresses.

To search for a person's e-mail address:

1. Choose Open Location or click the Open button on the toolbar.

2. Type **whowhere** in the text box and click Open to display the WhoWhere? home page. You can search by person or by organization.

3. If you're looking for a person, type the person's name in the text box in the middle frame **(Fig. 6.11)**.

4. If desired, scroll down to enter information about the person's organization, or location.

5. Click the Search button—you may have to scroll down in the middle frame to find it **(Figure 6.12)**. WhoWhere? displays the results as links, and divides them into three categories: highly, probably and possibly relevant **(Figure 6.13)**.

✓ Tips

- Click on a person's address to send her an e-mail message right away.

- To save an address, press the right mouse button and select Copy this Link Location in the submenu. Save the address as described on page 122.

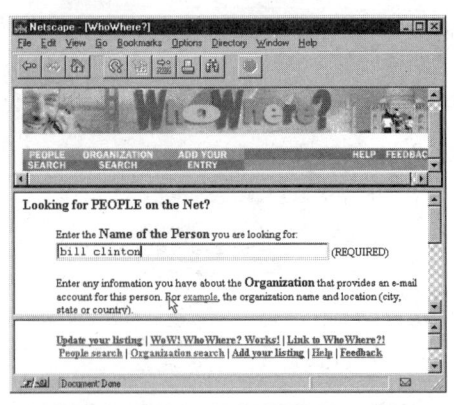

Figure 6.11 *In the middle frame, enter the name of the person whose e-mail address you want to find.*

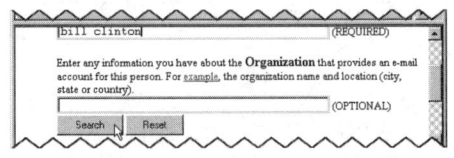

Figure 6.12 *Scroll down in the middle frame to find the Search button and click it.*

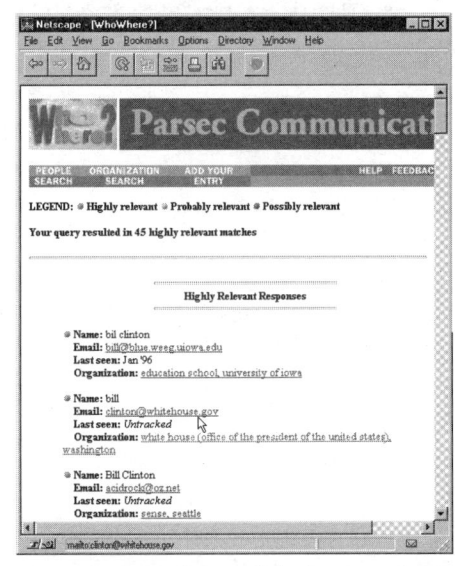

Figure 6.13 *Scroll through the list of matches to see if the person you were looking for is there. Click the name to send an e-mail message.*

Finding Stuff on the Web

Figure 6.14 *Click Organization Search in the top frame of the WhoWhere? home page.*

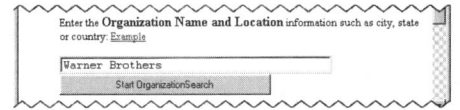

Figure 6.15 *Type the name of the organization in the text box in the middle frame and click Search.*

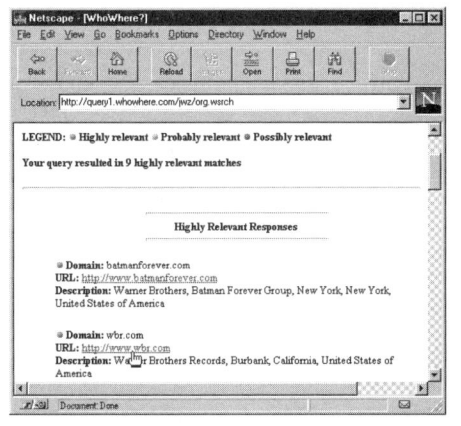

Figure 6.16 *In the list that appears, click the organization that you were looking for.*

Figure 6.17 *Once you click the link to the organization, Netscape shows its home page (in this case, Warner Brothers' home page).*

You can also use WhoWhere? to look for an organizations' Web site. Although many organizations have guessable URLs in the form of *www.organization.com*, others do not. WhoWhere? bridges the gap.

To find an organization:

1. Follow steps 1 and 2 on the previous page.

2. Click Organization Search in the top frame of the WhoWhere? home page **(Figure 6.14)**.

3. Type the name of the organization, and if desired, its location (city or state) in the text box **(Figure 6.15)**.

4. Click the Search button or press Return. WhoWhere? shows you the links to the pages that satisfy the search criteria **(Figure 6.16)**.

5. Click on the desired link. (Links to organizations tend to be Web pages as opposed to e-mail addresses.) The newly found page is displayed **(Figure 6.17)**.

✔ **Tip**

■ Before doing a search, try typing **www.organization.com** in the Open Location dialog box or in the Location field, where *organization* is the name of the company you're looking for.

Searching for people and organizations

59

Chapter 6

Finding an article in a newsgroup

There are over 14,000 newsgroups, and each of them receives from several to several hundred messages a day. Finding a message that deals with a particular topic can be difficult. You can use Deja News to search for newsgroup messages.

To do a quick search for an article in a newsgroup:

1. Choose Open Location or click the Open button on the toolbar.

2. Type **dejanews** in the text box and click Open.

3. In the Deja News home page that appears, type the search criteria, and click the Find button **(Figure 6.18)**.

4. Deja News lists the articles that fit the criteria **(Figure 6.19)**. Click an article that interests you to view that message. The message is shown in the browser, not the News window **(Figure 6.20)**.

5. If desired, you can reply to the posting by clicking Post Article. You'll be automatically switched to the News window. Or, e-mail a response to the writer by clicking Email Reply. A regular Message Composition window will appear.

✔ **Tip**

■ You can also refine requests further by clicking Power Search at the top of Deja News' home page.

Figure 6.18 *In Deja News' home page, type the keywords and click Find.*

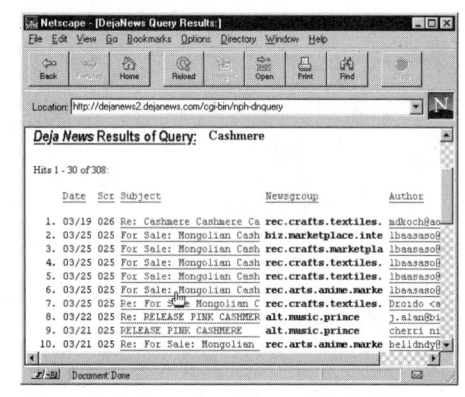

Figure 6.19 *Deja News shows the news postings that match your request. Click one to view it.*

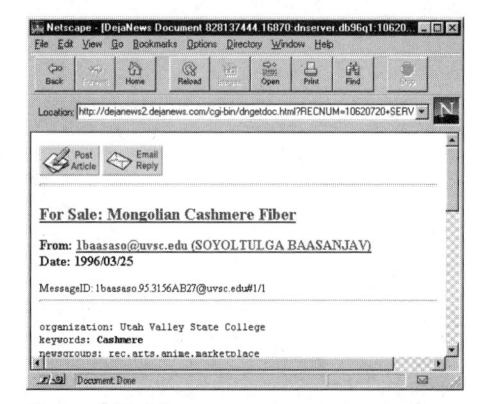

Figure 6.20 *The news posting appears in the browser window. To reply, click Post Article or Email Reply*

Finding Stuff on the Web

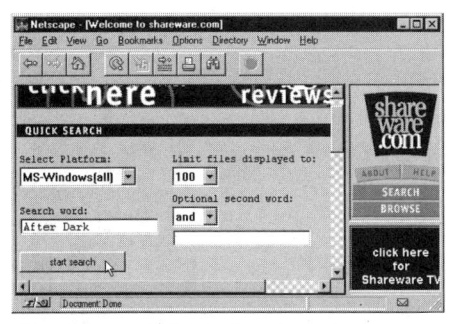

Figure 6.21 *Click Search to get to this main Search window, then choose the appropriate platform, the keywords (in this example, After Dark), the number of files you wish to display and an optional second keyword. Click Start search.*

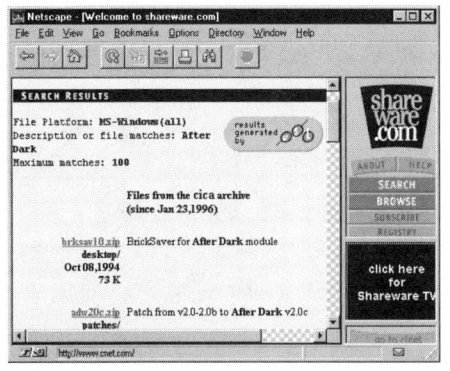

Figure 6.22 *The shareware programs or updates that satisfy the criteria given in the Search window (Figure 6.21) are listed in the central frame. Click one to see the available FTP sites.*

Figure 6.23 *When you click a file to download, shareware.com lists the FTP sites where you can find it. Click an FTP site to download the file.*

Finding shareware through the Web

Sometimes, the hardest part about downloading a file is finding it. One service that provides you with the FTP addresses for over 160,000 shareware programs (as well as commercial software updates) is shareware.com by C/net.

To find shareware through the Web:

1. Choose Open Location or click the Open button on the toolbar.

2. Type **shareware** in the text box and click Open. The C/net home page appears.

3. Click Search in either the left or top right frame to begin **(Figure 6.22)**.

4. Choose the desired platform in the Select platform submenu.

5. Type the appropriate keywords in the Search word submenu.

6. If desired, type a second key word and select And or Or.

7. Click Start search. The shareware files that satisfy the criteria given are listed in the central frame **(Figure 6.22)**.

8. Click the desired file to list the FTP sites where it can be found as well as its approximate download time **(Figure 6.23)**.

9. Click the desired FTP site to download the file. For more information on FTP transfers, consult *Downloading files* on page 42.

61

Chapter 6

Finding information in an open page

You've been reading this whole chapter thinking to yourself, "Hah, I know an easier way. What about the Find button on the toolbar?" The problem with the Find button is that it only searches within a particular page (or message or post). It doesn't search out on the Web. So, if you're looking for a particular word or phrase within a long document that you're already viewing, that's when you should use the Find button.

To find information in an open page:

1. Jump to the desired page.

2. Click the Find button on the toolbar **(Figure 6.24)** or choose Find in the Edit menu **(Figure 6.25)**. The Find dialog box appears.

3. Type the word or phrase that you wish to look for and click Find **(Figure 6.26)**. Netscape will highlight the first occurrence of the word, if any, in the currently open page **(Figure 6.27)**.

4. If desired, choose Find Next in the dialog box (if it's showing) to find the next occurrence of the search word or phrase. If the Find dialog box is not showing, choose Find Next in the Edit menu.

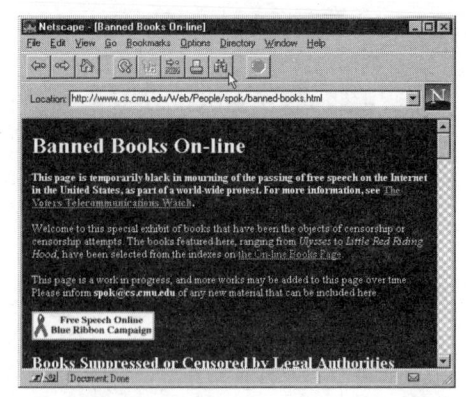

Figure 6.24 *Once you've found the page that contains the information, click the Find button to jump to the desired text.*

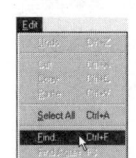

Figure 6.25 *You can also choose Find in the Edit menu.*

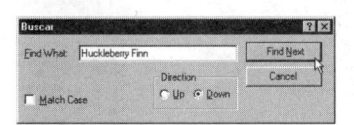

Figure 6.26 *Type the text you're looking for and click Find Next.*

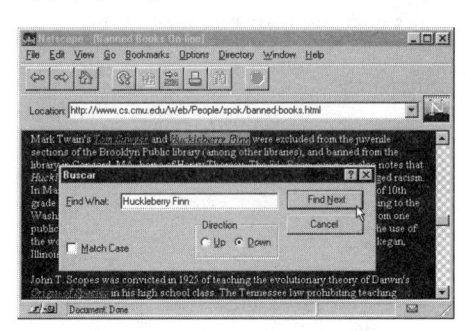

Figure 6.27 *Netscape highlights the found text. If this is the text you want, click on the page to make the browser active. If it's not, click Find Next to find the next occurrence.*

62

Finding Stuff on the Web

Checking out Netscape's pages

Some of Netscape's menu commands take you to particular pages on the Web (mostly on Netscape's own site). Some of these sites are kind of helpful. Some aren't.

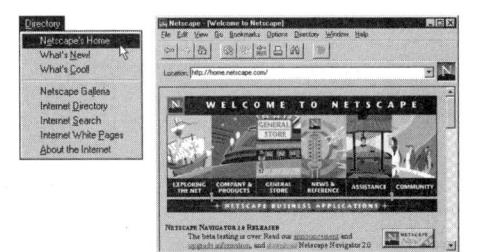

Figure 6.28 *Choose Netscape's Home in the Directory menu to jump to Netscape's home page.*

To find Netscape's home page:

Choose Netscape's Home in the Directory menu **(Figure 6.28)** or click the Netscape icon at the right side of the browser.

To find new pages (according to Netscape):

Choose What's New! in the Directory menu or click the What's New! button at the top of the browser **(Figure 6.29 and Figure 6.31)**.

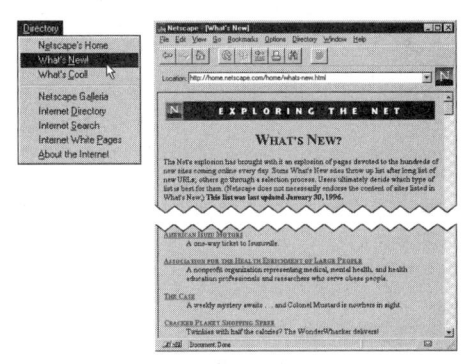

Figure 6.29 *Choose What's New! to see which sites Netscape has discovered lately.*

To find cool pages (according to Netscape):

Choose What's Cool! in the Directory menu or click the What's Cool! button at the top of the browser **(Figure 6.30 and Figure 6.31)**.

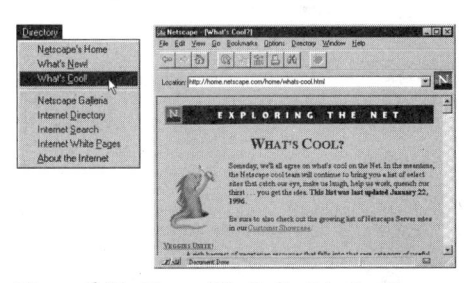

Figure 6.30 *Choose What's Cool! in the Directory menu to see what Netscape Corporations considers a "cool" page.*

To find servers built with Netscape servers software:

Choose Netscape Galleria in the Directory menu.

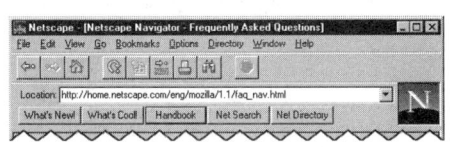

Figure 6.31 *You can also choose What's New! and What's Cool! (among other things) with the Directory buttons. Personally, I think they just take up much needed window space. To hide them, consult Controlling a browser's appearance on page 15.*

To search the Web with Netscape's search service:

Choose Internet Directory, Internet Search or Internet White Pages in the Directory menu. (For more information on finding Web pages, read the rest of this chapter.)

63

Chapter 6

Finding Netscape documentation

A couple of Netscape's built-in commands link you to help pages, including the documentation for Netscape itself.

To find the Netscape handbook:

Choose Handbook in the Help menu **(Figure 6.32)** or click the Handbook button at the top of the browser. Netscape's documentation will be displayed **(Figure 6.33)**. This is the same documentation you would get if you bought the manuals—although perhaps more up-to-date.

FAQ, which rhymes with *smack* and stands for Frequently Asked Questions, is a list of questions that Netscape has received over and over again. Your question may or may not be among them. Answers are included.

To find the Netscape FAQ:

1. Choose Frequently Asked Questions in the Help menu **(Figure 6.34)**.

2. Click the Netscape Navigator FAQ link **(Figure 6.35)**. Netscape's FAQs on Navigator are divided into several files.

3. Click on the FAQ link that interests you.

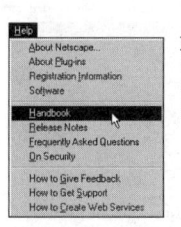

Figure 6.32 *Choose Handbook in the Help menu to view the Netscape documentation.*

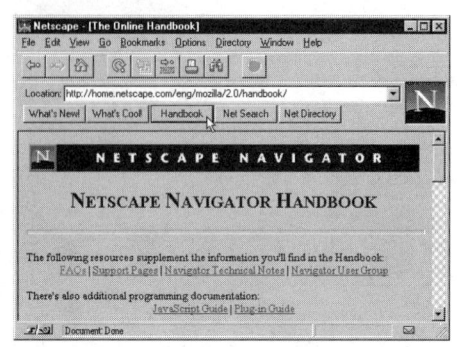

Figure 6.33 *The Handbook page has the advantage of always being the latest version available.*

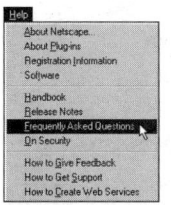

Figure 6.34 *Choose Frequently Asked Questions in the Help menu.*

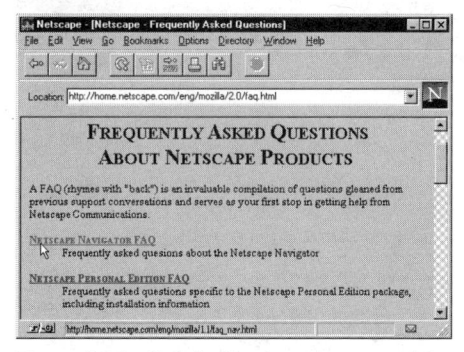

Figure 6.35 *Click the Netscape Navigator FAQ link to see if your question has already been answered in Netscape's files, in which you case you'll be able to quickly find a response.*

Finding Stuff on the Web

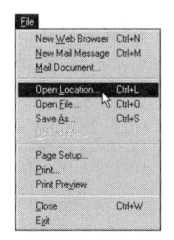

Figure 6.36 *Choose Open Location in the File menu (or click the Open button on the toolbar).*

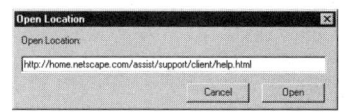

Figure 6.37 *Type the URL address for the support request form in the Open Location box.*

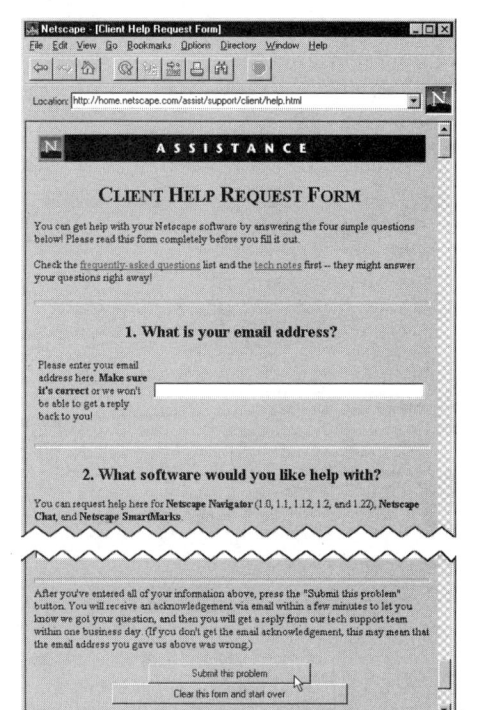

Figure 6.38 *Fill out the Client Help Request Form (it's long) and then click the Submit this problem button at the bottom of the page.*

Finding technical support

Netscape offers free technical support by telephone to users who have bought the Personal Edition of Netscape Navigator, or for users who have downloaded the LAN version by modem and then registered and paid for it. If you have not paid for Netscape, they will charge you $25 for the first 15 minutes, plus $2 for each additional minute.

To find technical support by telephone:

Call 1-800-320-2099.

Only registered LAN version Netscape users can get support via e-mail.

To find technical support online:

1. Choose Open Location in the File menu **(Figure 6.36)** or click the Open button. The Open Location dialog box appears **(Figure 6.37)**.

2. Type **http://home.netscape.com/assist/support/client/help.html**.

3. Fill out the form.

4. Click Submit this problem at the bottom of the page **(Figure 6.38)**. As long as you are a registered LAN version Netscape user, you should receive a notification in a couple of hours and a response within a few days.

✔ **Tip**

■ If you choose How to Get Support from the Help menu, you'll get referred to the handbook and the FAQs before you finally reach the form shown in Figure 6.38.

65

Chapter 6

Finding info about your Netscape software

Netscape's menus offer ways to get information about the software itself. You can find out what version you have, what plug-ins you have installed, what your registration number is, what upgrade options you have, and what new features have been added to the program since your version was released.

To get information about your Netscape software:

1. Choose About Netscape in the Help menu. The version number of your software is displayed **(Figure 6.39)**.

2. Click in the Netscape logo (in the About Netscape page) to see information about the software engineers who developed Netscape.

3. Choose About Plug-ins in the Help menu. A list of the currently installed plug-ins is displayed **(Figure 6.40)**.

4. Choose Registration Information in the Help menu. Your registration number is displayed **(Figure 6.41)**. If you have not yet registered your copy of Netscape, information on how to register will be shown.

5. Choose Software in the Help menu. Netscape displays its upgrades page **(Figure 6.42)**.

6. Choose Release Notes in the Help menu. A list of the new features included in your copy of Netscape appears **(Figure 6.43)**.

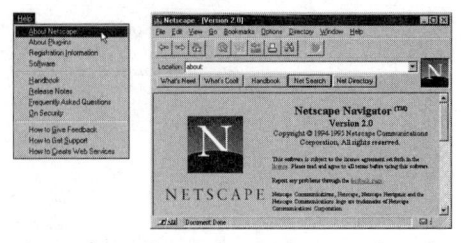

Figure 6.39 *Choose About Netscape in the Help menu to see what version you are using.*

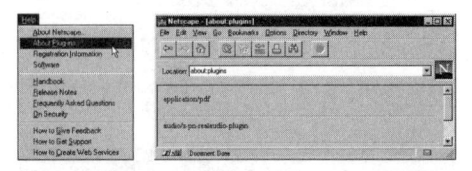

Figure 6.40 *Choose About Plug-ins in the Help menu to see which plug-ins you have installed.*

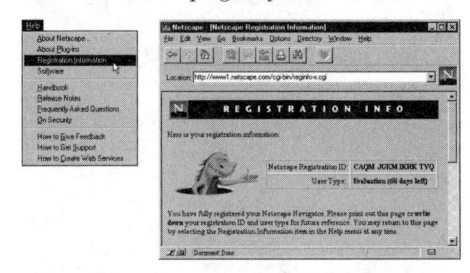

Figure 6.41 *Choose Registration Information to see your registration ID.*

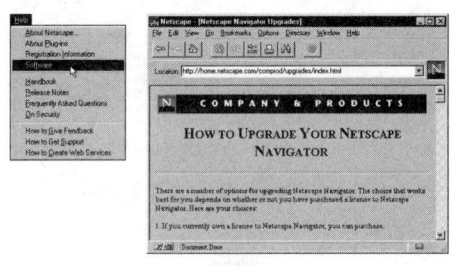

Figure 6.42 *Choose Software in the Help menu to see what upgrade options you have.*

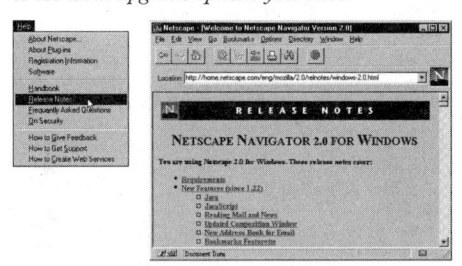

Figure 6.43 *Choose Release Notes to see a list of new features for your version of Netscape.*

Bookmarks

What is a bookmark?

There are approximately 4 million Web pages already in existence. If someday you should find a link to a gem of a page, you won't want to lose it. With Netscape you can store the URL addresses to your favorite sites as *bookmarks*. The next time you want to jump to that site, instead of trying to remember the circuitous route you took the first time, simply pull up your Bookmarks window **(Figure 7.1)**, double click and sail in. Or surf. Whatever.

The bookmarks that you create are listed in the Bookmarks window, which you can display on screen or hide at your convenience. They are also listed at the bottom of the Bookmarks menu for easy access **(Figure 7.2)**.

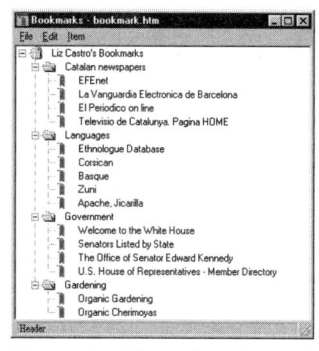

Figure 7.1 *The Bookmarks window helps you organize your favorite sites and get back to them with a simple double click.*

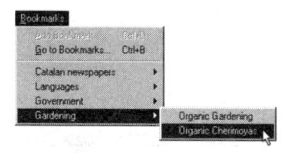

Figure 7.2 *The Bookmarks menu, in the main Netscape window lets you navigate to your favorite sites without pulling up the Bookmarks window.*

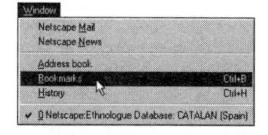

Figure 7.3 *Choose Bookmarks in the Window menu to open the Bookmarks window.*

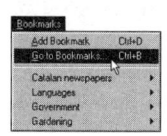

Figure 7.4 *Or choose Go to Bookmarks in the Bookmarks menu to open the Bookmarks window.*

To open the Bookmarks window:

Choose Bookmarks in the Window menu or choose Go to Bookmarks in the Bookmarks menu.

Chapter 7

Using bookmarks to navigate the Web

Bookmarks make it easy to find your way back to favorite sites. The truth is, typing URLs is a pain. It's easy to mix up lower and upper case letters, leave off a back slash, or simply misspell part of the address. Navigating with bookmarks is a breeze—double click and you're there.

To navigate with the Bookmarks window:

1. Choose Bookmarks in the Window menu or Go to Bookmarks in the Bookmarks menu. The Bookmarks window appears.

2. Double click the bookmark to jump to the corresponding Web page. You may also click once on the bookmark and choose Go to Bookmark in the Item menu **(Figure 7.5)**. The page is displayed in the browser **(Figure 7.7)**.

To navigate with the Bookmarks menu:

1. Choose the desired Web page from the Bookmarks menu in the main Netscape window **(Figure 7.6)**. The page is displayed in the browser **(Figure 7.7)**.

✔ Tip

- Double click a folder to open it and see its contents or to close it and hide its contents. You can tell that a folder is open by the icon of an open folder and by the symbol to its left. A plus sign indicates a closed folder while a minus sign indicates an open folder.

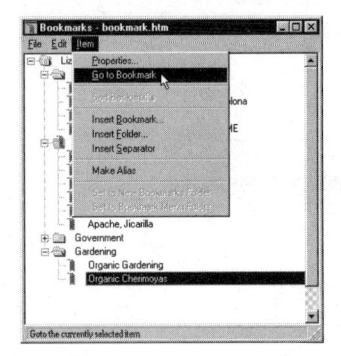

Figure 7.5 *Select a bookmark and choose Go to Bookmark or double click a bookmark to go to the corresponding page on the Web.*

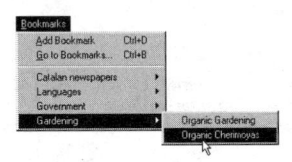

Figure 7.6 *If you don't have the Bookmarks window open, it may be faster to use the Bookmarks menu. Simply select the page desired to jump to it.*

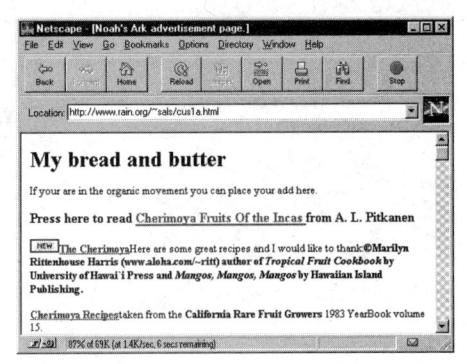

Figure 7.7 *The chosen page is displayed in the browser.*

Bookmarks

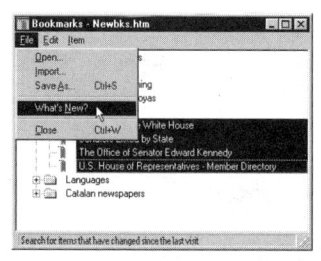

Figure 7.8 *Choose What's New? in the Bookmarks window's File menu. Here we've selected a few bookmarks to check.*

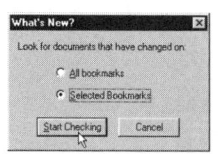

Figure 7.9 *Check All bookmarks to search the entire file or Selected Bookmarks to search the selected bookmarks. Choose Start Checking.*

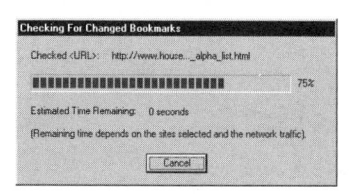

Figure 7.10 *A dialog appears in which you can watch Netscape's progress, or click Cancel if you get impatient.*

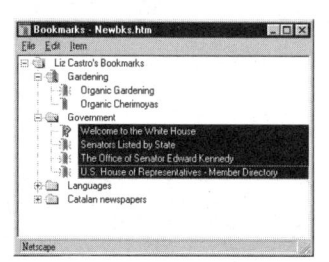

Figure 7.11 *Netscape marks changed pages with "bright" marks (all but the first bookmark in the selection). A question mark means the program can't tell if there have been changes or not (as in the* Welcome to the White House *bookmark).*

Checking what's new

Netscape can look through all your bookmarks, or through a selected group of them, and tell which pages have changed since your last visit.

To check what's new:

1. If desired, choose the bookmarks that you wish to check.

2. Choose What's New? in the Bookmarks window's File menu **(Fig. 7.8)**. The What's New? dialog box appears.

3. If you made a selection of bookmarks, click Selected Bookmarks **(Fig. 7.9)**. Otherwise, leave All Bookmarks checked. Click OK. Netscape connects to each of the pages listed in your bookmarks file to see if they've changed since your last visit.

4. A dialog box appears that charts Netscape's progress **(Figure 7.10)**. Click Cancel if you get tired of waiting. Changed bookmarks are displayed with "bright" marks **(Figure 7.11)**. Bookmarks that Netscape was unable to analyze are marked with a question mark.

✔ Tip

■ When you create a bookmark manually, Netscape marks it with a question mark, indicating that you have not visited it.

Chapter 7

Setting the New Bookmarks Folder

When you add a bookmark, it is automatically appended to the New Bookmarks Folder in the current bookmarks file. By default, Netscape sets up the principal folder to receive new bookmarks. However, you can choose any folder as the receiving folder, making it easy to add several bookmarks at a time to a particular category.

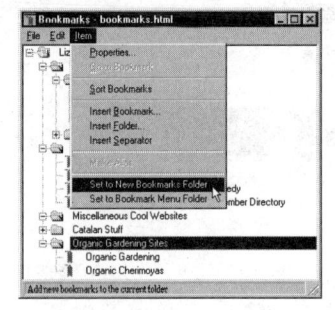

Figure 7.12 *Choose the folder that you want to add new bookmarks to and then choose Set to New Bookmarks Folder in the Item menu (in the Bookmarks window).*

To set the New Bookmarks Folder:

1. Click once on the folder to which new bookmarks should be added when you use the Add Bookmark command in the Bookmarks menu. You may choose any folder at any level in the Bookmarks window.

2. Choose Set to New Bookmarks Folder in the Item menu in the Bookmarks window **(Figure 7.12)**. The new New Bookmarks Folder is indicated by a folder with the bookmark icon inside it **(Figure 7.13)**.

Figure 7.13 *A bookmark icon appears in the folder that you have designated as the "New Bookmarks Folder".*

Bookmarks

Setting the Bookmarks Menu Folder

The Bookmarks menu is generated from the bookmarks in the Bookmarks window to give you rapid access to your bookmarks. You can choose which folder in the Bookmarks window is used to create the menu.

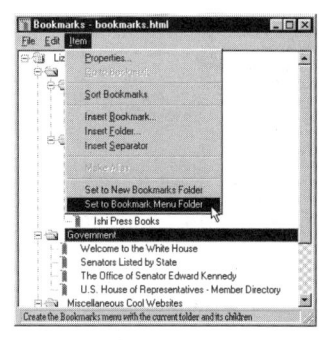

Figure 7.14 *To select the folder from which the Bookmarks menu will be generated, click the folder to select it, and then choose Set to Bookmark Menu Folder in the Item menu (in the Bookmarks window).*

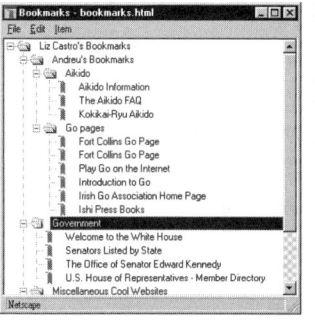

Figure 7.15 *The new "Bookmarks Menu Folder" has a menu icon on top of the folder icon.*

To set the Bookmarks Menu Folder:

1. Click once on the folder from which you want to generate the Bookmarks menu. You may choose any folder at any level of the Bookmarks window.

2. Choose Set to Bookmark Menu Folder in the Item menu in the Bookmarks window (**Figure 7.14**). A menu icon appears on top of the folder icon (**Figure 7.15**).

3. Display the Bookmarks menu to see the new configuration (**Figure 7.16**).

✔ Tip

■ OK, this isn't really a tip, just a complaint. The menu is called "Bookmarks" not "Bookmark" so why is the option called "Set to Bookmark Menu Folder"? Ask Netscape.

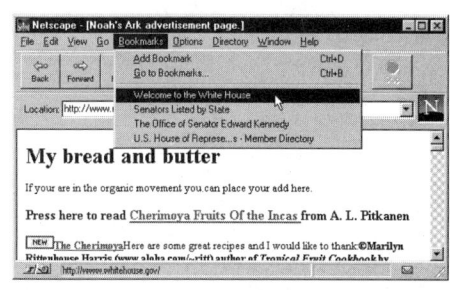

Figure 7.16 *The Bookmarks menu shows only those bookmarks that are contained in the folder that you've designated as the "Bookmarks Menu Folder".*

Chapter 7

Adding a bookmark from a Web site

The hardest part about creating a bookmark is finding a page that is worth going back to. Once you are there, adding a reference to the page is a snap.

To add a bookmark:

1. Navigate to the page whose URL you wish to save.

2. Choose Add Bookmark in the Bookmarks menu **(Figure 7.17)**. The title and URL of the Web page that you are currently browsing will be saved in a bookmark in the New Bookmarks Folder *(see page 70)* and will be automatically appended to the Bookmarks menu **(Figure 7.18)**.

✔ Tips

- You can also drag links from a page (or mail message or news posting) to the Bookmarks window.

- Right click a link and then choose Add Bookmark for this Link in the pop-up menu to add a link from a page without going to the page.

- When you add a link by dragging or choosing Add Bookmark for this Link in the pop-up menu, the URL (and not the title of the page) is used as the bookmark title. For information on changing the bookmark's title, consult *Editing a bookmark or folder* on page 76.

- When you create a bookmark, make sure it goes directly to the page you want, and not just to the site's home page.

Figure 7.17 *Once you have found a good page, simply choose Add Bookmark (Ctrl+D) from the Bookmarks menu to add the page to your bookmarks file.*

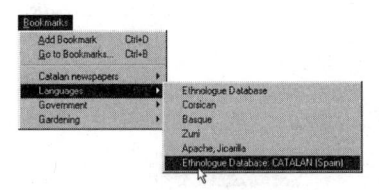

Figure 7.18 *The current page's title and URL are immediately added to the Bookmarks menu (as shown) and to the Bookmarks window.*

Figure 7.19 *Right click the link and choose Add Bookmark for this Link in the pop-up menu.*

72

Bookmarks

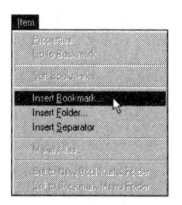

Figure 7.20 *Choose Insert Bookmark in the Item menu (in the Bookmarks window) to open the Bookmark Properties window.*

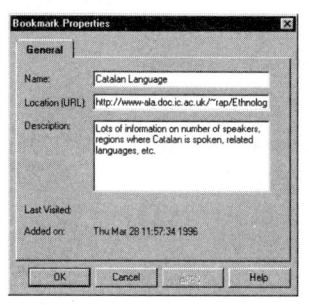

Figure 7.21 *The Bookmark Properties window contains information about the Title, URL and Location of a bookmark. You may edit a bookmark at any time by opening this window.*

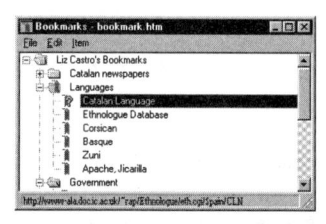

Figure 7.22 *The new bookmark appears in the Bookmarks window with a question mark next to it. The question mark means the bookmark either has not yet been visited, or may have new material.*

Adding a bookmark by hand

You don't need to connect to a page in order to add it to your bookmark file. As long as you know a page's URL—perhaps you've found a reference in a magazine—you can create a bookmark for the page manually.

Adding a bookmark by hand:

1. Open the Bookmarks window by choosing Bookmarks in the Window menu or Go to Bookmarks in the Bookmarks menu. The Bookmarks window appears.

2. Choose Insert Bookmark in the Item menu (in the Bookmarks window) **(Figure 7.20)**. The Bookmark Properties window appears **(Figure 7.21)**.

3. Type a title for the new bookmark in the Name text box. This title will appear in your Go menu and in your Bookmarks window.

4. Type (or copy) the URL for the page in the Location (URL) text box.

5. Finally, if desired, enter a short description of the page in the Description text box.

6. Click OK to add the bookmark to your bookmarks file **(Figure 7.22)**.

✔ Tips

- Type upper and lower case letters in URLs exactly as they were and beware of typos.

- You can add bookmarks manually without connecting to the Internet; thereby saving connect time and phone charges.

73

Chapter 7

Creating aliases of bookmarks

An alias is a sort of remote control. You can create aliases of your bookmarks in order to have access to your favorite sites in several locations in your bookmarks file. You use an alias exactly the same way you use a regular bookmark. The big difference is that if you change the URL or description of the original bookmark, the corresponding aliases are updated automatically.

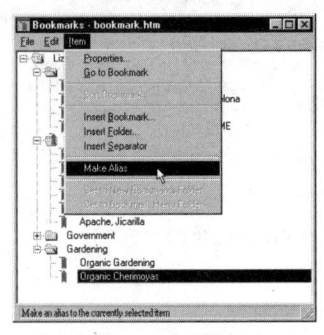

Figure 7.23 *After selecting the source bookmark, choose Make Alias in the Item menu (in the Bookmarks window).*

To create an alias:

1. Click once on the bookmark that you wish to create an alias of.

2. Choose Make Alias in the Item menu in the Bookmarks menu **(Fig. 7.23)**. The alias appears below the original bookmark **(Figure 7.24)**. If you open the Properties window of an alias, its URL is blank, since it depends on the URL of the parent bookmark.

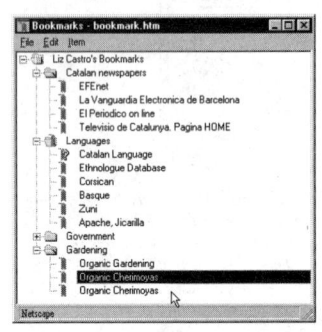

Figure 7.24 *The alias is created and placed below the selected bookmark. The alias appears identical to the original.*

3. Drag the alias to the new location **(Figure 7.25)**.

4. If desired, edit the alias to give it a new name or description. For more information, consult *Editing a bookmark or folder* on page 76.

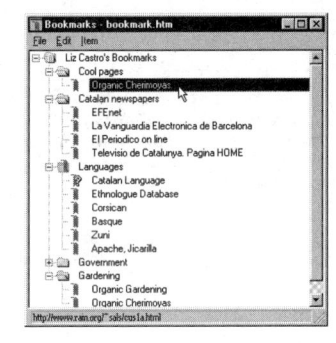

Figure 7.25 *Drag the new alias to another folder so that you can access the corresponding page from more than one place.*

✓ Tips

- You may not edit an alias' URL, since it comes directly from the bookmark. To change an alias' URL, change the URL of the *source* bookmark.

- If you change a bookmark's description, you won't see the change in the alias' Bookmark Properties window. However, if you open the bookmarks file as a Web page *(see page 81)*, the description will be updated correctly.

Bookmarks

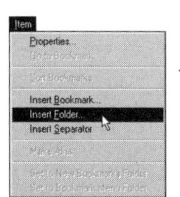

Figure 7.26 *To create a new folder for organizing your bookmarks, choose Insert Folder in the Item menu.*

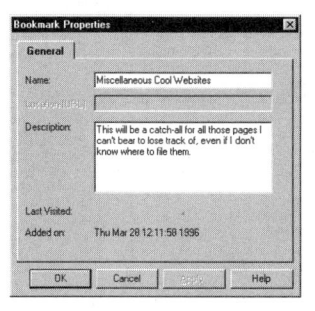

Figure 7.27 *Use the Bookmark Properties window to change the Name and Description of folders as well as bookmarks. You cannot associate a URL with a folder. (It wouldn't make sense anyway.)*

Figure 7.28 *The new folder appears directly below the folder you selected before choosing the Insert Folder command.*

Creating a bookmark folder

If you have a lot of bookmarks, sooner or later you will find that searching through your list is almost as troublesome as searching through the Web. The solution is a little organization. You can categorize your bookmarks and separate them into named folders.

To create a bookmark folder:

1. Open the Bookmarks window by choosing Bookmarks in the Window menu or Go to Bookmarks in the Bookmarks menu. The Bookmarks window appears. If you haven't created any folders yet, all the bookmarks will be in the default folder that Netscape creates for you.

2. Select the folder in which you wish to create the new folder.

3. Choose Insert Folder in the Item menu in the Bookmarks window **(Figure 7.26)**. The Bookmark Properties window appears **(Fig. 7.27)**.

4. In the Name field, type the name for your new folder.

5. In the Description field, enter a few words that define your category. This is a good way to help you remember what goes in this folder which, in turn, makes the folder more useful.

6. Click OK. The new folder appears in the Bookmarks window, below—that is, *inside*—the principal folder **(Figure 7.28)**.

7. Drag bookmarks or other folders to the new folder.

75

Chapter 7

Editing a bookmark or folder

When you add a bookmark with the Add Bookmark command, the title of the page is automatically used in the Bookmarks window to identify the bookmark. You may wish to give the bookmark a name that more clearly identifies its contents. In addition, you can change a bookmark's URL (perhaps, the creators of the page have moved it to a new server) or change its description.

To edit a bookmark:

1. Open the Bookmarks window by choosing Bookmarks in the Window menu or Go to Bookmarks in the Bookmarks menu. The Bookmarks window appears.

2. Click once on the bookmark that you wish to edit. Choose Properties in the Item menu (in the Bookmarks window) **(Figure 7.29)**. The Bookmark Properties window appears **(Figure 7.30)**.

3. Change the Name, URL and Description in the corresponding text boxes as desired **(Figure 7.31)**.

4. Click OK to save the changes. The bookmark's information is automatically updated in the Bookmarks window.

✔ Tip

- To delete a bookmark or folder (or separator) that you don't use anymore, select it and choose Delete in the Edit menu **(Figure 7.32)** or press Delete (not Backspace).

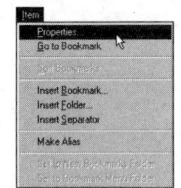

Figure 7.29 *Choose the Properties command in the Item menu to display the Bookmark Properties window.*

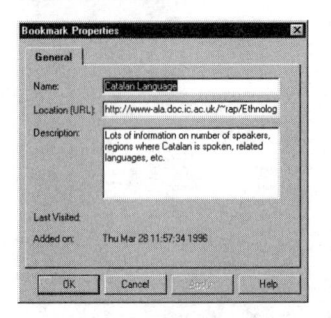

Figure 7.30 *In the Bookmark Properties window, you may change the Title to better identify the page's contents, update a page's URL, or add a description for the page.*

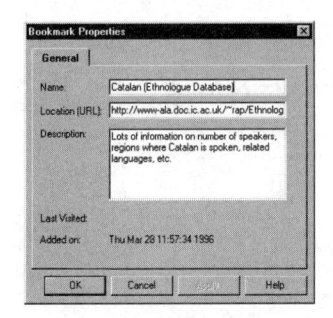

Figure 7.31 *Once you click OK to save the changes, the new data is automatically updated in the Bookmarks window and Bookmarks menu.*

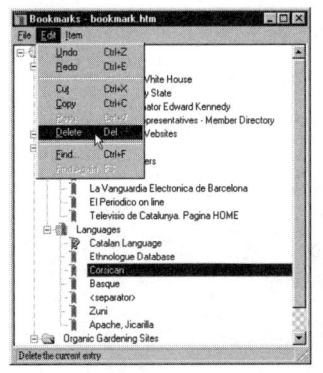

Figure 7.32 *To delete a bookmark, select it and then choose Delete from the Edit menu (in the Bookmarks window). You can also select the bookmark and then press the Delete key.*

Bookmarks

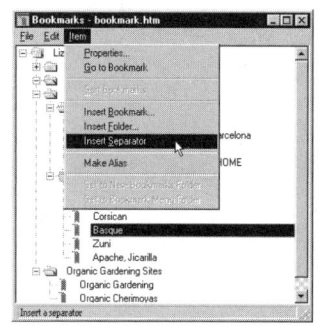

Figure 7.33 *To add a separator, first select the bookmark or folder below which you wish to insert the separator.*

Figure 7.34 *The separator appears below the currently selected item. You may insert separators at any level of the Bookmarks hierarchy.*

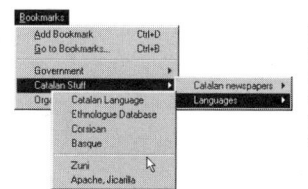

Figure 7.35 *Choose Insert Separator in the Item menu in the Bookmarks window.*

Adding a separator

If you have several folders, it may be helpful to have a visual clue that separates them. Since the Bookmarks menu is generated from your Bookmarks window, the separators that you include in the window will also appear in the menu.

To add a separator to your bookmarks window:

1. Click once on the folder or bookmark directly above the place where you wish to insert a separator.

2. Choose Insert Separator in the Item menu in the Bookmarks window **(Figure 7.33)**. A bookmark icon appears in the desired location with the word <*separator*> to its right **(Figure 7.34)**.

3. Click on the Bookmarks menu to see your new separator **(Figure 7.34)**.

✔ **Tip**

■ You are not limited to adding separators only between folders. You can insert a separator between any two objects in the Bookmarks window, regardless of their levels.

Chapter 7

Sorting your bookmarks file

If you have more than five or six bookmarks in a folder, or more than five or six folders in your bookmarks file, you may wish to alphabetize the items to make them easier to find.

To sort your bookmarks:

Choose Sort Bookmarks in the Item menu **(Figure 7.36)**. All of the folders and bookmarks will be sorted alphabetically **(Figure 7.37)**. Separators are placed at the top of the list.

✓ Tip

■ You can undo a sort; simply choose Undo in the Edit menu. (Be sure you choose the Undo command in the *Bookmarks window's* Edit menu and not the browser's Edit menu.)

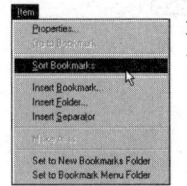

Figure 7.36 *Choose Sort Bookmarks in the Item menu (in the Bookmarks window).*

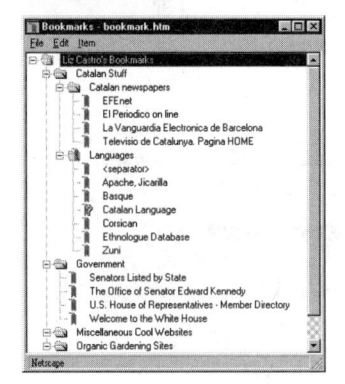

Figure 7.37 *The bookmarks are sorted alphabetically, in descending order.*

Bookmarks

Saving a bookmarks file

You can save a bookmarks file to give to friends, or simply to make a back-up copy. In fact, a bookmarks file is nothing more than an HTML page that you can browse as you would any other local file.

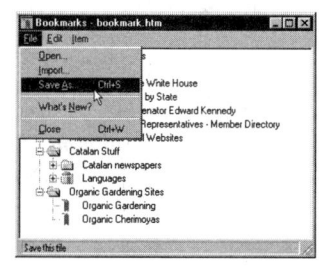

Figure 7.38 *To save a bookmarks file, perhaps to share it with friends or as a backup, choose Save As in the File menu in the Bookmarks window.*

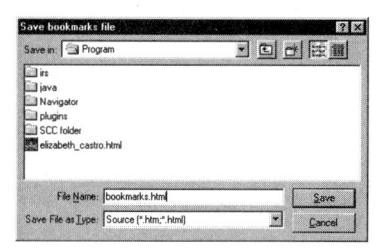

Figure 7.39 *In the Save bookmarks file dialog box, type the name for the new bookmarks file, and choose Source (*.htm) in the Save Files as Type pop-up menu. Then, click Save.*

To save a bookmark file:

1. Choose Save As in the File menu in the Bookmarks window **(Figure 7.38)**. A standard Save As dialog box appears **(Figure 7.39)**.

2. Give the file a name and choose the folder directory in which to save it.

3. Choose a file type for the bookmarks file. If you want to open the file with Netscape, choose Source (*.htm). To open the file in a word processor or text editor, choose Plain Text (*.txt).

4. Click OK to save the file.

✔ Tips

- If you tack on the extension .htm to the end of your bookmark file's name, you'll be able to open the file as a regular Web page *(see page 81)*.

- For example, if you save your bookmarks file with the proper extension (.htm), you'll be able to designate it as your home page. This way, each time you open Netscape, you will have your favorite sites just a click away. Fore more information, consult *Choosing a home page* on page 14.

Chapter 7

Opening a different bookmarks file

Although your bookmarks file is hidden from view when you close the Bookmarks window, it is not gone. Simply open the window again to see the bookmarks file again. If, however, you wish to open a *different* bookmarks file, you must follow these steps.

To open a different bookmarks file:

1. Open the Bookmarks window by choosing Bookmarks in the Window menu or Go to Bookmarks in the Bookmarks menu.

2. Choose Open in the File menu of the Bookmarks window **(Figure 7.40)**. A standard open dialog box appears **(Figure 7.41)**.

3. Navigate to the bookmarks file that you wish to open, and double click it to open it. The new bookmarks file will replace the current one in the Bookmarks window **(Figure 7.42)**. The old bookmarks file will remain intact in its former location.

✔ Tip

■ Saving and opening multiple bookmarks files is an ideal way to share hot site addresses. Since the bookmarks file is nothing more than a simple HTML file, you may also open it directly with Netscape—on PCs, Macs or even Unix machines—no matter what kind of computer the bookmark file comes from. *(See "Opening a bookmarks file as a Web page" on page 81.)*

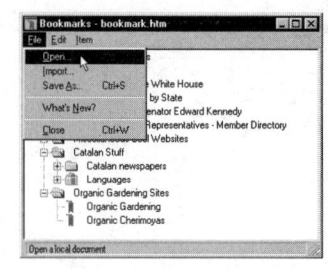

Figure 7.40 *To open a different bookmarks file, choose Open in the File menu in the Bookmarks window.*

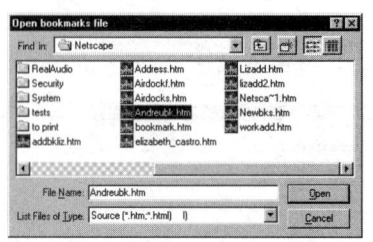

Figure 7.41 *In the standard Open dialog box that appears, choose the bookmarks file that you want to open.*

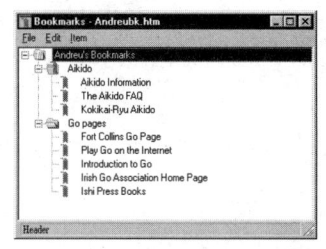

Figure 7.42 *The bookmarks in the new bookmarks file that you've just opened replace the ones from the old bookmarks file. The old bookmarks file remains intact on your disk.*

Bookmarks

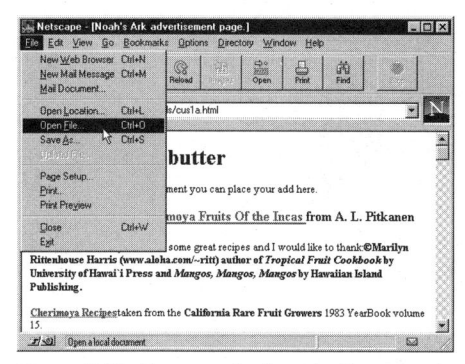

Figure 7.43 *To open a bookmarks file as a Web page, choose Open File in the File menu in the main Netscape window.*

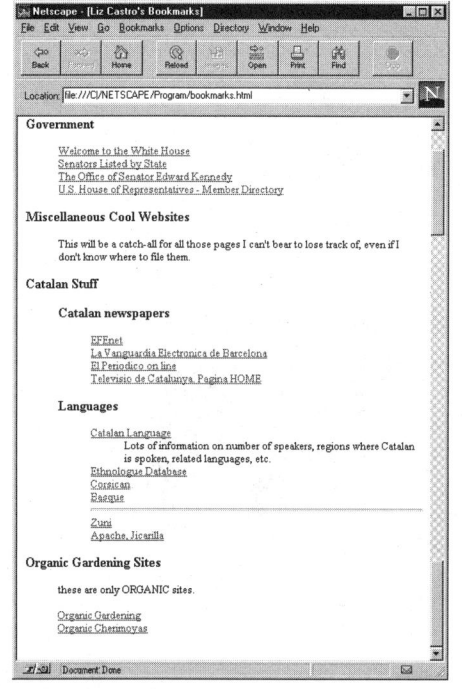

Figure 7.44 *The bookmarks file, complete with links to your saved sites, appears as a regular Web page.*

Opening a bookmarks file as a Web page

An easy way to see a bookmarks file without changing your regular bookmarks file is to open it as a Web page. Since the bookmarks file is in HTML format, like any other Web page, Netscape knows how to interpret it correctly, displaying folders in a large font, and making your bookmarks into links—automatically.

To open a bookmarks file as a Web page:

1. Save your bookmarks file, making sure to choose Source (*.htm) in the List Files of Type pop-up menu. For more information, consult *Saving a bookmarks file* on page 79.

2. Choose Open File in the File menu in the main Netscape window **(Figure 7.43)**.

3. Choose the desired file and click Open. The bookmarks file is loaded into Netscape just like any other Web page **(Figure 7.44)**.

✓ Tip

■ You can also designate a bookmarks file as a home page so that Netscape displays it automatically every time you launch the program. For more information, consult *Choosing a home page* on page 14.

81

Chapter 7

Importing bookmarks

If you wish, you may *add* the bookmarks in a bookmarks file to your current bookmarks file, instead of replacing the existing bookmarks.

To import bookmarks:

1. Open the Bookmarks windows by choosing Bookmarks in the Window menu or Go to Bookmarks in the Bookmarks menu. The Bookmarks window appears.

2. Choose Import in the File menu in the Bookmarks window **(Figure 7.45)**. The Import dialog box appears.

3. Choose the bookmarks file that you wish to import **(Fig. 7.46)** and click Open. The bookmarks in the imported file are added to the current Bookmarks window **(Figure 7.47)**.

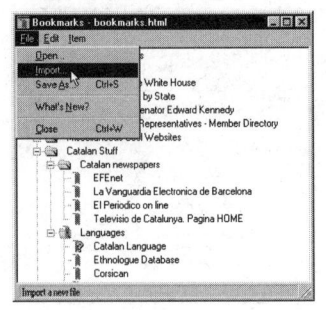

Figure 7.45 *To add bookmarks from another bookmark file to your current bookmark file, choose Import in the Bookmark window's File menu.*

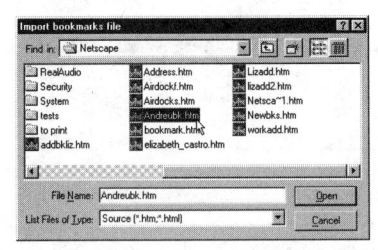

Figure 7.46 *In the Import dialog box that appears, choose the bookmarks file that you wish to import.*

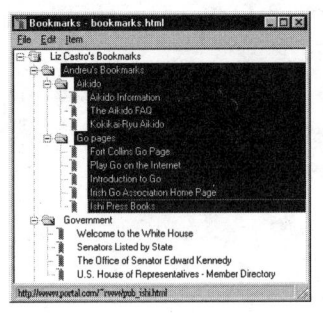

Figure 7.47 *The new bookmarks are added below the main folder in the current bookmarks file.*

The Mail Window

The Mail window is Netscape's central filing area for all incoming and outgoing correspondence. From the Mail window, you can get, read and send new mail, respond to mail, delete mail and file mail.

Not all mail is equal. The Mail window lets you flag important letters and marks all mail as read or unread, letting you choose to list all mail, or only that correspondence which you have not yet read.

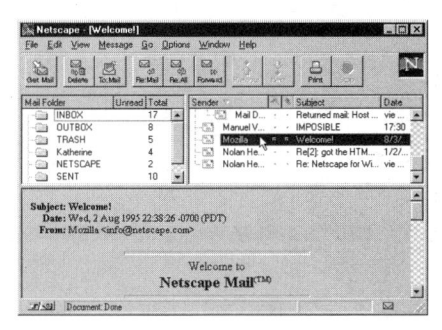

Figure 8.1 *You can change the size of each of the three panes in the Mail window, making them taller or shorter, or wider or narrower, according to the particular task at hand.*

The Mail window's filing system is fairly advanced, allowing you to create new folders for organizing incoming and outgoing correspondence, and to throw away those letters you no longer need.

Before you use the Mail or News windows, fill out the Server *(see page 236)* and Idenity information *(see page 237)*.

The parts of the Mail window

The Mail window is divided into three areas, or panes **(Figure 8.1)**. The top left pane contains the folders in which your mail is organized. New mail is automatically filed in the Inbox folder. Outgoing mail that has not yet been sent is filed in the Outbox folder.

When you click in one of the mail folders, a list of the messages contained in the folder appears in the top right pane of the Mail window. Each letter is identified by its Subject, Sender, Date, and whether it has been marked or read.

Once you click in one of the e-mail messages, the contents of the letter appears in the bottom pane.

Chapter 8

Opening the Mail window

The Mail window, together with the Browser and News windows, forms one leg of the Netscape triumvirate. You can have each type of window open at once, but to work with mail, the Mail window must be open and active.

To open the Mail window:

1. Choose Netscape Mail in the Window menu **(Figure 8.2)**. Netscape automatically checks your mail.

2. If the password dialog box appears, enter your password and click OK **(Figure 8.3)**. The Mail window appears **(Figure 8.4)**.

✔ Tip

■ You can also click the letter icon in the bottom right corner of all Netscape's windows to open the Mail window.

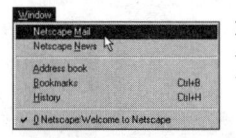

Figure 8.2 *To open the Mail window, choose Netscape Mail in the Window menu.*

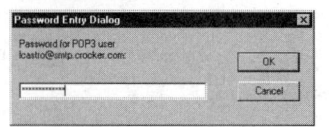

Figure 8.3 *If the Password Entry Dialog box appears, enter your password and click OK.*

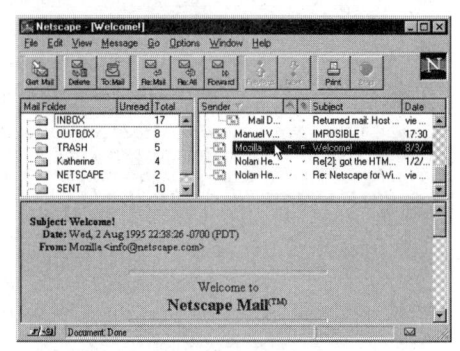

Figure 8.4 *The Mail window has three panes. The top left pane shows the folders, the top right pane shows the letters in each folder and the bottom pane shows the contents of each letter.*

Saving your mail password

You can save your mail password so that Netscape doesn't ask for it each time you open the Mail window.

To save your Mail password:

1. Choose Mail and News Preferences in the Options menu **(Figure 8.5)**.

2. Click the Organization tab. The Organization preferences appear.

3. Click Remember Mail Password in the General section **(Figure 8.6)**.

4. Click OK.

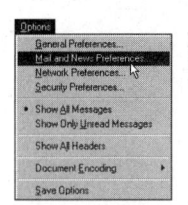

Figure 8.5 *Choose Mail and News Preferences in the Options menu.*

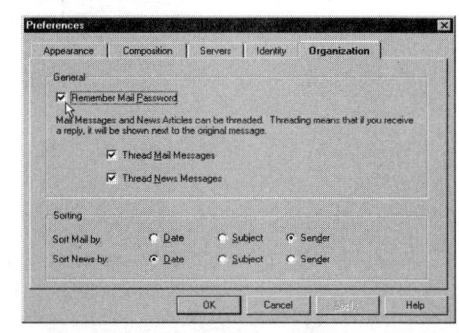

Figure 8.6 *Click the Organization tab and then click Remember Mail Password.*

The Mail Window

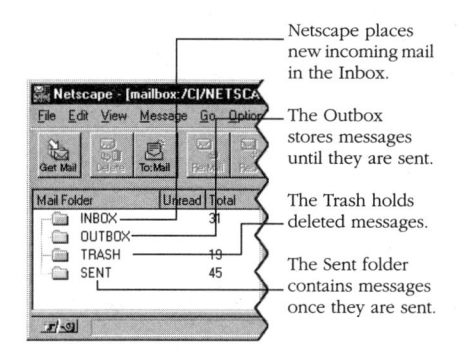

Figure 8.7 *The Mail window contains four folders by default. You may add others as desired.*

- Netscape places new incoming mail in the Inbox.
- The Outbox stores messages until they are sent.
- The Trash holds deleted messages.
- The Sent folder contains messages once they are sent.

The Mail window's four default folders

Netscape creates four default folders for filing mail: the Inbox, the Outbox, the Trash and the Sent folders **(Figure 8.7)**.

Netscape stores the new, incoming mail in the Inbox. Once you've read them, you can move them to a more specific folder *(see page 90)*. Or if you're lazy like me, you can just leave them there.

The Outbox holds mail that you've written but haven't yet sent. For example, you can write several messages without being connected to your Internet server and then send them all at once *(see page 108)*. If you change your mind about sending a message, simply move it from the Outbox folder.

Once you've actually sent a message, Netscape transfers it to the Sent folder. You can choose to file sent messages in another folder, or just leave them there.

Finally, the Trash folder holds mail that you've deleted. For more information on deleting files, consult *Deleting messages and folders* on page 91. You can retrieve messages from the Trash (it doesn't even smell bad) until you decide to empty it. Once you've emptied the trash *(see page 92)*, the messages are truly gone.

85

Chapter 8

Creating new folders

In addition to Netscape's default folders *(see page 85)*, you can create as many of your own as your hard disk space will allow. Folders are helpful for organizing your mail once you've received or sent it.

To create a new folder:

1. In the Mail window's File menu, choose New Folder **(Figure 8.8)**.

2. Enter a name for the folder in the dialog box that appears and click OK **(Figure 8.9)**. The new folder appears in the left pane of the Mail window **(Figure 8.10)**.

✔ Tips

- You can't create a folder inside another folder.

- It's a little tricky to change a folder's name once it's created. The easiest way is to create a new folder with the correct name and drag any messages to the new folder. The hard way is by finding the desired mail folder file (usually in the Mail folder inside the Netscape folder on your hard disk) and changing the name of both it and the corresponding .snm file.

- The Add Folder command is not for adding new folders, but rather for importing the contents of one folder into another.

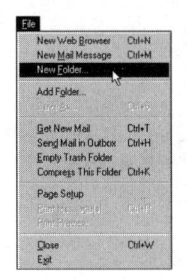

Figure 8.8 *Choose New Folder in the Mail window's File menu.*

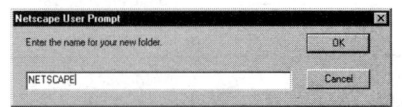

Figure 8.9 *In the dialog box, type the name for the new folder and click OK.*

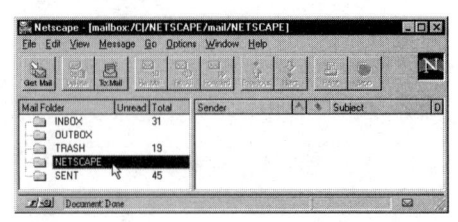

Figure 8.10 *The new folder appears in the upper left pane of the Mail window.*

The Mail Window

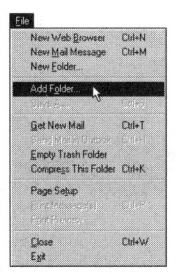

Figure 8.11 *Choose Add Folder in the Mail window's File menu.*

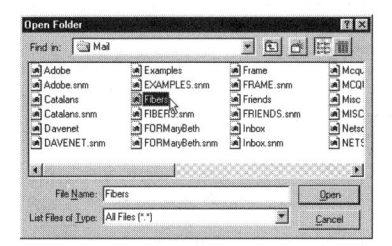

Figure 8.12 *Choose a mail folder file in the Open dialog box and click Open.*

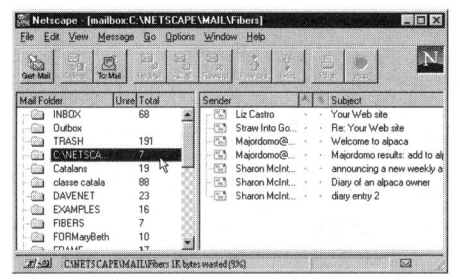

Figure 8.13 *The new mail folder appears in the left pane of the Mail window.*

Importing messages from another folder

Netscape stores all the messages in each folder in a single file. You can copy these mail folder files between computers and then open them to access the messages they contain. You can also open the mail folder files in your own Mail window to copy the messages into a new folder, but I'm not quite sure why you'd want to.

To import messages from another folder:

1. Choose Add Folder in the Mail window's File menu. The Open dialog box appears.

2. Find and select the mail folder file that you wish to import and click Open. The folder file is imported in the left pane of the Mail window.

3. Click the folder file to see the messages it contains.

✔ Tips

- Generally, mail folder files are stored in the Mail folder inside the Netscape folder. You will probably have to choose All Files in the Files of Type submenu to see them. Don't use the files that end in .snm, but rather the ones with no extension.

- The name of the new folder in the Mail window is the path to the selected mail folder file. To change the folder name, see the tip on the previous page.

Chapter 8

Selecting messages

There are several ways to select messages that make it easier to file, read or delete a particular group of messages.

To select more than one message:

Hold down Shift and click to add one or more messages that are next to the currently selected message **(Figure 8.14)**. Hold down Ctrl and click to add one or more messages that are not next to the currently selected one **(Figure 8.15)**.

You can also select all the flagged messages in a folder, perhaps prior to moving them to another folder en masse. For more information about flags, consult *Flagging messages* on page 94.

To select the flagged messages:

1. Select the desired folder.

2. Choose Select Flagged Messages in the Edit menu **(Figure 8.16)**. All the flagged messages in the currently selected folder are selected **(Figure 8.17)**.

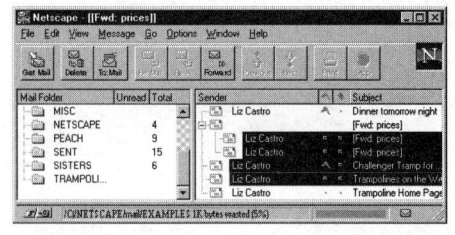

Figure 8.14 *Hold down Shift and click to select several messages in a row.*

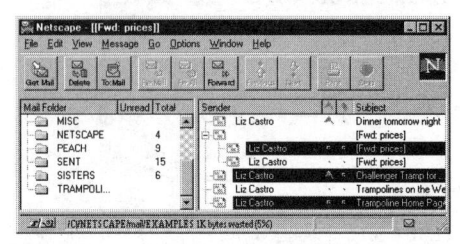

Figure 8.15 *Hold down Ctrl and click to select several messages that are not one after the other.*

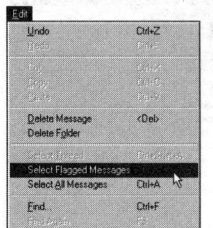

Figure 8.16 *Select a folder and then choose Select Flagged Messages in the Edit menu to select all the flagged messages in the folder.*

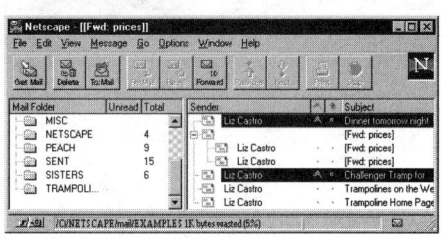

Figure 8.17 *All of the flagged messages are selected.*

88

The Mail Window

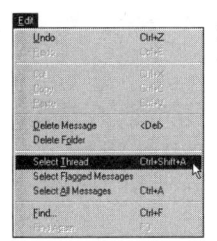

Figure 8.18 *Select a message and then choose Select Thread in the Edit menu to select all the related messages.*

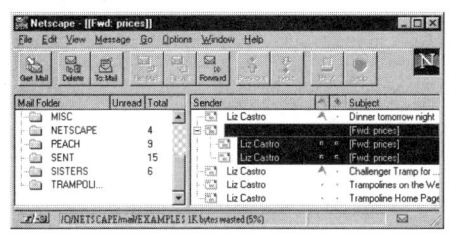

Figure 8.19 *All the messages related to the original message, that is, in the message's thread, are selected.*

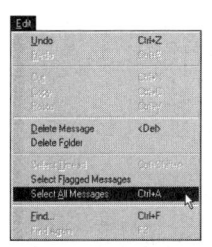

Figure 8.20 *Select a folder and then choose Select All Messages in the Edit menu to select every message in the folder.*

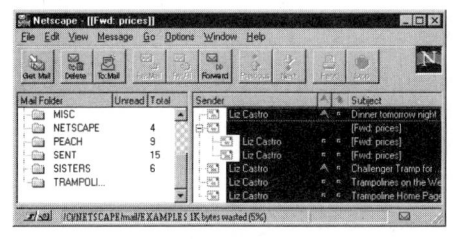

Figure 8.21 *All the messages in the folder are selected.*

You can also select all the messages in a thread (in a folder), in order to move, copy or delete them at once. For more information about threads, consult *Threading messages* on page 96.

To select a thread:

1. Select the folder that contains the thread.

2. Choose Select Thread in the Edit menu **(Figure 8.18)**. Each message that belongs to the thread is selected **(Figure 8.19)**.

Finally, you can select all the messages in a folder.

To select all the messages in a folder:

1. Select the desired folder.

2. Choose Select All Messages (Ctrl+A) in the Edit menu **(Figure 8.20)**. All the messages in the chosen folder are selected **(Figure 8.21)**.

✔ **Tips**

- You can't select messages in more than one folder at a time.

- Once you've selected a group of messages, you can move or copy them to another folder, or delete them. For more information on moving and copying messages, consult *Moving and copying messages* on page 90. For more information on deleting messages, consult *Deleting messages and folders* on page 91.

89

Chapter 8

Moving and copying messages

Generally, in order to keep things organized, you move messages from Netscape's default folders (e.g., the Inbox and Sent folders) to the folders you have created. *Copying* moves the message to the new folder and leaves a copy in the old one.

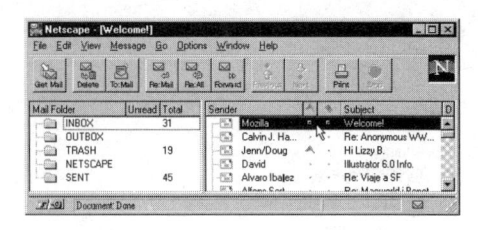

Figure 8.22 *Select the desired message.*

To move messages to a different folder:

1. Select the message(s) **(Figure 8.22)**.

2. Choose the desired destination folder under Move in the Message menu **(Fig. 8.23)**. The message disappears from the current folder and is transferred to the selected one **(Fig. 8.24)**.

Figure 8.23 *Choose the destination folder in the Move submenu in the Message menu.*

To copy messages to a different folder:

1. Select the message(s) **(Figure 8.22)**.

2. Choose the desired destination folder under Copy in the Message menu **(Figure 8.25)**. The message remains in the current folder and is also copied to the selected one **(Fig. 8.26)**.

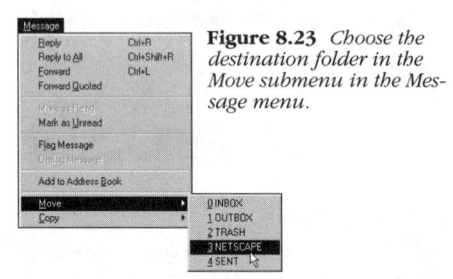

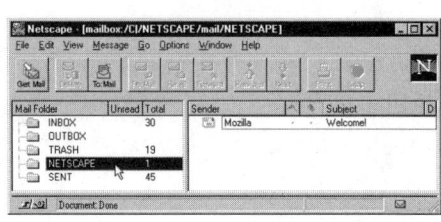

Figure 8.24 *The message is removed from its earlier location (the Inbox now has only 30 messages) and placed in the desired folder.*

✓ Tips

- You can also drag messages from one folder to another. Hold down Ctrl while you drag to copy.

- Use the special selecting commands *(see page 88)* to select more than one message before moving or copying.

- You cannot move or copy messages to the Outbox folder. The only way to place messages there is by sending them with Deferred Delivery selected. For details, consult *Composing messages offline* on page 108.

Figure 8.25 *Choose the desired folder in the Copy submenu in the Message menu.*

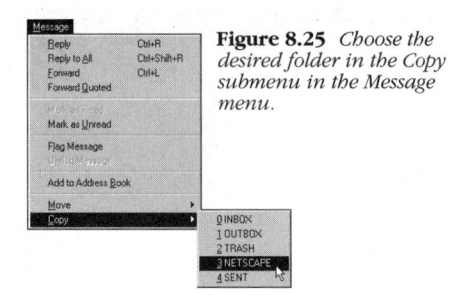

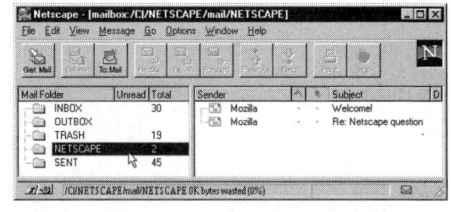

Figure 8.26 *The message remains in the previous location (the Inbox still has 30 messages), and is copied to the selected folder (which now has 2).*

90

The Mail Window

Deleting messages and folders

Once you no longer need a message, you can delete it in order to conserve space on your hard disk and keep your Mail window reasonably neat.

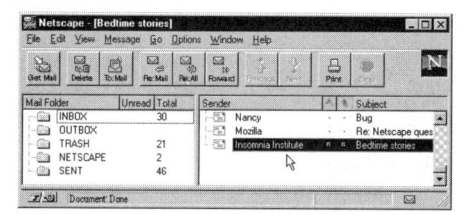

Figure 8.27 *Choose the message you wish to delete.*

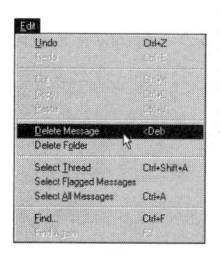

Figure 8.28 *Choose Delete Message in the Edit menu (or press the Delete key).*

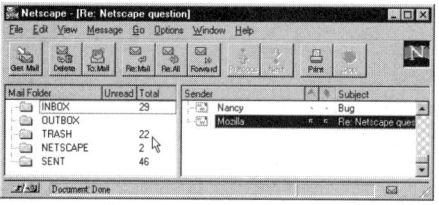

Figure 8.29 *The message disappears from the current folder and is placed in the Trash.*

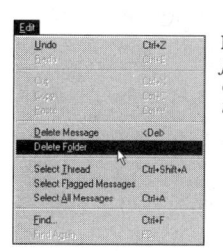

Figure 8.30 *To delete a folder, select it and then choose Delete Folder in the Edit menu.*

To delete a message:

1. Select the desired message(s) **(Figure 8.27)**.

2. Choose Delete Message from the Edit menu or press Delete—not Backspace **(Figure 8.28)**. No alert box will appear to confirm the deletion. The message simply disappears from the current folder and is moved to the Trash folder **(Figure 8.29)**.

You can only delete a folder after you've deleted all the messages it contains.

To delete a folder:

1. Select the desired folder.

2. Choose Delete Folder in the Edit menu or press Delete—not Backspace **(Figure 8.30)**. No alert box will appear to confirm the deletion. The folder simply disappears forever.

✔ Tips

- To recover a message you've deleted, simply drag it out of the Trash folder.

- You can also drag a message to the Trash folder to delete it.

- Press Ctrl+Z immediately after deleting one or more messages or a folder to restore the items to their previous location.

91

Chapter 8

Conserving disk space

When you delete a message, it is not permanently deleted, but instead is placed in the Trash folder. You can retrieve an item from the Trash folder at any time before emptying it *(see page 90)*. Empty the trash to permanently remove the messages it contains.

To empty the Trash folder:

Choose Empty Trash Folder in the File menu **(Fig. 8.31)**. No alert box appears, nor will the Undo command make your messages come back. The Trash folder simply appears empty **(Figure 8.32)**.

Another way to reduce the amount of space taken up by your folders and messages is by compressing your folders.

To compress a folder:

1. Select the folder you wish to compress **(Figure 8.33)**.

2. Choose Compress this Folder in the File menu **(Figure 8.34)**. The folder is compressed **(Figure 8.35)**.

✔ Tips

- The amount of space you can recover by compressing a folder is shown in the status area of the Mail window when the folder is selected.

- Emptying the trash automatically compresses all the folders.

- Compressing a folder does not affect any of the messages it contains. It simply recovers wasted space that is generated when you move messages from one folder to another.

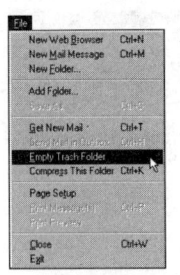

Figure 8.31 *To permanently remove the deleted messages, choose Empty Trash Folder in the File menu.*

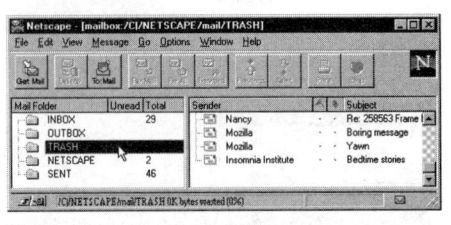

Figure 8.32 *The Trash folder is empty.*

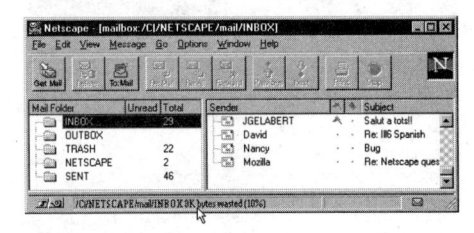

Figure 8.33 *Select a folder. The amount of data wasted is shown in the status area at the bottom of the window.*

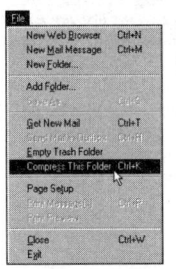

Figure 8.34 *Choose Compress This Folder in the File menu.*

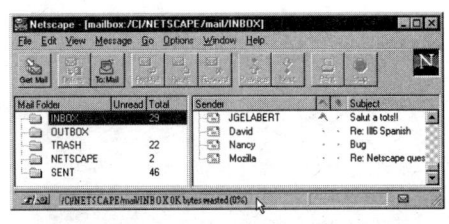

Figure 8.35 *The status area indicates that the compressed folder no longer wastes disk space.*

The Mail Window

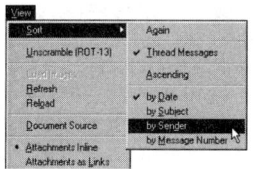

Figure 8.36 *Choose By Sender under Sort in the View menu to put the messages in order by sender.*

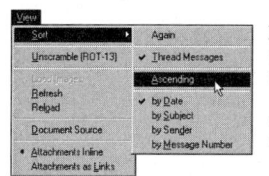

Figure 8.37 *Choose Ascending under Sort in the View menu to choose the direction in which to sort.*

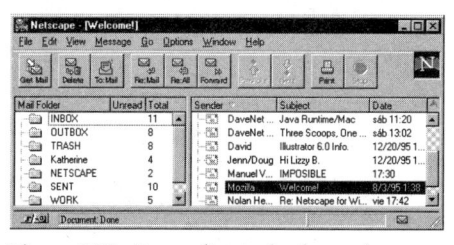

Figure 8.38 *Descending order, by sender.*

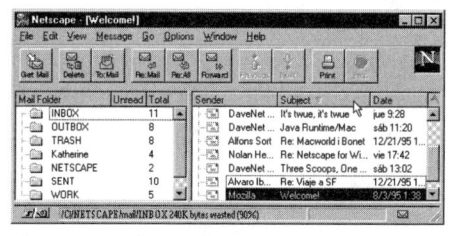

Figure 8.39 *Descending order, by Subject. Notice that "Re:" is ignored.*

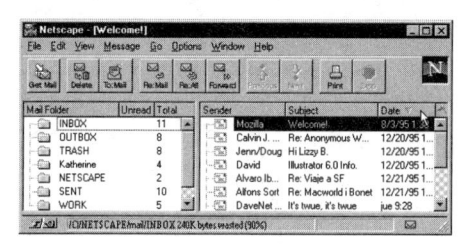

Figure 8.40 *Descending order, by date.*

Putting your messages in order

You can view your messages in order of Sender, Subject or Date, or even by Message Number. They may be sorted in ascending or descending order, although the latter is the default option. Mail folders (and newsgroups) are always displayed in alphabetical order.

To put your messages in order:

1. Select By Date, By Subject, By Sender or By Message Number under Sort in the Mail window's View menu **(Figure 8.36)**. The messages are sorted according to the criteria chosen.

2. Toggle the Ascending option under Sort in the View menu to list the letters in ascending (when the option is checked) or descending order **(Figure 8.37)**.

✔ **Tip**

■ You can also click the column heading (Sender, Subject, or Date) to sort your messages by the contents of that column **(Figure 8.38, Figure 8.39, and Figure 8.40)**. To sort by Message number, you have to use the menu.

93

Chapter 8

Flagging messages

In a busy mailbox, it's sometimes hard to keep your eye on an important piece of mail. One easy way to make a message stand out is to mark or flag it.

To flag or unflag a message:

1. Select the desired message in the right pane of the Mail window **(Figure 8.41)**.

2. Choose Flag Message in the Message window **(Figure 8.42)**. A checkmark next to the command indicates that the message is flagged. Choose the command again to toggle it. A little red flag appears in the Flagged column next to the flagged message **(Figure 8.43)**. The flag disappears when you unflag the message.

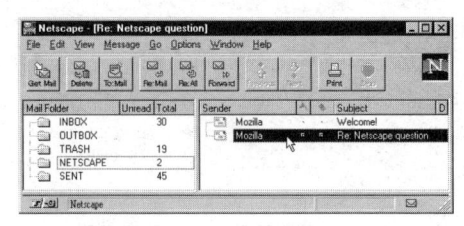

Figure 8.41 *Select the message you wish to flag.*

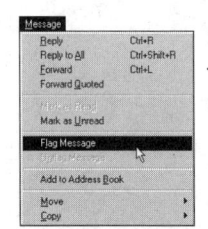

Figure 8.42 *The new folder appears in the upper left pane of the Mail window.*

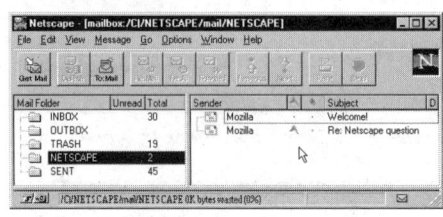

Figure 8.43 *A little red flag appears next to the message.*

✔ Tips

- You can flag a message (or remove its flag) by clicking in the Flagged column next to the desired message.

- You can navigate through only the flagged messages using the First Flagged, Next Flagged, and Previous Flagged commands in the Go menu. For more information on getting from message to message, consult *Navigating through your messages* on page 104.

94

The Mail Window

Marking mail as read or unread

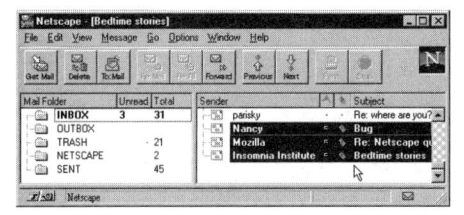

Figure 8.44 *Choose the unread messages that you wish to mark as read.*

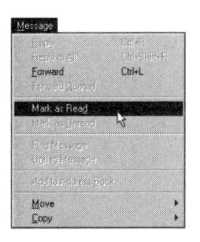

Figure 8.45 *Choose Mark as Read in the Message menu.*

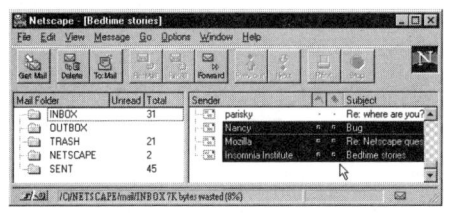

Figure 8.46 *The newly "read" messages appear in plain text and the green diamonds disappear.*

When you receive new mail, Netscape marks it with a green diamond so that you know that it's new. Once you've read a message, the mark disappears. You can choose to restore the Unread mark to remind yourself to return to that message at a later date. You can also mark mail as read, even if you haven't read it—perhaps because you can tell from the Subject line that the message is not of interest to you.

To mark mail as read or unread:

1. Select the desired messages in the Mail window's right pane **(Fig. 8.44)**.

2. In the Message menu, choose Mark as Unread or Mark as Read **(Fig. 8.45)**. A green diamond appears next to messages that are unread and disappears for messages that you've read or marked as read **(Figure 8.46)**.

✔ Tips

- You can also mark a message as read or unread by clicking in the Read column (the one with the green diamond) next to the desired message.

- You can navigate through the unread messages using the First Unread, Next Unread, and Previous Unread commands in the Go menu. For more information about navigating, consult *Navigating through your messages* on page 104.

- You can mark a single message as read without opening it (which automatically marks it as read). The trick is to click right on the diamond, not on the title of the message.

95

Chapter 8

Threading messages

Netscape can relate all the replies (and replies to replies) that are generated from a single original message into a wonderful invention called a *thread*. This makes it easy to follow a particular conversation from start to finish even if you have a busy mailbox. You can choose to view your e-mail in threads, or as individual messages.

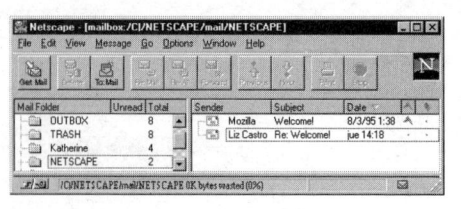

Figure 8.47 *Unthreaded messages appear independently in the Mail window's right pane.*

To thread messages:

1. Choose Thread Messages under Sort in the Mail window's View menu **(Figure 8.48)**. The option will have a check next to it when it is active. Choose the option again to toggle it. Each message that is related to another will appear underneath the parent message, connected by a dotted, hierarchical line **(Figure 8.49)**.

2. Click the minus sign next to a threaded message group to hide the replies beneath it. Click a plus sign next to a threaded message group to reveal the replies beneath it **(Figure 8.50)**.

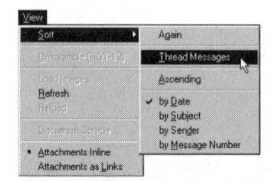

Figure 8.48 *Choose Thread Messages under Sort in the View menu to relate messages with similar subjects.*

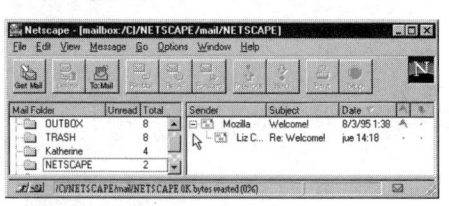

Figure 8.49 *Threaded messages appear in hierarchical form with the original message at the top and replies below and to the right.*

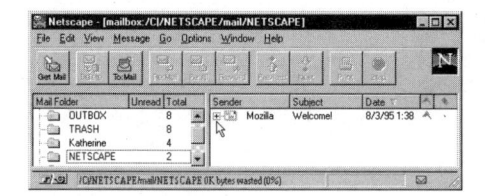

Figure 8.50 *Click the minus sign to the left of the original message's letter icon to hide the replies. Click it again (it will have turned into a plus sign as shown above) to show the replies.*

The Mail Window

Changing the size of the panes

You can change the size of each of the three panes, according to the task at hand. For example, if you're filing mail, you'll want the two upper panes as large as possible **(Figure 8.53)**. On the other hand, if you're reading a series of messages, it will be better to make the lower pane as large as possible **(Figure 8.54)**.

To change the size of the panes:

1. Place the pointer over one of the separators between the panes. The cursor changes into a double-headed arrow **(Figure 8.51)**.

2. Click with the mouse and drag to make the panes larger or smaller **(Figure 8.52, Figure 8.53, and Figure 8.54)**.

✔ Tips

- You can resize the entire window by dragging in the usual way.

- If you make the panes so short that not all the contents can be seen at once, scroll bars will appear to let you get to the hidden items. This does not happen if you make a pane too narrow; in that case, the hidden material stays out of sight.

- When you change the width of the panes, either by moving the pane separator as described above or by changing the window size, the width of the *columns* is not affected. For more information, consult *Changing the columns* on page 98.

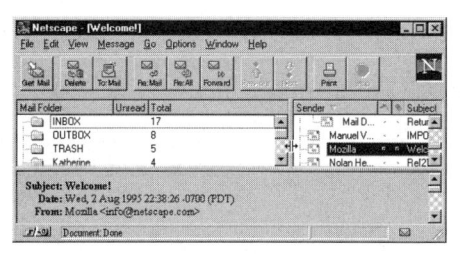

Figure 8.51 *To reduce the amount of wasted space in the left pane, place the pointer on the pane's border, click and drag to resize.*

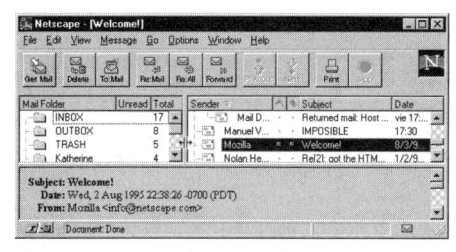

Figure 8.52 *Now there is more room in the right pane to display more information.*

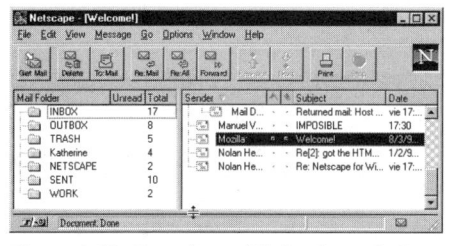

Figure 8.53 *Drag the middle border to the bottom to hide the contents of messages (and have more room for folder and message titles).*

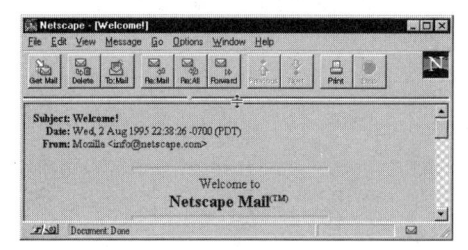

Figure 8.54 *Drag the middle border to the top to hide the folders and message titles and thus have more space for the message itself.*

97

Chapter 8

Changing the columns

There is a lot of information jammed into eight columns between two panes in the Mail (and News) window. You can adjust the width or order of the columns to suit your particular task.

To change the column width:

1. Place the cursor on the left border of the column's title **(Figure 8.55)**.

2. Drag to adjust the size of the column **(Figure 8.56)**.

You may find it easier to organize your messages if the columns are arranged in a special order. For example, you could put the Marked and Read columns to the left of the Sender column.

To change the column order:

Click in the desired column's title and drag it to the new position **(Figure 8.57)**. The other columns are adjusted accordingly.

✔ Tip

■ If you aren't interested in a particular column's data, drag it to the rightmost position in the pane. Then, either make the other columns larger or the pane or window smaller so that the undesired columns are hidden from view.

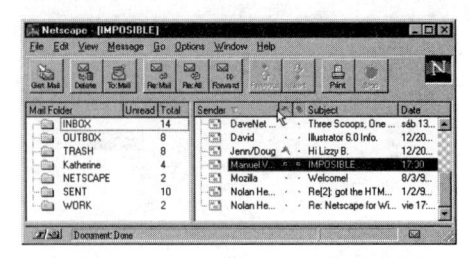

Figure 8.55 *Some of the Senders' names are cut off. To make the Sender column wider, click the right border of the column and drag to resize.*

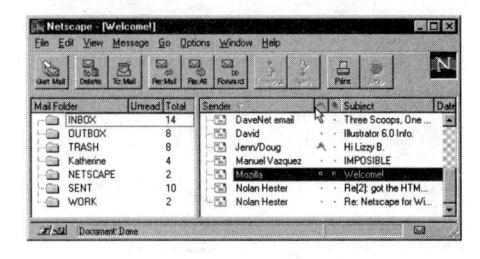

Figure 8.56 *Once the column is wider, the Senders' complete names can be seen.*

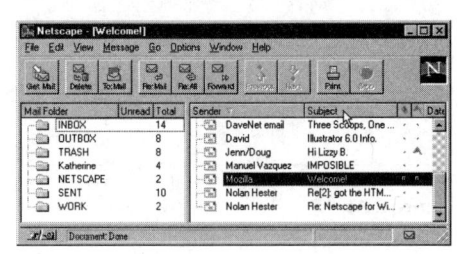

Figure 8.57 *To move the Subject column next to the Sender column, simply click the Subject header and drag to the right of the Sender header.*

The Mail Window

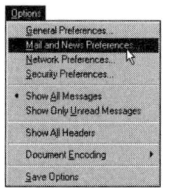

Figure 8.58 *Choose Mail and News Preferences in the Options menu.*

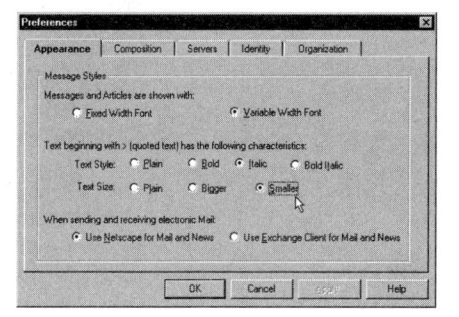

Figure 8.59 *Click the Appearance tab at the top left corner of the window to show the Appearances preferences. Then choose the desired font type and style.*

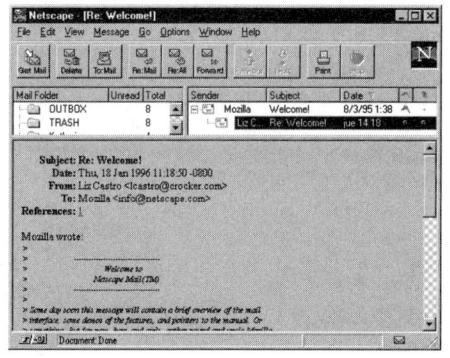

Figure 8.60 *Notice how the entire note is displayed in a Variable Width Font (Times in this case) and that the quoted part of the note is in italics.*

Changing your messages' appearance

You can change the appearance of messages in the Mail (and News) window to make them easier to read.

To change your messages' appearance:

1. Choose Mail and News Preferences in the Options menu **(Figure 8.58)**. The Mail and News Preferences window appears.

2. Click the Appearance tab at the top, left corner of the window to show the Appearance preferences **(Fig. 8.59)**.

3. In the first section, choose Fixed Width Font to show your messages in a font like Courier and Variable Width Font to show your messages in a font like Times or Helvetica.

4. In the second section, choose a style and a size for the quoted text in your messages.

5. Click OK to close the Preferences window. The messages in the Mail (and News) window will now appear with the type of font selected. Quotes will appear with the style selected **(Figure 8.60)**.

✔ Tips

- You can specify the actual fonts in the Fonts tab of the General Preferences dialog box *(see page 223)*.

- Unfortunately, these options have no effect on the Message Composition window (where they would be particularly handy).

Reading and Sending Mail

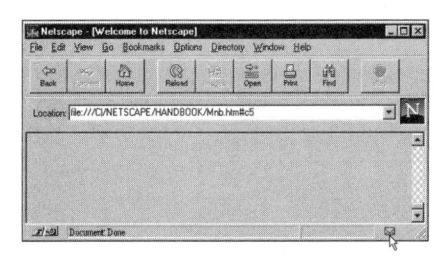

Figure 9.1 *Click the letter icon in the lower right corner of the Netscape window to retrieve your mail from the server.*

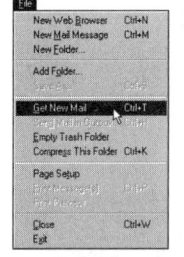

Figure 9.2 *Another way to check your mail is by choosing Get New Mail in the Mail window's File menu.*

Figure 9.3 *Last but not least, you can also click the Get Mail button at the left of the toolbar to check your mail.*

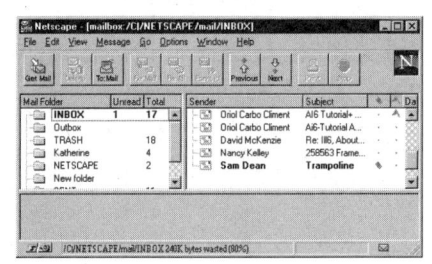

Figure 9.4 *Regardless of the method you use, Netscape places new mail in the Inbox, and shows both the Inbox and the message title in bold.*

You can use Netscape to compose and send new mail, or to read or reply to mail that you've received from others.

Getting new mail

Once you have a new e-mail address, checking to see if someone has actually sent you something becomes almost an obsession. Luckily, Netscape gives you several ways to check your electronic mailbox.

To get new mail from the browser or News window:

Click the letter icon in the bottom right corner of the screen **(Figure 9.1)**. Netscape will open the Mail window, ask for your password if necessary *(see page 84)*, consult your server, and finally show you your new mail (if you have any).

If you've already opened the Mail window, you can click the mail icon or choose the command from the menu.

To get new mail from the Mail window:

1. Choose Get New Mail in the Mail window's File menu **(Figure 9.2)**. The new mail, if any, will be displayed in the Inbox folder **(Figure 9.4)**.

✓ Tip

■ You can also click the Get Mail button on the Mail window's toolbar to get mail **(Figure 9.3)**.

Chapter 9

Having Netscape check for mail periodically

When you are connected to the Internet, you can have Netscape check for mail every few minutes all on its own and alert you when you've received something. Obviously, if you're not connected, Netscape won't be able to tell if you have mail.

To have Netscape check for mail periodically:

1. Choose Mail and News Preferences in the Options menu **(Figure 9.5)**. The Preferences dialog box appears.

2. Click the Servers tab at the top of the dialog box.

3. At the bottom of the Mail section, click Every and then press the Tab key **(Figure 9.6)**.

4. Enter a number next to the Every text box to determine how often Netscape will check the server for mail.

5. Click OK to close the Preferences dialog box.

✓ **Tips**

- Netscape doesn't automatically copy mail from the server, it just checks to see if there is any. If there is, it notifies you with an exclamation point next to the letter icon **(Figure 9.7)**. You still have to *get* your mail *(see page 101)*.

- If you don't want Netscape constantly checking for mail, choose Never in step 3.

- Netscape will only check for mail automatically if you have saved your mail password *(see page 84)*.

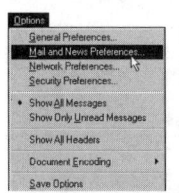

Figure 9.5 *Choose Mail and News Preferences from the Options menu.*

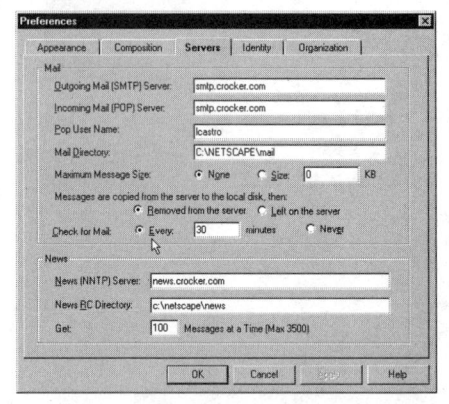

Figure 9.6 *First click Servers at the top of the box. Then select Every next to Check for Mail and type a number in the minutes box.*

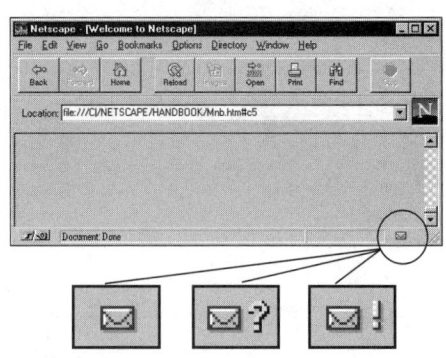

Figure 9.7 *A plain letter icon means you have no letters waiting on the server. A question mark means Netscape can't tell if you have any mail waiting (you're probably not connected). An exclamation point means you have mail waiting on the server.*

102

Reading and Sending Mail

Reading mail

Once you have received new mail, you can open it and read it. You can also re-read mail received earlier, or read mail that you have sent to others.

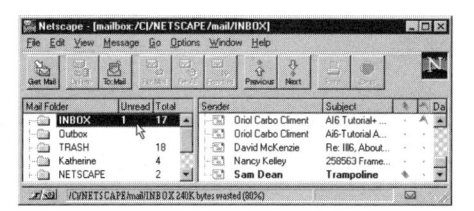

Figure 9.8 *New mail is placed in the Inbox, and both the Inbox and the message titles themselves are shown in bold face. Click a message title in the right pane to open it.*

To read mail:

1. Click the folder in the top left pane that contains the e-mail you want to read **(Figure 9.8)**. You'll find new mail in the Inbox folder. The contents of the folder appear in the top right pane.

2. Click the message that you want to read **(Figure 9.9)**. The contents of the message appear in the bottom pane of the window.

3. Use the scroll bars in the lower pane to move around in the note.

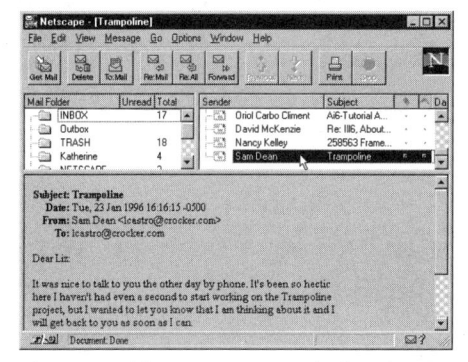

Figure 9.9 *The new message is displayed in the lower pane of the Mail window. (I've also made the entire Mail window longer here, so as to be able to see all three panes.)*

✓ Tips

- You can have the Mail window display only those messages that you haven't read yet by choosing Show Only Unread Messages in the Options menu **(Figure 9.10)**.

- You can show additional information about a message **(Figure 9.11)**, including the route it took to get to you (which is sometimes useful for exposing fraudulent messages), by choosing Show All Headers in the Options menu.

- Thankfully, the Mail window can be rearranged according to the task at hand. When reading, make the bottom pane as large as possible. When filing, make the upper panes larger. For more information on changing the panes, consult *Changing the size of the panes* on page 97.

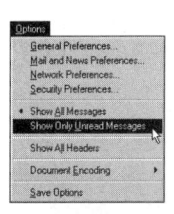

Figure 9.10 *To hide all but the unread messages in the upper right pane of the Mail window, choose Show Only Unread Messages in the Options menu.*

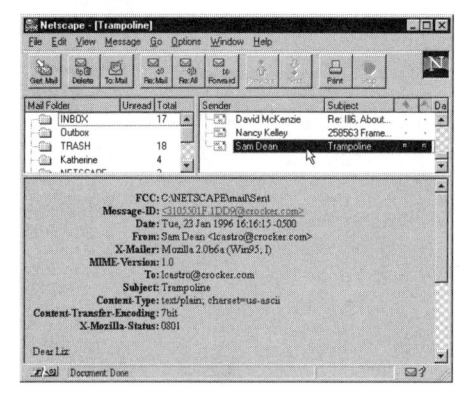

Figure 9.11 *The additional information includes the route the message took to get to you, as well as other technical details.*

Chapter 9

Navigating through your messages

Netscape's Go menu makes it easy to move from one message to the next.

To open the next message:

Choose Next Message in the Go menu or press the down arrow **(Figure 9.12)**.

To open the previous message:

Choose Previous Message in the Go menu or press the up arrow.

✓ Tips

- The up and down arrows only work if the cursor is in the upper-right pane of the window. If you've clicked in the lower pane, the up and down arrows simply navigate you through that particular message.

- You can jump to the first unread message by choosing First Unread in the Go menu. Jump to the next and previous unread messages by choosing Next Unread and Previous Unread, respectively **(Fig. 9.13)**. (*Next* in this case means *below* the current message. *Previous* means *above* the current message, and does not refer to the unread message you read before the current one.) For more information, consult *Marking mail as read or unread* on page 95.

- Jump to the first flagged message by choosing First Flagged in the Go menu **(Fig. 9.14)**. Jump to the next and previous flagged messages by choosing Next Flagged and Previous Flagged. For more information, consult *Flagging messages* on page 94.

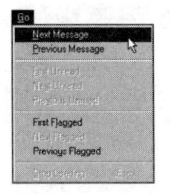

Figure 9.12 *Click Next Message or Previous Message in the Go menu to move from one message to another.*

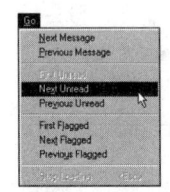

Figure 9.13 *Choose any of the Unread commands (First Unread, Next Unread or Previous Unread) to navigate only among those messages that you have not yet read.*

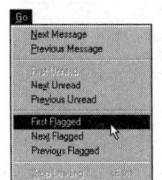

Figure 9.14 *Choose First, Next or Previous Flagged to navigate among the marked messages.*

Reading and Sending Mail

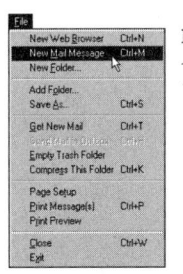

Figure 9.15 *Choose New Mail Message in the File menu to start a new e-mail message.*

Figure 9.16 *You can also click the To: Mail button on the toolbar to start a new message.*

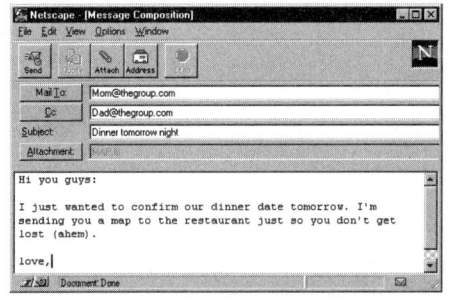

Figure 9.17 *In the Message Composition window, type the recipient's address in the Mail To field, type a Subject, add an Attachment and type the contents of the message.*

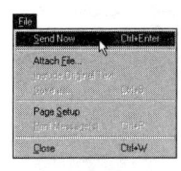

Figure 9.18 *Once your satisfied with the message, choose Send Now in the File menu. (For deferred delivery, consult Composing messages offline on page 108.)*

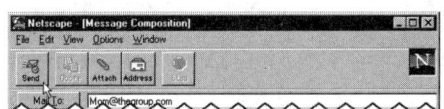

Figure 9.19 *You can also send a finished message by clicking the Send button at the top left of the Message Composition window.*

Composing a new message

Somehow, e-mail is a thousand times easier to write than a conventional letter.

To compose a new message:

1. Choose New Mail Message in the File menu **(Figure 9.15)** or click the To: Mail button **(Fig. 9.16)**. A fresh Message Composition window appears.

2. Type the recipient's address in the Mail To field. Separate multiple addresses with a comma **(Fig. 9.17)**.

3. Type the address(es) where you wish to send "carbon" copies in the Cc box.

4. Type a subject for the message. The subject is important; as the most visible part of the message, it is often used as the criteria for filing.

5. Click the Attachment button to attach a file or URL to the message *(see page 116)*.

6. Type the contents of the message in the area at the bottom of the window.

7. Choose Send in the File menu or click the Send button to send the message **(Figure 9.18 and Figure 9.19)**.

✓ Tips

- Click the Address button (or any of the Mail To, Cc, etc. buttons) to make the Address book appear.

- By default, your messages are sent immediately. For information on deferred sending, consult *Composing messages offline* on page 108.

- Double click a name in the Address book to open a new message automatically addressed to that person.

105

Chapter 9

Viewing or hiding the parts of a message

A message can have up to nine sections: From, Reply To, Mail To, Mail Cc, Mail Bcc, Newsgroups, Followups To, Subject, and Attachment. You can show or hide any combination of these message parts.

To view or hide parts of a message:

1. Choose New Mail Message in the File menu to open the Message Composition window **(Figure 9.20)**. By default, you'll see the Subject, Mail To, Cc, and Attachment fields.

2. Choose the desired message part from the View menu **(Figure 9.22)**. When the option has a checkmark, that message part will be visible **(Figure 9.23)**. You can also choose Show All in the View menu to view all nine message parts.

✔ Tip

■ Some of the message parts are self explanatory. Others are not so clear. *From* is your e-mail address. *Reply To* is the address where replies should be sent. *Mail Cc* is for sending a "carbon" copy of the message to others. *Mail Bcc* is for sending a copy to others without the recipient's knowing. *Newsgroups* shows the newsgroup to which you wish to post the message (see page 146).

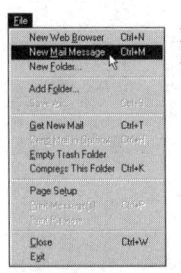

Figure 9.20 *Choose New Mail Message in the File menu to open the Message Composition window.*

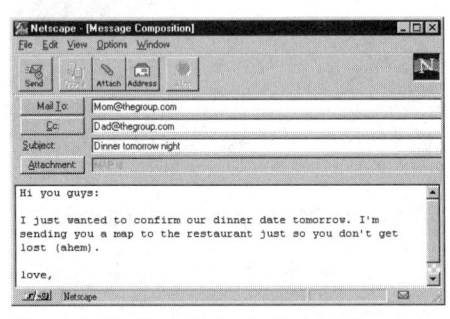

Figure 9.21 *By default, the Message Composition window shows the Mail To, Cc, Subject, and Attachment fields as well as the contents.*

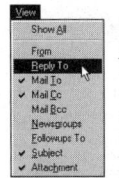

Figure 9.22 *Choose the message part that you wish to see in the View menu. Visible parts are shown with a checkmark. (Choose a checked item to uncheck it and hide it in the Message Composition window.)*

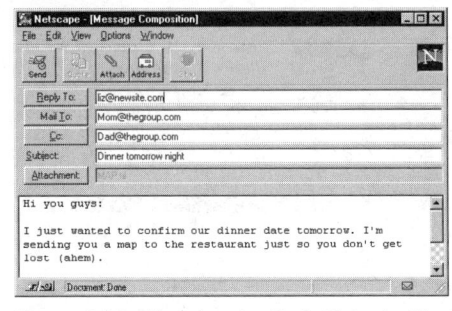

Figure 9.23 *After choosing Reply To in the View menu, the corresponding field is displayed in the Message Composition window.*

Reading and Sending Mail

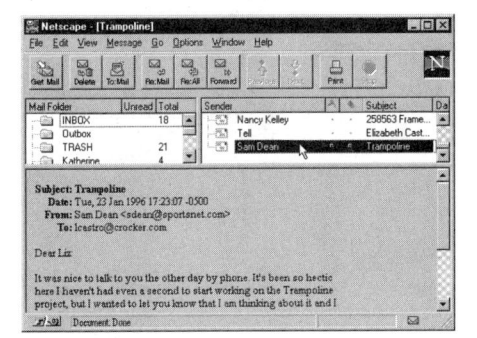

Figure 9.24 *Select the message to which you wish to reply.*

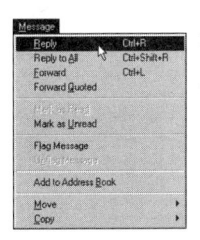

Figure 9.25 *Choose Reply in the Mail window's Message menu.*

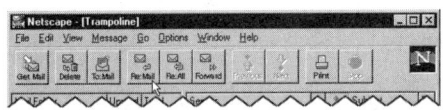

Figure 9.26 *You can also click the Re: Mail button in the middle of the toolbar.*

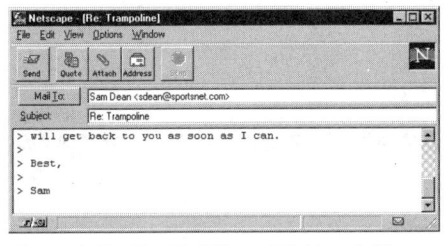

Figure 9.27 *The Mail To and Subject fields are automatically filled in and the contents may contain a quoted version of the original message.*

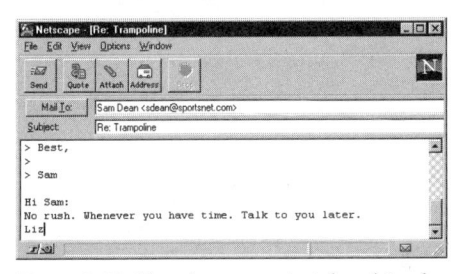

Figure 9.28 *Type the new material and Send.*

Replying to a message you've received

Replying to someone else's message instead of creating a new message *(see page 105)* has certain advantages: the addressing is done automatically and you can choose to quote the original letter in your reply.

To reply to a message you've received:

1. Select the message to which you wish to reply **(Figure 9.24)**.

2. Choose Reply in the Message window **(Figure 9.25)** or click the Re: Mail button on the toolbar **(Figure 9.26)**. The Message Composition window appears. The Mail To box is automatically filled in. The original letter may or may not be quoted in the message area *(see page 111)*. The subject area contains the original subject preceded by "Re:" **(Figure 9.27)**.

3. Type the body of the message **(Figure 9.28)**.

4. Click the Send button or choose the Send command in the File menu *(see page 105)*. Unless you have chosen Deferred Delivery in the Options menu *(see page 108)*, your reply is sent immediately.

✓ Tip

- If the original message was addressed to more than one person, you can reply to all of them at once by selecting Reply to All in the Message menu, or by clicking Re: All on the toolbar.

Chapter 9

Composing messages offline

If you have a dial-up Internet connection, you can compose messages offline and then send them all together once you've connected. Not only does this save a lot of money, but it'll let you relax as you write.

To compose messages offline:

1. Disconnect from the Internet without quitting Netscape (or launch Netscape without connecting to the Internet).

2. Choose New Mail Message in the File menu or select a message and choose Reply in the Message menu **(Figure 9.29)**. The Message Composition window appears.

3. In the Message Composition window's Options menu, choose Deferred Delivery **(Figure 9.30)**.

4. Compose the message as usual *(see page 105)*.

5. Choose Send Later in the File menu or click the Send button in the Message Composition window **(Figure 9.31 and Figure 9.32)**. The message is stored in the Outbox.

6. When you're ready to send the message(s) consult *Sending the messages in the Outbox* on page 109.

✔ Tips

- To return to immediate sending, open the Message Composition window and choose Immediate delivery in the Options menu.

- If you change your mind about sending a message in the Outbox, simply drag it to another folder *(see page 86)* or delete it *(see page 91)*.

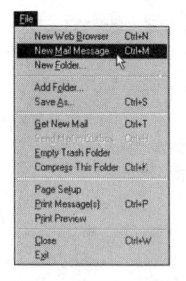

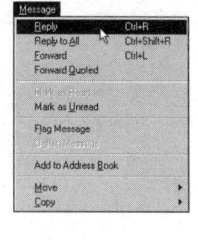

Figure 9.29 *Either choose New Mail Message in the File menu, or select a message and choose Reply or Reply to All in the Message menu.*

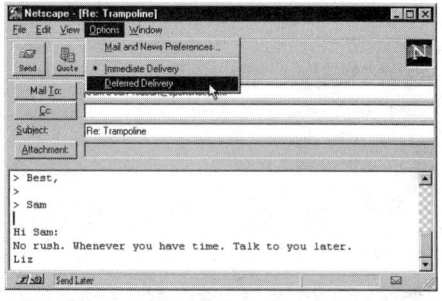

Figure 9.30 *Choose Deferred Delivery in the Message Composition's Options menu to hold off sending your messages until later (presumably when you've connected up again).*

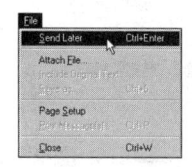

Figure 9.31 *When you've finished composing your message, choose Send Later in the File menu.*

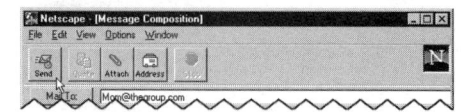

Figure 9.32 *You can also click the Send button on the toolbar. Although its title doesn't change the Send (Later) button does acquire a little clock to indicate that you've chosen Deferred Delivery.*

Reading and Sending Mail

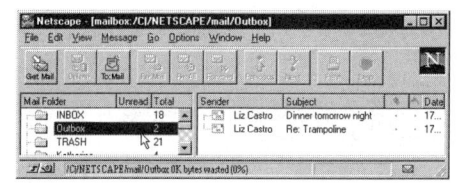

Figure 9.33 *As you compose messages offline and "send" them as described on page 108, they are stored in the Outbox.*

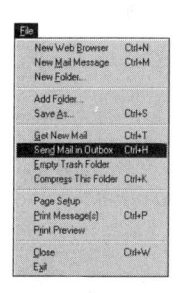

Figure 9.34 *Once you've connected to the Internet and are ready to send your messages, choose Send Mail in Outbox in the File menu.*

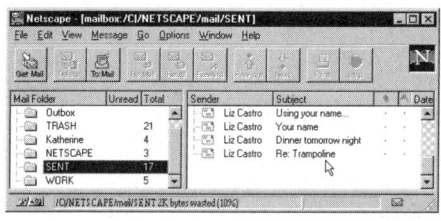

Figure 9.35 *Once you send the messages in the Outbox, they are moved from the Outbox folder to the Sent folder.*

Sending the messages in the Outbox

If you've composed several messages offline—both e-mail and news *(see page 149)*—you can choose to send them when it is convenient for you.

To send the messages in the Outbox:

1. If desired, click the Outbox in the Mail window to see which messages you've stored for later delivery.

2. Open your Internet connection.

3. With the Mail window active, choose Send Mail in Outbox in the File menu **(Figure 9.34)**. All your stored mail and news postings are sent. Netscape automatically transfers sent messages to the Sent folder **(Figure 9.35)**. For more information on the Sent folder, consult *The Mail window's four default folders* on page 85.

4. Close your Internet connection, if desired.

✔ Tip

- If the Send Mail in Outbox option does not appear, make sure the Netscape Mail window is open and active.

109

Chapter 9

Editing messages in the Outbox

Unfortunately, it's not as easy as it should be to edit a message once you've stored it in the Outbox for deferred delivery *(see page 108)*. In fact, you can't really edit it at all. Instead, you can open it, copy out the good parts and create a new message.

To edit a message in the Outbox:

1. Open the Outbox folder and click the message to display its contents in the bottom pane of the window.

2. Select the entire message with the mouse **(Figure 9.36)**.

3. Choose Copy or press Ctrl+C in the Edit menu **(Figure 9.37)**.

4. Follow the instructions for composing a message offline *(see page 108)*.

5. Choose Paste in the Edit menu (or press Ctrl+V) when you're ready to paste the contents of the old message into the new one **(Figure 9.38)**.

6. Delete the old message from the Outbox as described on page 91.

✓ Tip

- If you change your mind about sending any message that you've stored in the Outbox for deferred delivery, you can move *(see page 90)* or eliminate the message *(see page 91)* so that it does not reach the recipient. Of course, you have to do this before actually connecting up and sending the message.

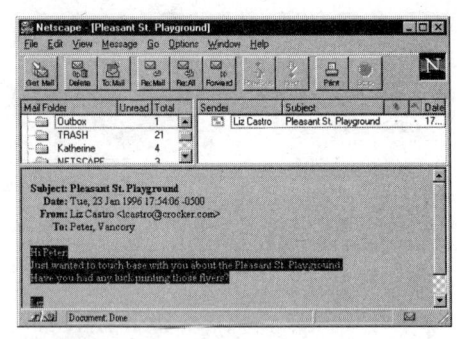

Figure 9.36 *Choose the message you want to edit. Then highlight the message with the mouse.*

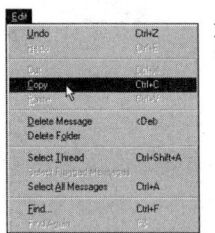

Figure 9.37 *Choose Copy in the Edit menu.*

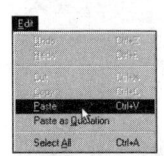

Figure 9.38 *Once you've created the new message and placed the cursor in the contents field, choose Paste in the Edit menu.*

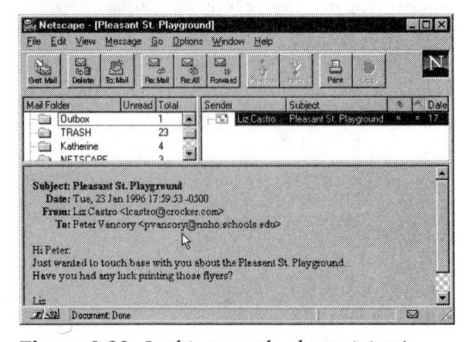

Figure 9.39 *In this example, the recipient's address was incorrect while the contents remained the same.*

110

Reading and Sending Mail

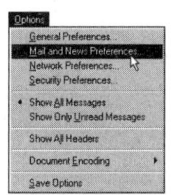

Figure 9.40 *Choose Mail and News Preferences in the Options menu.*

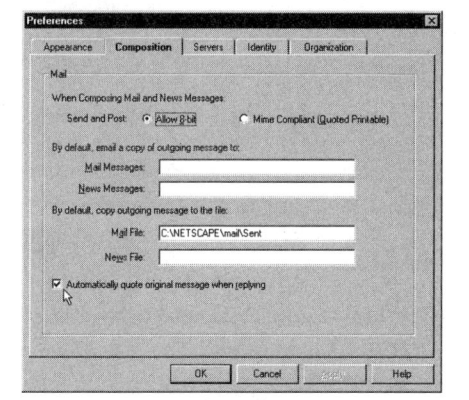

Figure 9.41 *Click the Composition tab and then check Automatically quote original message when replying at the bottom of the window.*

Quoting every message

When you reply to a message, you can have Netscape automatically "quote" the original correspondence, so that the recipient readily knows what you are responding to. Each line of a quoted message is preceded with a greater than sign (>), by Internet convention, and the original author's name is inserted at the beginning of the quote.

To quote every message:

1. Choose Mail and News Preferences in the Options menu **(Figure 9.40)**. The Preferences dialog box appears.

2. Click the Composition tab at the top of the window. The Composition preferences appear **(Figure 9.41)**.

3. Mark the option Automatically quote original message when replying at the bottom of the dialog box **(Fig. 9.41)**. Leave the option unchecked if you don't want Netscape to include a copy of the original message every time you reply.

4. Click OK to close the Preferences dialog box. From now on, each message you reply to will automatically include a copy of the original message.

✓ Tip

- You can choose how the quoted material appears in the Mail window (although not in the Message Composition window). For more details, consult *Changing your messages' appearance* on page 99.

111

Chapter 9

Quoting individual messages

Having Netscape quote every message you reply to can get a little tiresome, especially if the original messages are often long. You can turn off Netscape's automatic quoting and then quote messages individually, when desired.

To quote individual messages:

1. Generally, you will have turned Netscape's automatic feature off, as described on page 111, unchecking the option in step 3 **(Figure 9.42)**.

2. Reply to a message in the normal way **(Figure 9.43 and Figure 9.44)**. See page 107 for details. The Message Composition window appears.

3. In the Message Composition window click the Quote button or choose Include Original Text in the File menu **(Figure 9.45 and Figure 9.46)**. The original message appears in the message area, labeled with the original author's name. Each line of a quote is preceded by greater than signs (>), as is the convention on the Internet.

4. You may cut out parts of the quote if you don't wish to quote the entire original message. Simply select them with the mouse and choose Cut from the Edit menu, or press Backspace.

✔ **Tip**

■ You can change the way a quote is displayed in the Mail window, but unfortunately, not in the Message Composition window. For more details, consult *Changing your messages' appearance* on page 99.

Figure 9.42 *Uncheck the Automatically quote original messages option in the Composition tab of the preferences dialog box (cf Figure 9.41).*

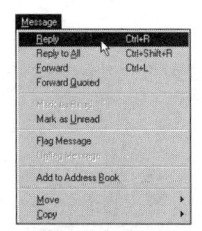

Figure 9.43 *Choose Reply or Reply to All in the Message menu.*

Figure 9.44 *Or click the Re: Mail or Re: All buttons on the toolbar.*

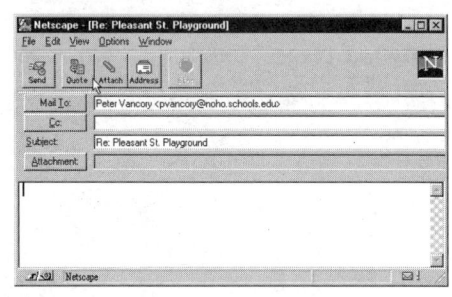

Figure 9.45 *The Mail To and Subject fields are automatically filled in. Click the Quote button to quote the original message.*

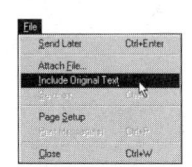

Figure 9.46 *Or choose Include Original Text in the Message Composition window's File menu.*

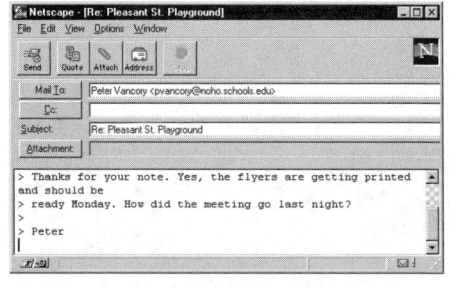

Figure 9.47 *The original message is quoted.*

Reading and Sending Mail

Custom quoting

If you don't want to quote the entire message, or if you want to quote several parts of various messages, you can use Netscape's custom quoting feature to add greater than signs at the beginning of each line of text.

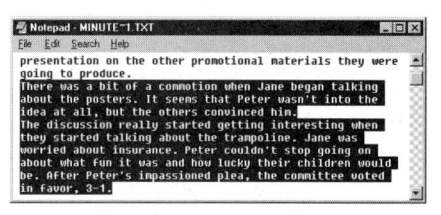

Figure 9.48 *Select the material you wish to quote in the original document. (This is from Notepad.)*

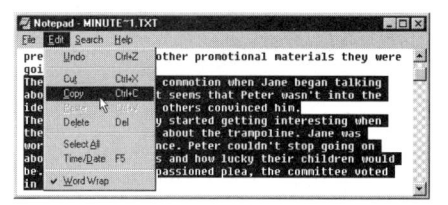

Figure 9.49 *Choose Copy to copy the material to the clipboard.*

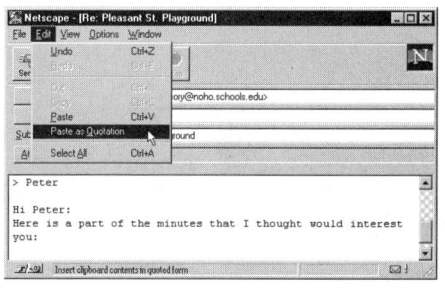

Figure 9.50 *Switch back to the Message Composition window, and choose Paste as Quotation in the Edit menu.*

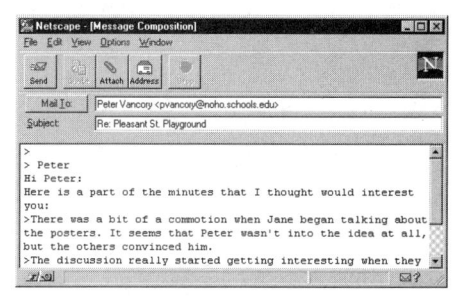

Figure 9.51 *The copied material is pasted in the contents area with a greater than sign (>) at the beginning of each line (well, paragraph).*

To quote a part of a message:

1. Select the text that you wish to quote **(Figure 9.48)**. The text may be from any file; it doesn't have to be from a message received with Netscape.

2. Choose Copy (Ctrl+C) in the Edit menu **(Figure 9.49)**.

3. With the Message Composition window active in Netscape, choose Paste as Quotation in the Edit menu **(Fig. 9.50)**. The copied text will be pasted with a greater than sign at the beginning of each line **(Fig. 9.51)**.

✔ Tip

- Netscape actually inserts a greater than sign (the Internet recognized symbol for quoted text) at the beginning of each *paragraph*. Since most electronic mail is made up of one line paragraphs, this system works fine for quoting from messages. If you paste text from other programs, you may notice that there is only one greater-than sign at the beginning of each paragraph. In this case, either insert the additional symbols manually, or copy each line individually.

113

Chapter 9

Forwarding a message

Sometimes you will receive e-mail that either isn't for you or that you would like to share with others. The easiest way to share mail you have received with other people is to forward it.

To forward a message as an attachment:

1. Select the message that you wish to forward in the Mail window **(Figure 9.52)**. The contents of the message appear in the lower pane.

2. Select Forward in the Message menu **(Fig. 9.53)**. The Message Composition window appears. The Subject is automatically set to "[Fwd: title of original message]" and the original message is attached to the new message.

3. Enter the recipient's address in the Mail To box.

4. Fill in the other message parts as desired.

5. Add any personal comments about the forwarded material in the message area.

6. Click the Send button or choose the Send command in the File menu.

✔ Tips

- You can also click the Forward button on the toolbar to forward a message **(Figure 9.54)**.

- A forwarded message appears below the main message, much like an attached document **(Figure 9.55)**.

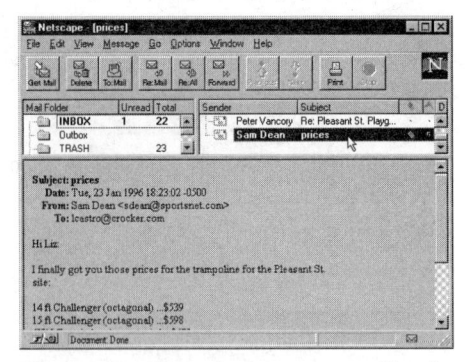

Figure 9.52 *Choose the message you wish to forward.*

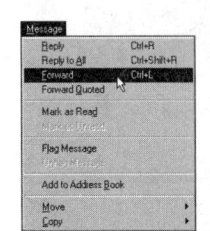

Figure 9.53 *Choose Forward in the Message menu.*

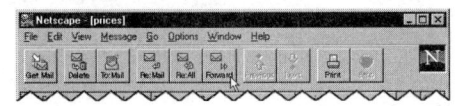

Figure 9.54 *Or, click the Forward button.*

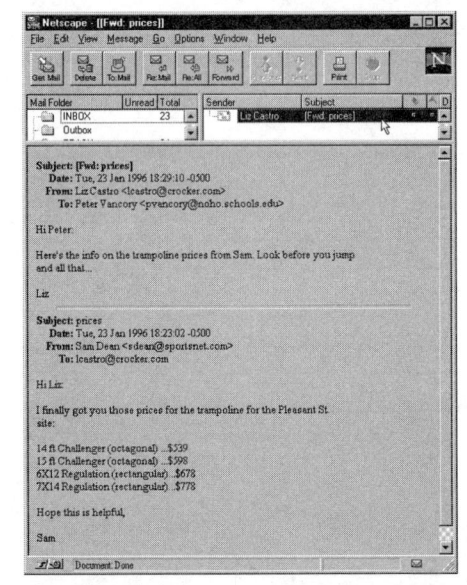

Figure 9.55 *A forwarded message appears below the new portion of the current message.*

Reading and Sending Mail

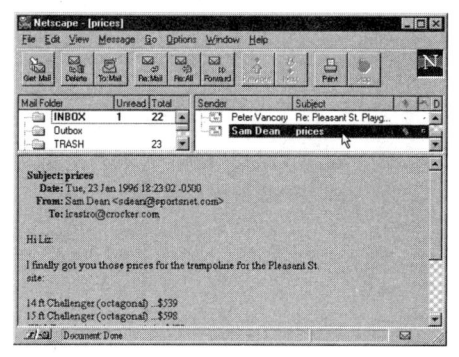

Figure 9.56 *Choose the message you wish to forward.*

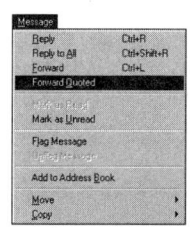

Figure 9.57 *Choose Forward Quoted in the Message menu.*

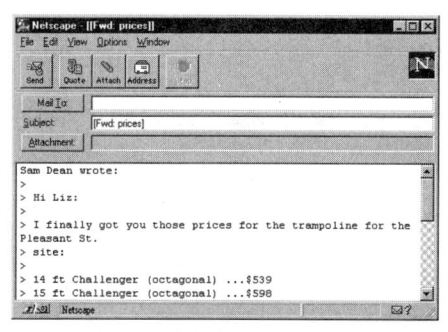

Figure 9.58 *The forwarded message appears as a quote (with >) in the contents area.*

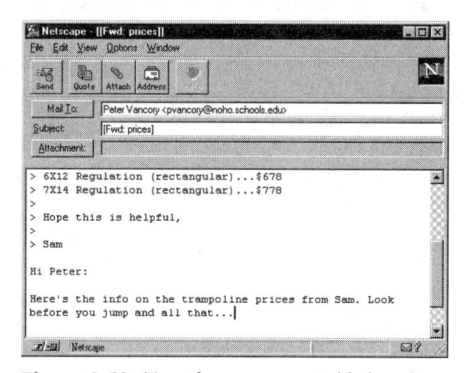

Figure 9.59 *Type the new material below the quoted message.*

Forwarding a message as a quote

You can also forward a message as a quote.

To forward a message as a quote:

1. Select the message that you wish to forward in the Mail window **(Figure 9.56)**. The contents of the message appear in the lower pane.

2. Select Forward Quoted in the Message menu **(Figure 9.57)**. The Message Composition window appears. The Subject is automatically set to "[Fwd: title of original message]" and the original message is quoted in the message area **(Figure 9.58)**.

3. Enter the recipient's address in the Mail To box.

4. Fill in the other message parts as desired.

5. Add any personal comments about the forwarded material in the message area below the quoted, forwarded message **(Figure 9.59)**.

6. Click the Send button or choose the Send command in the File menu.

115

Chapter 9

Attaching files to a message

Electronic mail does not limit you to letters; you can send packages too. You can attach any kind of file to a message—including images or even programs. You can also attach a URL to a message, giving the recipient direct access to a Web page *(see page 117)*.

To attach a file to a message:

1. Choose New Mail Message in the File menu or select a message and choose Reply in the Message menu. The Message Composition window appears.

2. Choose Attach File in the File menu **(Figure 9.60)** or click the Attach button.

3. In the Attachments dialog box that appears, click Attach File **(Fig. 9.61)**.

4. In the dialog box that appears, select the file that you wish to send with the message and click OK **(Figure 9.62)**.

5. Back in the Attachments dialog box, choose As Is to send the file in its current form or choose Convert to Plain Text to send the file as text **(Figure 9.63)**.

6. Click OK. The file's path appears in the Attachments box in the Message Composition window **(Fig. 9.64)**.

7. Compose the rest of the message.

✓ Tip

■ Click the Attach button to add or edit an attached file.

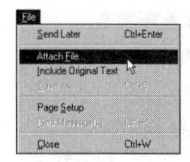

Figure 9.60 *From the Message Composition window, choose Attach File in the File menu.*

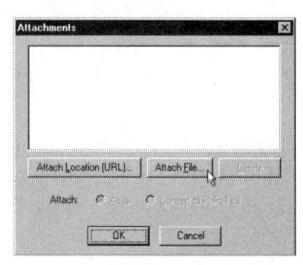

Figure 9.61 *Click the Attach File button in the Attachments dialog box.*

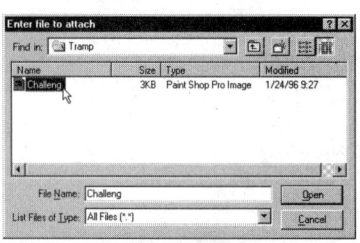

Figure 9.62 *Choose the desired file and click Open.*

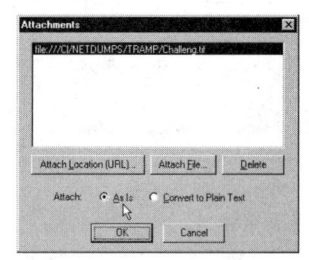

Figure 9.63 *The selected file appears in the Attachments dialog box. Click As is or Convert to Plain Text and then click OK.*

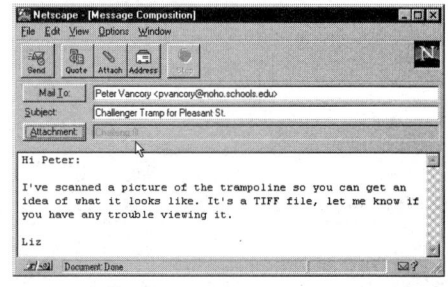

Figure 9.64 *The attached file appears in the Attachment field in the Message Composition window.*

116

Reading and Sending Mail

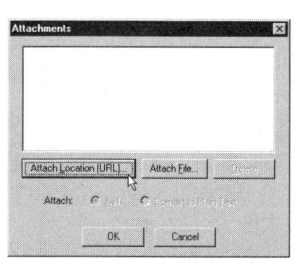

Figure 9.65 *Click Attach Location (URL) in the Attachments dialog box.*

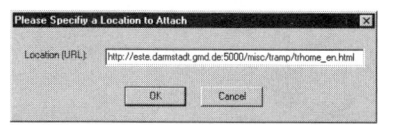

Figure 9.66 *Type or paste the URL and click OK.*

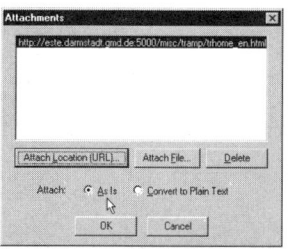

Figure 9.67 *The URL appears in the Attachments dialog box. Click As Is to send it with HTML tags and Convert to plain text to send it without.*

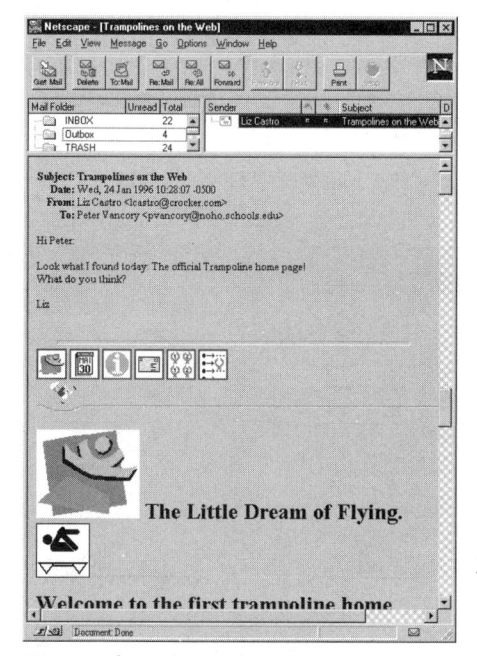

Figure 9.68 *As long as the recipient views the message with Netscape, the URL appears within the message just like any other Web page.*

Attaching a URL to a message

If you find a great Web page on the Net and want to share it with someone, instead of sending the page's address in text form, you can send them the actual page within your message. As long as they use Netscape to view your message, the page will appear just as if they had jumped to it themselves.

To attach a URL to a message:

1. From the Message Composition window, choose Attach File or click the Attach button.

2. In the Attachments dialog that appears, click Attach Location (URL) **(Figure 9.65)**.

3. Type or paste the desired URL in the dialog box that appears and click OK **(Figure 9.66)**.

4. In the Attachments dialog box, choose As Is to send the page with HTML tags; choose Convert to Plain Text to send it without **(Fig. 9.67)**. For more information about tags, consult *Saving a Web page* on page 46.

5. Repeat steps 3–5 for each URL you wish to attach.

6. Click OK to close the dialog box. The URL appears in the Attachments box in the Message Composition window.

7. Compose the rest of the message as usual *(see page 105)*.

✓ Tip

- If you're not sure what program the recipient uses for e-mail, send the page without tags.

117

Chapter 9

Mailing a document

Earlier versions of Netscape allowed you to mail a Web page directly from the browser. Although Netscape's mail features have expanded, the old command remains. The effect is virtually identical to attaching a URL *(see page 117)*. The only difference is that the actual URL, as a link, is added to the note above the page itself.

To mail a document:

1. In the browser, jump to or open the desired Web page.

2. Choose Mail Document in the File menu. The Message Composition window appears with the Web page automatically attached and the URL as a link in the body of the message.

3. Edit and send the message as usual *(see page 105)*. The mailed document appears both as a link and as an attachment to the recipient.

✓ Tip

■ You can also mail an individual frame. Simply select the frame and the Mail Document command turns into Mail Frame in the File menu.

Figure 9.69 *Jump to (or open) the desired page and select Mail Document in the File menu.*

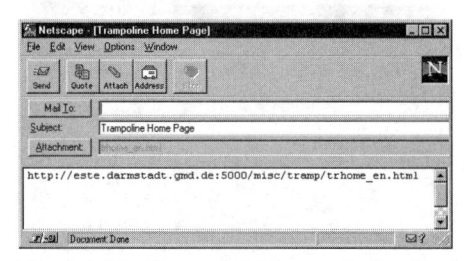

Figure 9.70 *The page's URL is attached and added to the contents of the message. Add the name and contents and send as usual.*

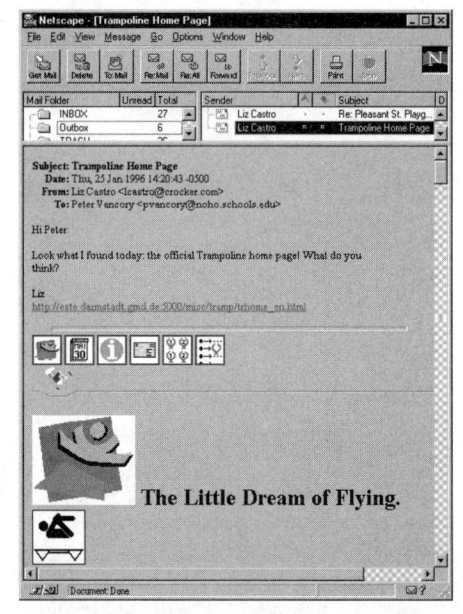

Figure 9.71 *The link to the page and the page itself appear below the message.*

Reading and Sending Mail

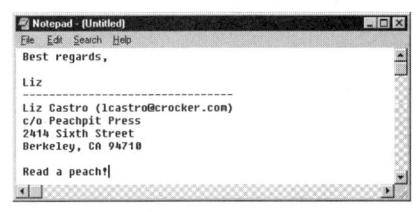

Figure 9.72 *A signature typically contains your name, e-mail and snail mail addresses, and a pithy quote. This one was created with Notepad.*

Figure 9.73 *Choose Save As in the text editor's File menu.*

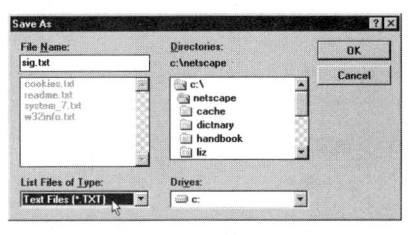

Figure 9.74 *Save the signature file as a Text File (*.TXT).*

Creating a signature file

One of the nice traditions of e-mail writing is adding a few lines at the bottom of the note that tell who you are, and sometimes what you do and where you're from. You can create a signature in any word processor, including Notepad or Wordpad.

To create a signature:

1. Open a word processor or text editor. Write, Notepad or WordPad are fine.

2. Create your signature as desired **(Figure 9.72)**. A signature typically contains your name, e-mail and snail mail addresses, and a pithy quote. You can also add ASCII images.

3. Choose Save As in the text editor's File menu **(Figure 9.73)**.

4. Give the file a name and choose the Text (*.TXT) format in the Save As dialog box. Click OK **(Fig. 9.74)**.

5. To use the signature file, consult *Using a signature file* on page 120.

✔ Tip

■ Although a signature is limited to text characters, you can be creative about how to use them. Some people even make pictures out of text characters, or more simply, add famous quotes and sayings to their signatures.

119

Chapter 9

Using a signature file

Once you've created a signature file *(see page 119)*, Netscape can automatically add it to each message that you send. All you have to do is tell Netscape where the signature file is.

To use a signature file:

1. In Netscape, choose Mail and News Preferences in the Options menu **(Figure 9.75)**.

2. In the Preferences dialog box that appears, click the Identity tab **(Figure 9.76)**.

3. At the bottom of the Identity preferences tab, click Browse.

4. Choose the desired signature file in the dialog box that appears and click Open **(Figure 9.77)**. The file's path will appear in the Identity preferences tab **(Figure 9.78)**.

5. Click OK to close the Identity tab. The next time you write a message, Netscape will include your signature automatically **(Figure 9.79)**.

✓ Tips

- If the signature file does not appear in the Open dialog box when you try to choose it, you probably didn't save it in Text Only (or ASCII) format *(see page 119)*.

- If you move the signature file, or change its name, or the name of the folder it's in, Netscape won't be able to find it and will simply stop adding it to your messages. Unfortunately, Netscape won't tell you there's a problem, so you have to watch it.

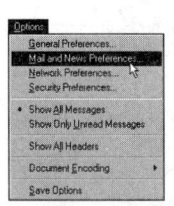

Figure 9.75 *Choose Mail and News Preferences in the Options menu.*

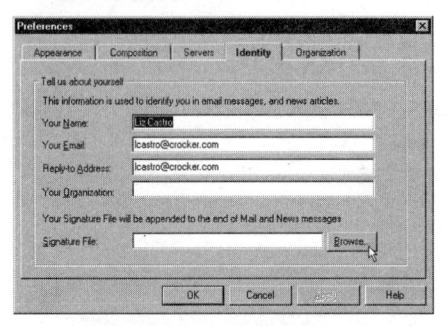

Figure 9.76 *Click the Identity tab and then the Browse button to choose a signature file.*

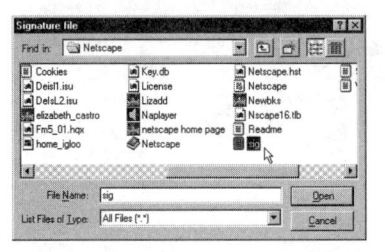

Figure 9.77 *Choose the desired signature file and click Open.*

Figure 9.78 *The path to the selected signature file now appears in the Identity preferences tab.*

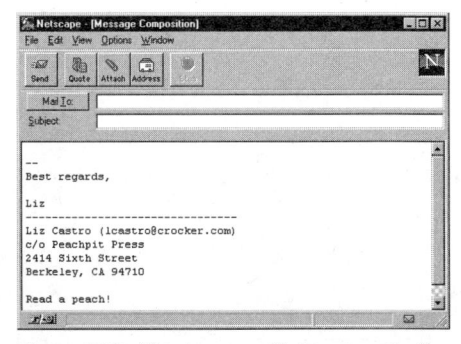

Figure 9.79 *The signature file is automatically copied to each new Message Composition window.*

120

The Address Book

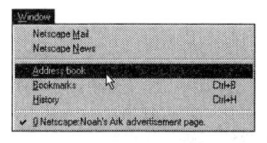

Figure 10.1 *Choose Address Book in the Window menu to open the Address Book.*

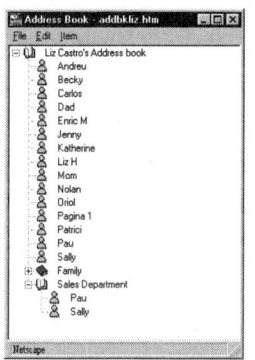

Figure 10.2 *The Address Book helps you keep track of those long and complicated e-mail addresses.*

The Address Book window

Netscape lets you save e-mail addresses in the Address Book, a window that you can let float on the screen beside the main Netscape window or hide at your convenience.

The Address Book includes not only the e-mail addresses themselves, but also the recipient's name, a description, and a nickname if desired. The Address Book always lists addresses by their names, in alphabetical order.

An Address Book can also contain *mailing lists* that make it easy to send messages to more than one person at a time. Because a mailing list is actually a collection of *aliases* of addresses and not the addresses themselves, you can include an address in as many mailing lists as desired.

To open the Address Book:

Choose Address Book in the Window menu **(Figure 10.1)**. The Address Book appears **(Figure 10.2)**.

Chapter 10

Adding an address

E-mail addresses tend to be long and hard to remember. You can store e-mail addresses in the Address Book together with the recipient's name, a description and a nickname.

To add an address to the Address Book:

1. Open the Address Book window by choosing Address Book in the Window menu.

2. Choose Add User in the Item menu **(Figure 10.3)**. The Address Properties dialog box appears.

3. Enter a short, descriptive, easy-to-remember word for the Nickname **(Figure 10.4)**. You can use the nickname to call up the person's name and e-mail address in a message.

4. Press the Tab key and enter the Name of the person or organization that corresponds to the e-mail address. The Name will appear on all correspondence that you send out, and it will identify the incoming and outgoing mail in the Mail window.

5. Press the Tab key to advance the cursor to the E-mail Address field. Type the e-mail address carefully. One mistyped digit or letter can keep your mail from getting to its destination.

6. Press the Tab key to advance the cursor to the Description field. If desired, enter a description for the address.

7. Click OK. The new address appears in the Address book in alphabetical order.

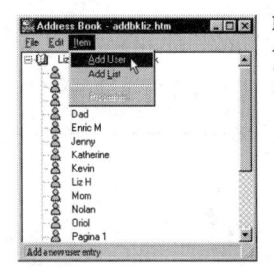

Figure 10.3 *In the Address Book, choose Add User in the Item menu.*

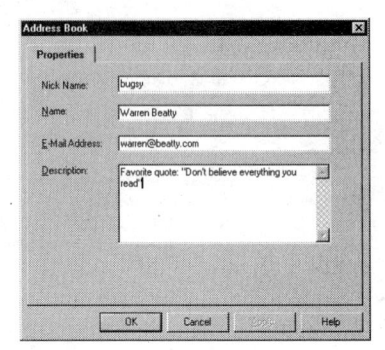

Figure 10.4 *The Address Book dialog appears in which you can enter the desired information.*

122

The Address Book

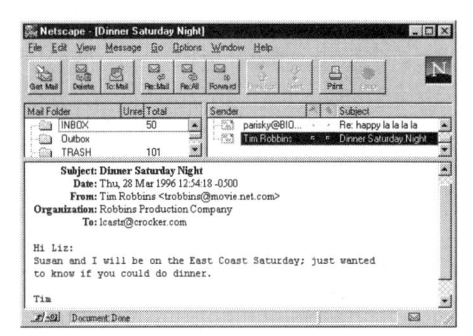

Figure 10.5 *Select the letter from the person whose address you wish to add to your Address Book.*

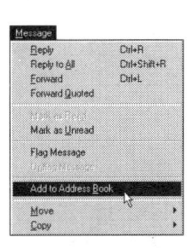

Figure 10.6 *Choose Add to Address Book in the Mail window's Message menu.*

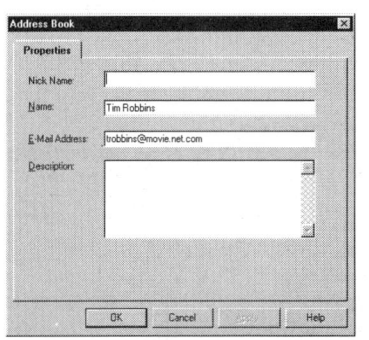

Figure 10.7 *The sender's name and e-mail address are entered in the Address Book dialog box automatically. Enter a nickname and description, if desired, and click OK.*

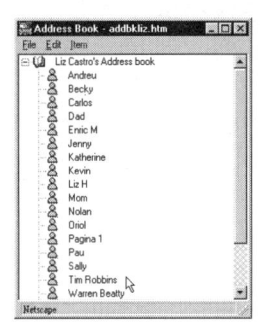

Figure 10.8 *The new address appears in the Address Book.*

Adding an address from an incoming message

You can add the address of anyone who has sent you a message. Adding an address in this way ensures that the address is not misspelled.

To add an address from incoming messages:

1. Open the message from which you wish to copy the sender's address **(Figure 10.5)**.

2. Choose Add to Address Book in the Message menu **(Figure 10.6)**. The Address Book dialog box appears with the name and address automatically filled in.

3. Add a nickname and description if desired **(Figure 10.7)**. For more information, consult *Adding an address* on page 122.

4. Click OK. The new address is added to your Address Book **(Figure 10.8)**.

✔ Tips

- It is possible (and not very hard as you can see by Figure 10.5) to send mail with a false address. If the sender has not used a real address, you won't be able to use it to write them back irate notes.

- You can add messages from news postings using this same technique.

123

Chapter 10

Creating a mailing list

The Address Book lets you create a mailing list, similar to the aliases in the Bookmarks window, that lets you send e-mail messages to a whole group of people at the same time.

To create a mailing list:

1. Open the Address Book by choosing Address Book in the Window menu.

2. Choose Add List in the Item menu **(Figure 10.9)**. The Address Book dialog box appears.

3. Enter a short, descriptive, easy-to-remember word for the Nickname **(Figure 10.10)**. You will be able to use the nickname to invoke the list.

4. Type a name for the mailing list in the Name field. A mailing list's name is like a nickname for *all of the addresses* the list contains. As such, it does not appear on any of your correspondence but instead is replaced by the addresses of each person on the list.

5. In the Description field, type a few words that define the list's members.

6. Click OK to save the changes.

7. Shift-click the addresses that you wish to add to the mailing list **(Fig. 10.11)**.

8. Drag the names to the new list's icon. Aliases of the addresses are added to the new list while the addresses themselves remain unchanged and in their original positions **(Figure 10.12)**.

✓ Tip

- You can add new names to the mailing list at any time. Simply drag them on top of the list's icon as in step 8.

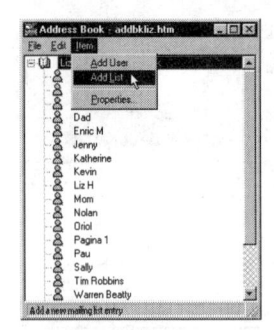

Figure 10.9 *In the Address Book, choose Add List in the Item menu.*

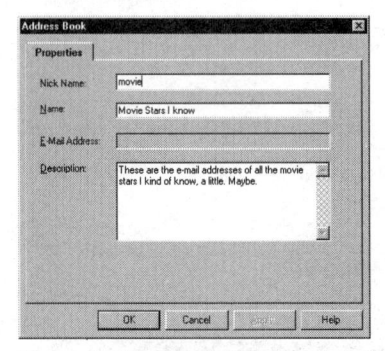

Figure 10.10 *In the Address Book dialog box, enter the nickname, name and description for the mailing list.*

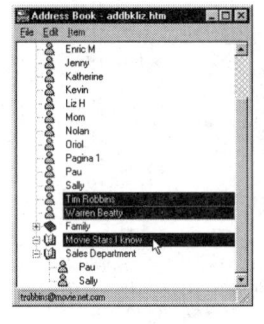

Figure 10.11 *Select the addresses you wish to add to the mailing list. Use Shift to add multiple, sequential addresses. Use Control to add non-sequential ones. Then drag the selection to the new mailing list.*

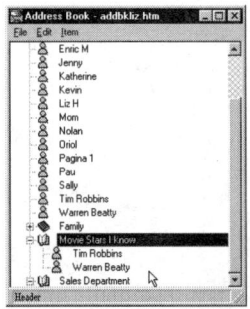

Figure 10.12 *The new mailing list appears in the Address Book with its contents below. Double click to hide (or show) its addresses.*

The Address Book

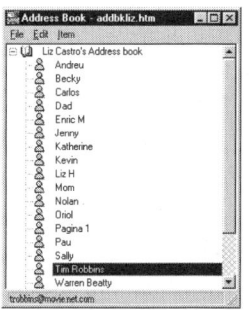

Figure 10.13 *In the Address Book, select the desired address by clicking it once. Select additional addresses with Shift (if they're touching in the list) or Control (if they're not).*

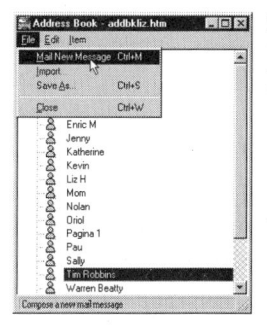

Figure 10.14 *Choose Mail New Message in the File menu.*

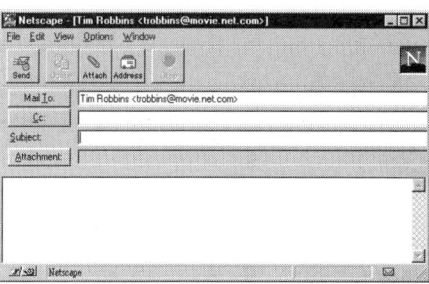

Figure 10.15 *A pre-addressed Message Composition window appears.*

Using an address or list

The beauty of the Address Book is that you can send e-mail to someone without having to type his address. A list lets you e-mail *several* people at once.

To use an address:

1. Select the desired address or list in the Address Book **(Figure 10.13)**.

2. Choose Mail New Message in the File menu **(Figure 10.14)**. The Message Composition window appears, and is automatically addressed to the person selected in step 1 **(Figure 10.15)**.

3. Compose the message as usual.

✔ Tips

- You can double click an address to open a new, automatically addressed Message Composition window.

- Add an address (or more than one by selecting several first) to an existing mail message by dragging it from the Address Book to the desired field.

- You can tell which field you are dragging an address to by watching the light blue line that appears below the field.

- Once in the Message Composition window, click any of the address buttons (Mail to:, Cc:, etc.) to access the Address Book.

- You can also type the nickname in a field in the Message Composition window to add an address to that field. The full address appears when you press Tab to go to the next field.

125

Chapter 10

Changing or deleting an address or list

You may need to change an entry in your address book, for example, if the person changes online services, or to add descriptive information or a nickname.

To change an address or list:

1. Click once on the address or list to select it and then choose Properties in the Item menu **(Figure 10.16)**.

2. In the Address Book dialog box that appears, change the values in the fields as desired **(Figure 10.17 and Figure 10.18)**.

3. Click OK to save the changes.

Getting rid of unused addresses or lists is simple and essential. The cleaner you keep your address book, the easier it will be to find the addresses you *do* use.

To delete an address or list:

1. Select the item you wish to delete in the Address Book by clicking it once.

2. Choose Delete in the Edit menu in the Address Book window, or press the Delete key—not the Backspace key **(Figure 10.19)**. The address or list disappears from the Address Book.

✔ Tip

■ No alert appears when you delete an address. If you delete an address by mistake, choose Undo immediately to restore it.

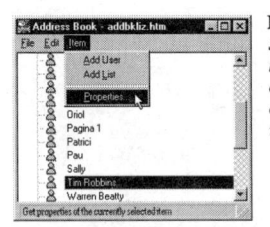

Figure 10.16 *Select the address or list that you wish to change. Then choose Properties in the Item menu.*

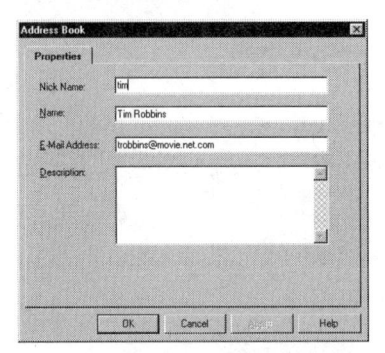

Figure 10.17 *If you've selected an individual address, the Address dialog box appears. Edit the address as desired.*

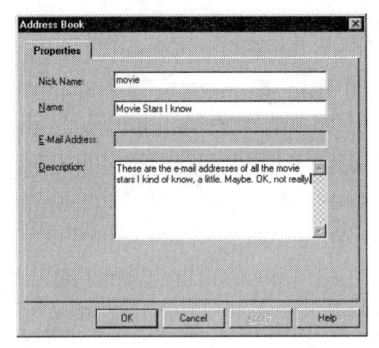

Figure 10.18 *If you've selected a list to change, an almost identical Address Book dialog box appears in which to make the changes. The only field you can't change (of course) is the E-mail Address field.*

Figure 10.19 *Choose Delete in the Address Book's Edit menu or press the Delete key (not Backspace).*

The Address Book

Figure 10.20 *Choose Find in the Address Book's Edit menu.*

Figure 10.21 *Type the search criteria and click OK.*

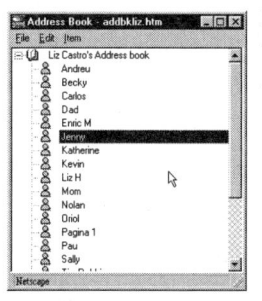

Figure 10.22 *Netscape highlights the first address that satisfies the criteria. Why is this address highlighted? Check out Figure 10.23.*

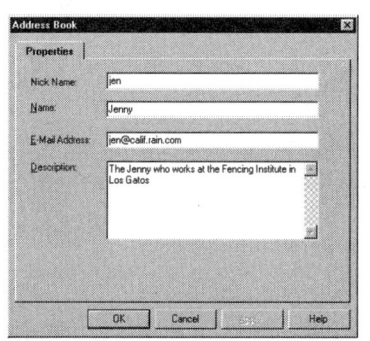

Figure 10.23 *The address found in Figure 10.22 contained the search criteria in its Description field.*

Figure 10.24 *To find the next address that satisfies the criteria, choose Find again in the Address Book's window.*

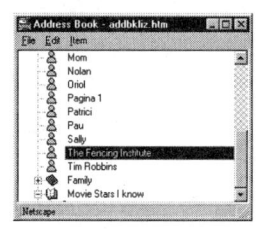

Figure 10.25 *The next address that contains the search criteria (this time in the Name itself) is highlighted.*

Finding an address

If you have many entries in your Address Book, it may be hard to find just the address you're looking for. You can search the contents of the Address Book to find the information you need quickly.

To find an address:

1. Choose Find in the Address Book's Edit menu **(Figure 10.20)**.

2. In the dialog box that appears, type the text that you wish to search for and click OK **(Figure 10.21)**. Netscape highlights the first entry that satisfies the search criteria **(Figure 10.22)**.

3. If the selected address is not the one you're looking for, choose Find Again in the Address Book's Edit menu **(Figure 10.24)**. The next entry that satisfies the search criteria is highlighted **(Figure 10.25)**.

4. Repeat step 3 until you've found the desired address.

✓ Tip

- Netscape searches in each of the fields in each address. If it's not obvious why a certain address has been highlighted, it's probably because the search criteria was found in one of the fields that is not directly visible from the Address Book window—like Nickname, E-mail Address or Description **(Figure 10.23)**.

127

Chapter 10

Saving an address book

You can save an address book in order to share it with others or simply to make a back-up copy. In fact, an address book is nothing more than an HTML page that you can browse as you would any other local file.

To save an address book:

1. Choose Save As in the Address Book's File menu **(Figure 10.26)**. The Save dialog box appears **(Fig. 10.27)**.

2. Give the file a name and choose the directory in which to save it.

3. Choose a file type for the address book. If you want to open the file with Netscape, choose Source (*.htm). To open the file in a word processor or text editor, choose Text (*.txt).

4. Click OK to save the file.

✓ Tips

- If you tack on the extension .htm to the end of your address book's name, you'll be able to open the file as a regular Web page *(see page 130)*. Each of the addresses in the address book is converted into a link on the Web page.

- Yes, that is the Save *bookmarks* file that appears, but it works fine.

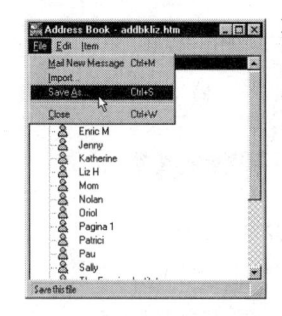

Figure 10.26 *Choose Save As in the Address Book's File menu.*

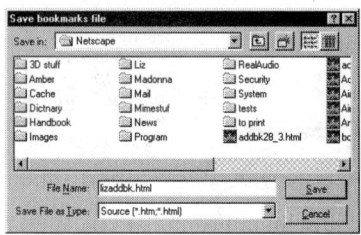

Figure 10.27 *In the Save dialog box, give the Address Book file a name, choose Source (to save it with HTML tags) or Text (to save it without HTML tags) and then click OK.*

128

The Address Book

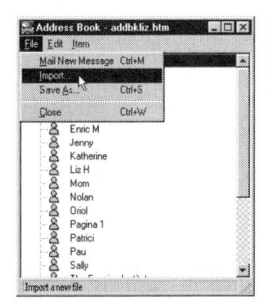

Figure 10.28 *Choose Import in the Address Book's File menu.*

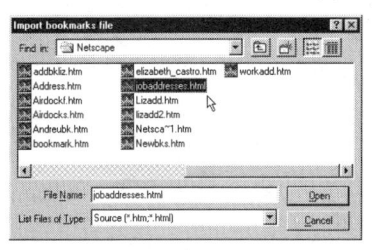

Figure 10.29 *Select the desired address book file and click Open.*

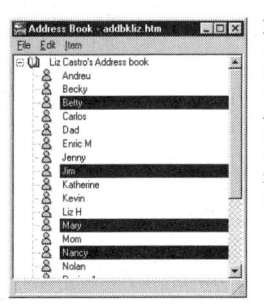

Figure 10.30 *The new addresses are added to the existing ones in the Address Book window. Addresses with the same names are not replaced, simply added.*

Importing an address book

You can import the addresses from a saved address book file into your current Address Book. For example, you can save the address book file on your computer at work and then import it into your Address Book at your home computer.

To import an address book:

1. Choose Import in the Address Book's File menu **(Figure 10.28)**. The Import dialog box appears.

2. Choose the address book file that you wish to import and click Open **(Figure 10.29)**. The addresses in the imported file are added to the current Address Book **(Figure 10.30)**.

✔ Tips

■ Currently, Netscape does not replace or update names that already exist. It simply adds the new entries. The only unique part of an address is the nickname. If an incoming address has the same nickname as an existing address, the incoming address' nickname will be lost.

■ Yes, that is the Import *bookmarks* file dialog box, but it works just fine.

129

Chapter 10

Opening an address book as a Web page

An easy way to see an address book without changing your regular address book is to open it as a Web page. Since the address book is in HTML format, like any other Web page, Netscape knows how to interpret it correctly, displaying all the addresses as links which can be clicked on to send a message to the corresponding person.

To open an address book as a Web page:

1. Save your address book, making sure to choose Source (*.htm) in the List Files of Type pop-up menu. *(See "Saving an address book" on page 128.)*

2. Choose Open File in the File menu in the main Netscape window **(Figure 10.31)**.

3. Choose the desired file and click Open **(Figure 10.32)**. The address book file is loaded into Netscape and each address is automatically converted into a link **(Fig. 10.33)**.

✔ **Tip**

■ You can use this technique to create a Web page that elicits feedback from your readers. Save an address book that contains all of the public relations or technical support people in your company. Then include the address book cum Web page in your site. Your readers will have instant e-mail access to all of the people in the address book.

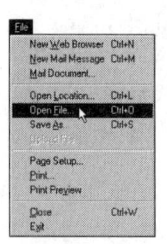

Figure 10.31 *In the main Netscape File menu, choose Open File.*

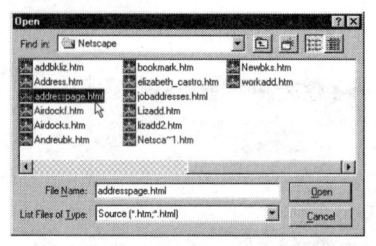

Figure 10.32 *In the Open dialog box, choose the desired address book file that you wish to open.*

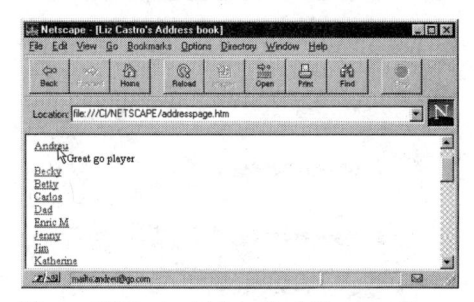

Figure 10.33 *An Address Book file opened as a Web page appears with each address as a link. Users can click the address to send a message to the corresponding person. (This isn't my real Address Book, I confess.)*

The News Window

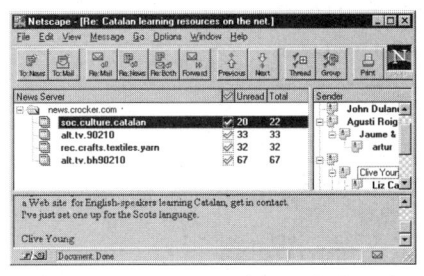

Figure 11.1 *The upper left pane (enlarged here) lists the news hosts and available newsgroups.*

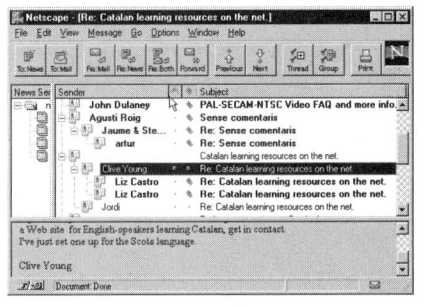

Figure 11.2 *When you click a newsgroup, its postings are displayed in the upper right pane of the News window (enlarged here).*

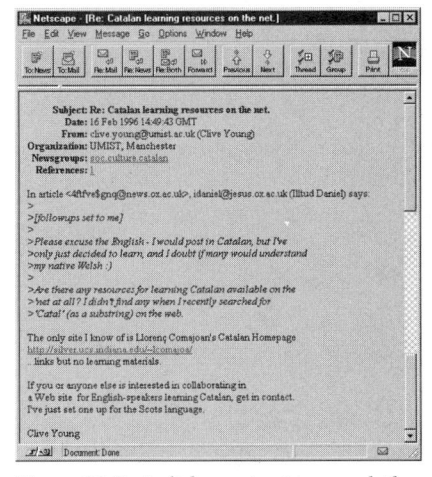

Figure 11.3 *A click on a posting reveals the message in the lower pane (enlarged here).*

The News window is Netscape's central command area for displaying the newsgroups available through your server and the postings that belong to each one. From the News window, you can view and subscribe to newsgroups, and read and reply to postings or create your own.

There is an enormous amount of traffic in the newsgroups. The News window lets you flag postings that are important and mark an individual posting, a thread or even an entire newsgroup as read, so that it doesn't appear the next time you view the newsgroup.

The parts of the News window

The News window is divided into three areas, or panes. The top left panel **(Figure 11.1)** lists the newsgroups, and gives the number of unread and total messages in each, and whether you're subscribed. You can choose to view *all* the newsgroups, the *new* newsgroups, only the newsgroups you've *subscribed to* or only the newsgroups you've subscribed to that *have new messages*.

When you click in one of the newsgroups, a list of the postings it contains appears in the top right pane of the News window **(Figure 11.2)**. Each posting is identified by its Subject, Sender, Date, and whether it has been marked or read.

Once you click a posting, the contents of the message appears in the bottom pane of the News window **(Figure 11.3)**.

Chapter 11

Using the News window

The most important difference between the News window and the Mail window is that the former shows newsgroups and postings while the latter shows folders and e-mail. Overall, however, their functions are virtually identical:

To get around in the News window, consult *Navigating through your messages* on page 104.

To resize the News window and its individual panes, consult *Changing the size of the panes* on page 97. To resize the columns or change their order, consult *Changing the columns* on page 98.

To choose a font for viewing News messages, consult *Changing your messages' appearance* on page 99.

To sort your postings, consult *Putting your messages in order* on page 93. To view your postings in hierarchical order, instead of strictly by date or sender, consult *Threading messages* on page 96.

To open the News window:

Choose Netscape News in the Window menu **(Figure 11.4)**. The News window is displayed with the news host (if any) listed in the top left pane. (For more information about news hosts, consult *Opening a news host* on page 134.)

To close the News window:

Click the close box in the upper right window of the News window or double click the News icon in the upper left corner of the News window **(Figure 11.5 and Figure 11.6)**.

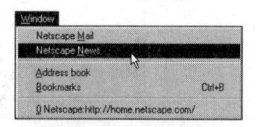

Figure 11.4 *Choose Netscape News in the Window menu to open the News window.*

Figure 11.5 *Click the standard Window buttons to adjust the window. From left to right: Minimize, Maximize and Close.*

Figure 11.6 *Or double click the Netscape news icon in the upper left corner to close the News window.*

The News Window

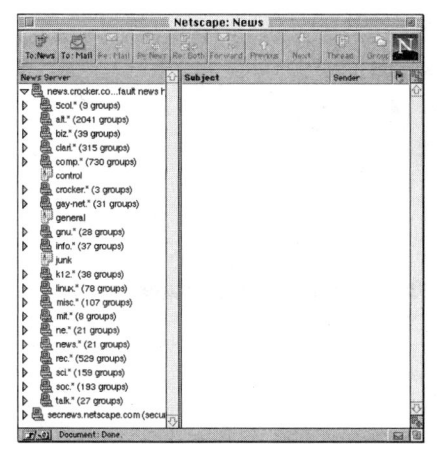

Figure 11.7 *A news host may offer several different categories of newsgroups. Click a triangle to see the individual newsgroups in each section.*

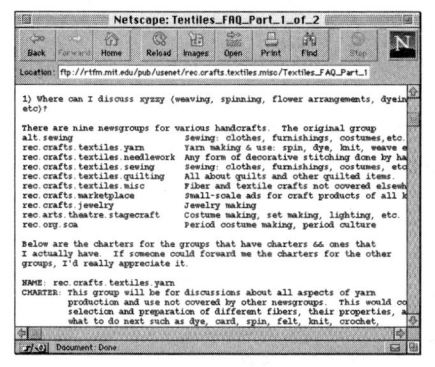

Figure 11.8 *A FAQ (this one is from rec.crafts.textiles) tells what topics are discussed in a particular newsgroup and gives general information about those topics.*

Where newsgroup names come from

There are several major categories of newsgroups: alt (*alternative*, includes a wide variety of groups from alt.sex to alt.appalachian), comp (*computer*, with every program and operating system imaginable), news (*newsgroups*, most contain information about newsgroups themselves), rec (*recreation*, from rec.arts.cinema to rec.games.go to rec.sport.fencing), sci (*science*, from sci.archaeology to sci.virtual-worlds), and soc (*society*, includes the soc.culture newsgroups that discuss different countries and their customs). Your server will probably have access to several more categories, including specialty or local groups.

One good way to find out what a newsgroup is about is by reading its FAQ or *frequently asked questions* file, if it has one. Each newsgroup's FAQ is generally posted to the newsgroup once a month. You can find many of them at **ftp://rtfm.mit.edu/pub/usenet/newsgroup.name** where *newsgroup.name* is the full name of the newsgroup in question.

133

Chapter 11

Opening a news host

Most people have access to only one news server or host. In general, the news host's name is *news.service-provider-name.com* (or .edu). If you're not sure, contact your Internet service provider. You must open at least one news host so that Netscape knows where to connect to get the data for the newsgroups.

To open a new newsgroup host:

1. With the News window active, choose Open News Host in the File menu **(Figure 11.9)**.

2. In the dialog box that appears, type the name of your news server—something like **news.provider.com**. Consult your Internet provider if you're not sure **(Figure 11.10)**.

3. Click OK. Netscape contacts the news host and, if you have the proper access privileges, shows the news host folder in the left pane of the News window **(Figure 11.11)**.

✓ Tips

■ Some news hosts restrict access to certain users. Others let anyone connect to see the newsgroups it contains. For example, to see the newsgroups offered to the public by Netscape Communications, open the news host **secnews.netscape.com**. (The name of the Netscape newsgroup is **netscape.navigator**.)

■ You can open as many news hosts as you have access to.

■ To eliminate a news host, select it and choose Remove News Host in the File menu **(Figure 11.12)**. The news host disappears.

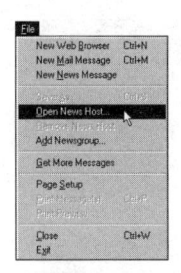

Figure 11.9 *Choose Open News Host in the File menu to set up a new newsgroup server.*

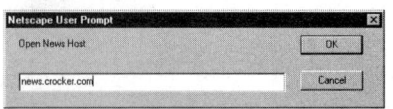

Figure 11.10 *In the dialog box that appears, type the name of the news host (generally "news" followed by the server name).*

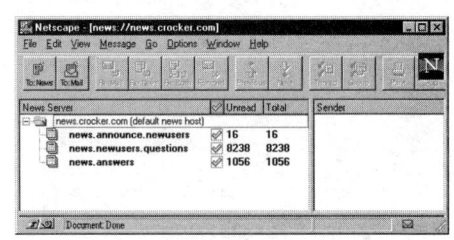

Figure 11.11 *The news host appears in the upper left pane of the News window. Sometimes there will already be a few newsgroups showing, but usually you'll have to download the whole list (see page 135).*

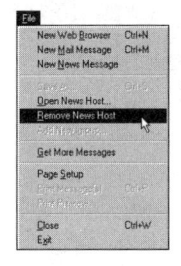

Figure 11.12 *To eliminate an old or unused news host from the left pane, choose Remove News Host in the File menu.*

134

The News Window

Getting a list of all newsgroups

Your Internet service provider decides which newsgroups you have access to and which you don't. Some commercial online services like CompuServe and AOL have gotten a bit of press lately about their efforts to censor certain newsgroups. By downloading the full list from the server, you can see exactly what you get. It also makes it easy to browse through them and subscribe to the ones that interest you (see page 139).

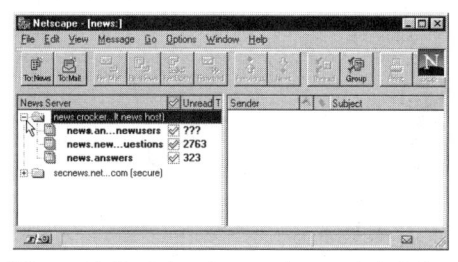

Figure 11.13 *Select the news host and click the plus sign next to its name to open it.*

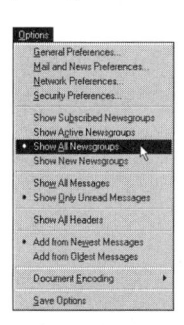

Figure 11.14 *Choose Show All Newsgroups in the Options menu.*

To get a list of all newsgroups:

1. Select a news host and then click the plus sign next to the news host's name to open it (**Figure 11.13**).

2. Choose Show All Newsgroups in the Options menu (**Figure 11.14**). If this is the first time that you've selected this option with this news host, it may take a few minutes. All of the available newsgroups are listed in the upper left pane (**Figure 11.15**).

✓ Tips

- Viewing all the newsgroups is useful for finding new newsgroups. You can then create a subset of newsgroups that interest you and hide the rest. For more information on choosing a subset, consult *Subscribing to a newsgroup* on page 139. For more details on hiding the newsgroups that don't interest you, consult *Showing only subscribed newsgroups* on page 140.

- Click the plus sign next to a name with an asterisk to see all the newsgroups in that category. Click the minus sign to hide them.

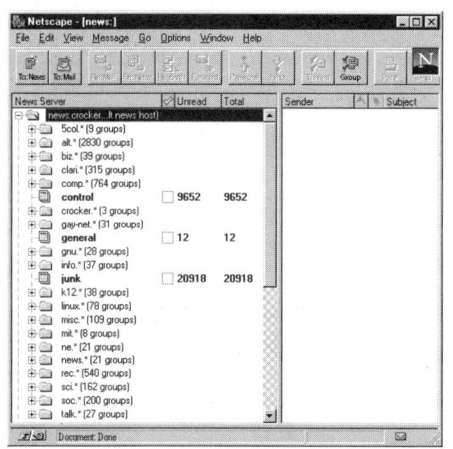

Figure 11.15 *All of the newsgroups that the news host contains are displayed, divided into categories. Click the plus sign next to a newsgroup folder (which has an asterisk in its name) to see the "subnewsgroups" it contains.*

135

Chapter 11

Getting a list of new newsgroups

New newsgroups are added all the time. All it takes is a group of people who write a charter, elicit votes from the potential public and then distribute the new newsgroups to the Internet. You can display the newsgroups which have been added since the last time you checked.

To get a list of new newsgroups:

1. Select the desired news host and click the plus sign to its left.

2. With the News window active, choose Show New Newsgroups in the Options menu **(Figure 11.16)**. A message will appear that tells you how many new newsgroups have been added, if any, since the last time you used this command.

3. Click OK **(Figure 11.17 and Figure 11.18)**. The new newsgroups are displayed at the end of the current newsgroup list **(Figure 11.19)**.

✔ Tip

■ You are not automatically subscribed to new newsgroups. For more information on subscribing, consult *Subscribing to a newsgroup* on page 139.

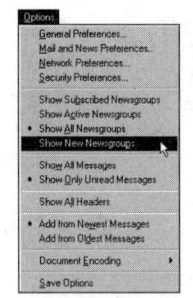

Figure 11.16 *With the News window active, choose Show New Newsgroups in the Options menu.*

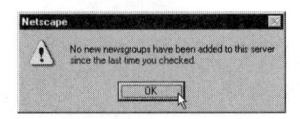

Figure 11.17 *Netscape will show an alert if no newsgroups have been created since the last time you checked.*

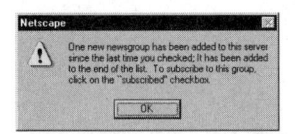

Figure 11.18 *If new newsgroups have been created since the last time you checked, Netscape will tell you how many there are and then display them at the bottom of the current list.*

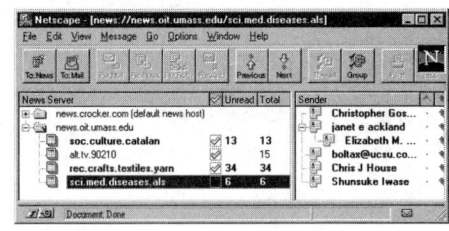

Figure 11.19 *Netscape lists the new newsgroup (sci.med.diseases.als) at the end of your current list. You are not automatically subscribed to it.*

The News Window

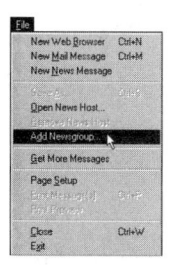

Figure 11.20 *With the News window active, choose Add Newsgroup in the File menu.*

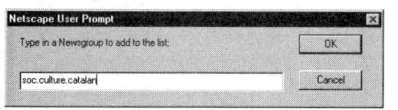

Figure 11.21 *In the dialog box that appears, type the full name of the newsgroup that you want to view.*

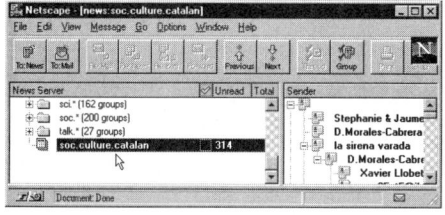

Figure 11.22 *The new newsgroup appears at the end of the list in the left pane. You are not automatically subscribed to it.*

Viewing a newsgroup by name

If you know the name of a newsgroup, you don't have to sort through the full list in order to view it.

To view a newsgroup when you know its name:

1. With the News window active, choose Add Newsgroup in the File menu **(Figure 11.20)**.

2. In the dialog box that appears, type the full name of the newsgroup that you want to view **(Figure 11.21)**.

3. Click OK. The newsgroup appears in the left pane of the News window **(Figure 11.22)**.

✓ **Tip**

■ You are not automatically subscribed to a newsgroup when you view it. For more information, consult *Subscribing to a newsgroup* on page 139.

137

Chapter 11

Viewing a newsgroup from other windows

You can view, and then subscribe to, a newsgroup from the browser or the Mail window. If you know the newsgroup's name, you can type it in the Location field in the browser. In addition, if you encounter a link to the newsgroup, either on a Web page or in an e-mail message, you can click the link to view the newsgroup.

To use the Location field in the browser to view a newsgroup:

1. In the main Netscape window, type **news:newsgroup.address** in the Location field, where *newsgroup.address* is the complete name of the newsgroup that you wish to view **(Figure 11.23)**. Netscape automatically displays the News window with the selected newsgroup at the bottom of the list in the left pane.

2. Click the newsgroup's name to display the messages in the right pane of the News window **(Figure 11.24)**.

To jump to a newsgroup from a Web page or e-mail:

1. Click the link on the Web page or e-mail message **(Figure 11.25)**. The News window opens and displays the newsgroup in the left pane.

2. Click the newsgroup's name to view its messages in the right pane **(Figure 11.26)**.

✔ Tip

- You are not automatically subscribed to a newsgroup when you view it *(see page 139)*.

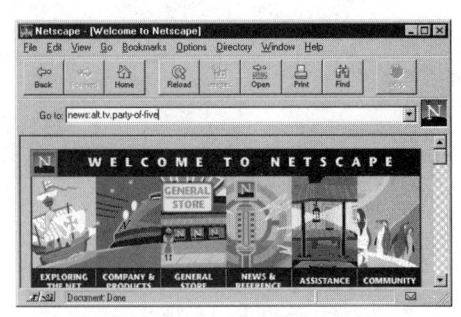

Figure 11.23 *Type* **news:** *followed by the newsgroup's name in the Location field in the main Netscape window.*

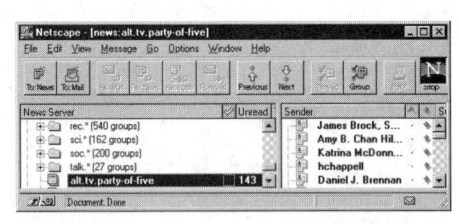

Figure 11.24 *The newsgroup appears at the bottom of the list and its messages appear in the right pane.*

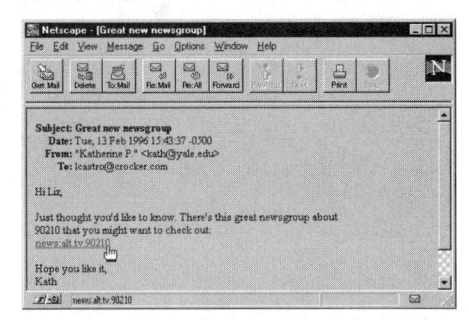

Figure 11.25 *Click a link to a newsgroup from a Web page or an e-mail message.*

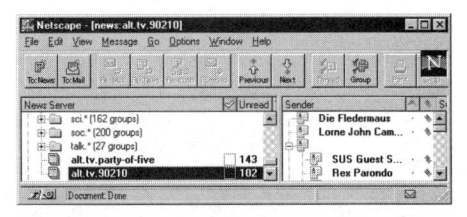

Figure 11.26 *Netscape automatically switches to the News window and shows the newsgroup in the left pane at the bottom of the list with its messages in the right pane.*

The News Window

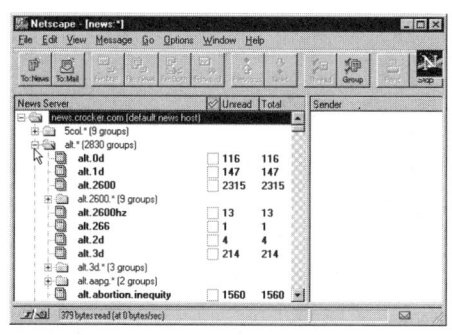

Figure 11.27 *Scroll around in the list of newsgroups in the left pane until you see the one that you want to subscribe to. Click the plus sign next to folders to open them (or click the minus sign to hide their contents).*

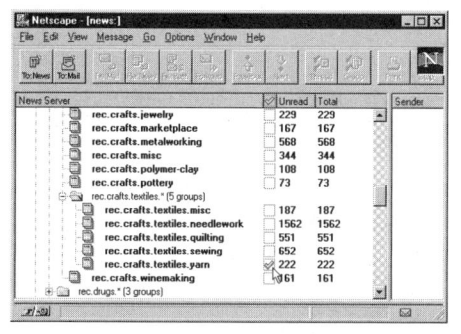

Figure 11.28 *Click the box next to the newsgroup's name to subscribe to it. A yellow checkmark will appear.*

Subscribing to a newsgroup

You can browse through the postings in any newsgroup from the full list *(see page 135)*. However, since there are over 14,000 individual newsgroups, it is handy to select a few that you wish to follow and hide the rest. Selecting a newsgroup is called *subscribing* to it.

To subscribe to a newsgroup:

1. Use the techniques described on the preceding pages to show the desired newsgroup in the upper left pane of the News window **(Figure 11.27)**.

2. Click in the Subscribed column (the one headed by ☑), directly to the right of the newsgroup's name **(Figure 11.28)**. A yellow checkmark appears next to the newsgroup to show that you have subscribed to it.

To cancel a subscription to a newsgroup:

Click the yellow checkmark next to a newsgroup's name to cancel a subscription. The yellow checkmark disappears.

✔ Tip

- You can subscribe to as many newsgroups as you like. The idea, of course, is to subscribe to the ones that you will actually read, and then hide the rest. You can always go back to the main list.

139

Chapter 11

Showing only subscribed newsgroups

Once you have subscribed to each newsgroup in which you are interested, you can hide the rest. You can also choose to view only the newsgroups to which you are subscribed that have new messages (since the last time you checked).

To show only the newsgroups that you have subscribed to:

1. Select a news host in the News window.

2. Choose Show Subscribed Newsgroups in the Options menu **(Figure 11.29)**. The extra newsgroups are hidden and only the newsgroups that you have subscribed to are shown **(Figure 11.30)**.

Some of the newsgroups to which you have subscribed may have many new messages added each day. Others may not see any action during weeks. You can choose to display only those newsgroups to which you have subscribed that have *new* messages.

To show only the newsgroups with new messages:

1. Select a news host in the News window.

2. Choose Show Active Newsgroups in the Options menu **(Figure 11.31)**. Only the newsgroups to which you are subscribed that have new messages are displayed **(Figure 11.32)**.

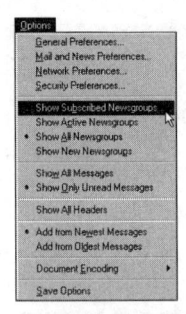

Figure 11.29 *With the News window open, choose Show Subscribed Newsgroups in the Options menu.*

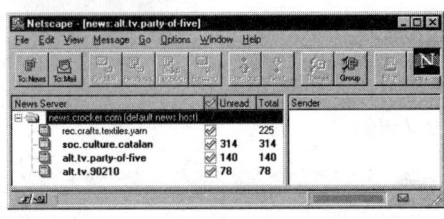

Figure 11.30 *Only the newsgroups that you have subscribed to (marked by a yellow checkmark) are shown in the left pane of the News window.*

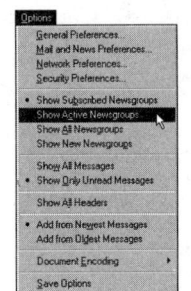

Figure 11.31 *With the News window active, choose Show Active Newsgroups in the Options menu.*

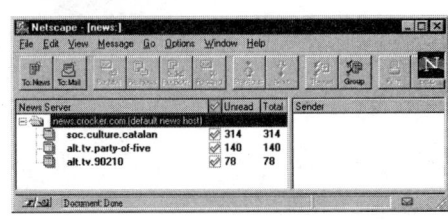

Figure 11.32 *Netscape only shows those newsgroups that you're subscribed to that have messages that you haven't read yet. (Notice that the rec.crafts.textiles.yarn newsgroup that appeared in Figure 11.30 does not appear here, because it has no unread messages.)*

The News Window

Marking messages as read

Some newsgroups get an awful lot of traffic. If you don't have enough time to read every message, you can mark them as read so that they don't appear the next time you open that newsgroup.

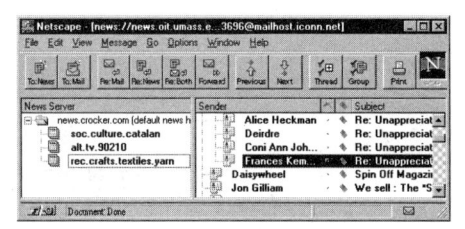

Figure 11.33 *The new unread messages appear in bold face with a green diamond.*

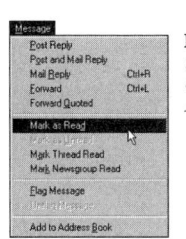

Figure 11.34 *After selecting the desired message(s), choose Mark as Read in the Message menu.*

To mark messages as read:

1. Select the messages that you wish to mark as read **(Figure 11.33)**.

2. Choose Mark as Read or Mark as Unread in the Message menu **(Figure 11.34)**. Read messages no longer appear in boldface, nor do they carry a green diamond **(Figure 11.35)**.

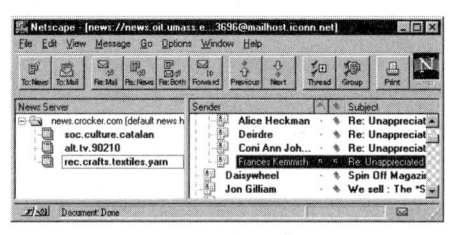

Figure 11.35 *The message marked as read is no longer shown in bold face, and loses its diamond.*

To mark a thread as read:

1. Select a message in the thread. You don't need to select all of them.

2. Choose Mark Thread as Read in the Message menu **(Figure 11.36)**. The messages in the thread no longer appear in boldface, nor do they have a green diamond **(Figure 11.37)**.

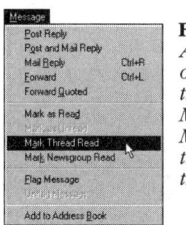

Figure 11.36 *After selecting any one message in the thread, choose Mark Thread Read in the Message menu (left) or click the Mark Thread button on the toolbar (right).*

✓ Tips

- You can hide read messages. For more information, consult *Hiding read messages* on page 143.

- You can also click the Mark Thread button on the toolbar to mark a thread as read. Click the green diamond next to any message to mark it as read. Click it again to mark it as unread.

- For more information about threaded messages, consult *Threading messages* on page 96.

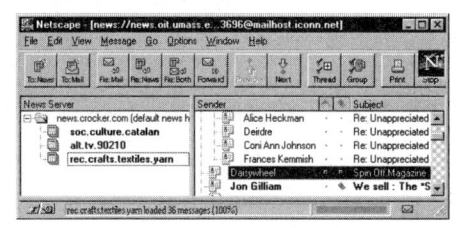

Figure 11.37 *All the messages in the thread are marked as read and, as such, are shown in plain text without the green diamond.*

141

Chapter 11

Marking an entire newsgroup as read

Sometimes you'll want to mark an entire newsgroup as read so that the next time you open the newsgroup you'll be sure that the messages are new.

To mark an entire newsgroup as read:

1. Select the newsgroup—or any message in the newsgroup—that you wish to mark as read **(Figure 11.38)**.

2. Choose Mark Newsgroup Read in the Message menu **(Figure 11.39)**. All the messages in the newsgroup are marked as read **(Figure 11.40)**.

✔ Tip

- You can also click the Mark Group button on the toolbar to mark a group as read **(Figure 11.41)**.

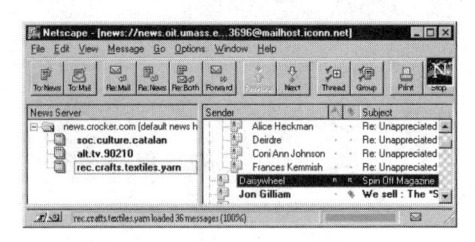

Figure 11.38 *Choose a newsgroup that you wish to mark as read. (You can also click a message within the newsgroup.)*

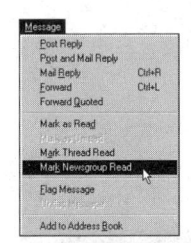

Figure 11.39 *Select Mark Newsgroup Read in the Message menu.*

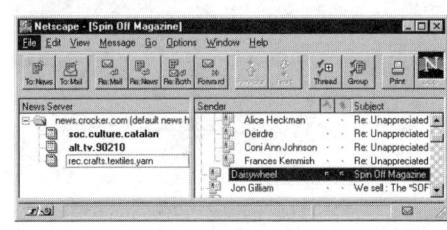

Figure 11.40 *All the messages in the newsgroup are marked as read, and are shown in plain text without the green diamond.*

Figure 11.41 *You can also click the Mark Group button to mark a newsgroup as read.*

The News Window

Hiding read messages

Once you've read a message, you can make it disappear so that it's easier to find the messages you *haven't* read yet.

To hide read messages:

Choose Show Only Unread Messages in the Options menu **(Figure 11.43)**. The messages that you've read—or marked as read—disappear **(Figure 11.44)**.

To show both read and unread messages:

Choose Show All Messages in the Options menu **(Figure 11.45)**. Both the messages that you've read as well as those you haven't appear in the right pane.

✔ Tip

- If you had already selected Show Only Unread Messages in the Options menu, and then read a few messages, the messages don't disappear as you read them. In fact, selecting the option again has no effect. First, you have to select Show All Messages and *then* choose Show Only Unread Messages. Seems like a bug to me.

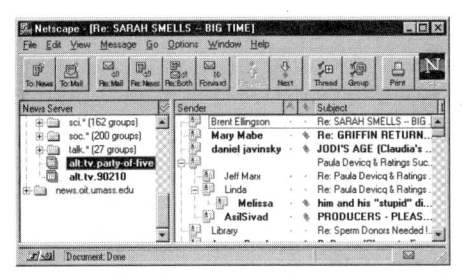

Figure 11.42 *When you read a message or mark it as read, the boldface lettering and green diamond disappear.*

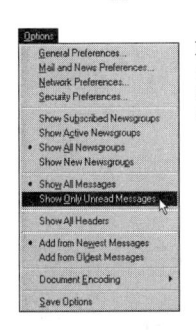

Figure 11.43 *Choose Show Only Unread Messages to view both the read and unread messages.*

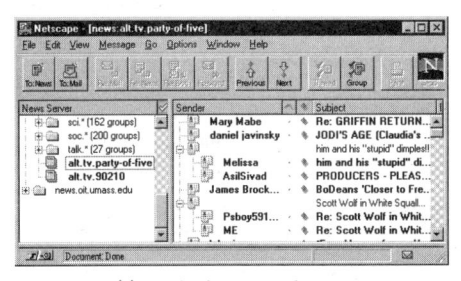

Figure 11.44 *Only the unread messages are shown.*

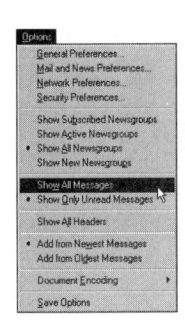

Figure 11.45 *Choose Show All Messages in the Options menu.*

Chapter 11

Getting more messages

Although some newsgroups can contain hundreds or even thousands of messages at a time, Netscape will only load a certain number of these to start. For example, the newsgroup may contain 1,238 messages but Newsgroup will load only 100 at a time. Once you're through with the first one hundred, you can load in more.

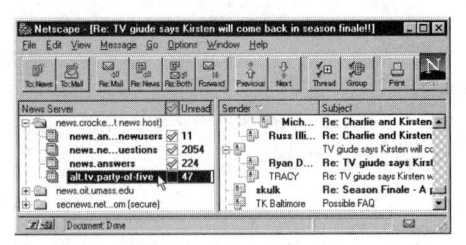

Figure 11.46 *Select the desired newsgroup (or any message it contains).*

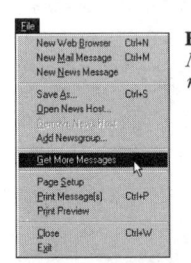

Figure 11.47 *Choose Get More Messages in the File menu.*

To get more messages:

1. Select the desired newsgroup (or any message that it contains **(Fig. 11.46)**.

2. Choose Get More Messages in the File menu **(Fig. 11.47)**. Netscape displays the new set of messages **(Fig. 11.48)**.

To change the number of messages loaded at a time:

1. Choose Mail and News Preferences in the Options menu. The Preferences box appears. Click the Server tab.

2. Type a new number in the text box next to Get xx messages at a time **(Figure 11.49)**.

3. Click OK to close the dialog box.

✔ Tips

■ While your postings may be in order of Sender or Subject, the new postings shown are always in order of date. Threading also affects the display.

■ In the Options menu, choose Add from Newest Messages if you want to load in messages starting with the most recently posted ones. Choose Add from Oldest Messages if you want to load in messages starting from the oldest ones.

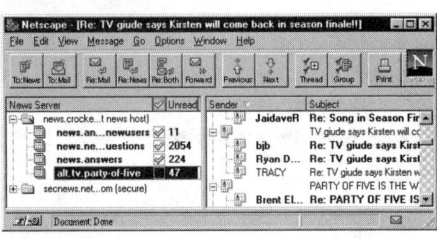

Figure 11.48 *More messages are displayed in the right pane.*

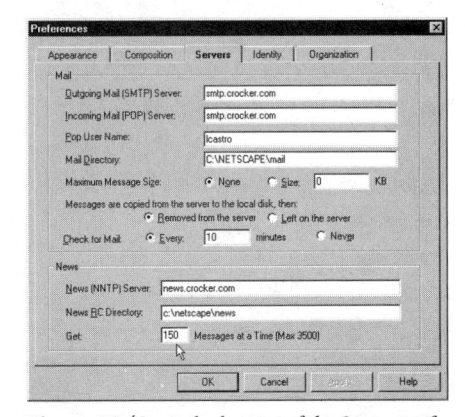

Figure 11.49 *At the bottom of the Server preferences tab, type a number next to Get xx Messages at a time (Max 300).*

Reading and Posting News

The main difference between working with newsgroups and using e-mail is that newsgroup postings disappear while mail remains on your hard disk.

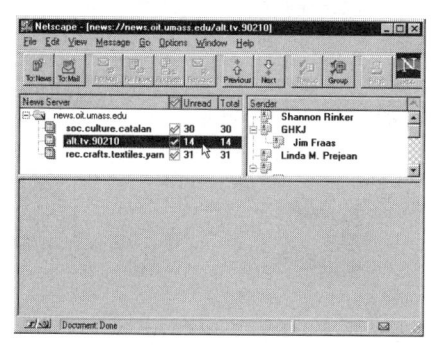

Figure 12.1 *Click the newsgroup's name in the left pane of the News window.*

Reading the postings in a newsgroup

You don't have to subscribe to a newsgroup *(see page 139)*, in order to read the postings that it contains.

To read a newsgroup's postings:

1. Click the newsgroup in the left pane of the News window **(Fig. 12.1)**. The postings are shown in the right pane of the News window.

2. Click a posting in the right pane to display its contents in the lower pane of the News window **(Figure 12.2)**.

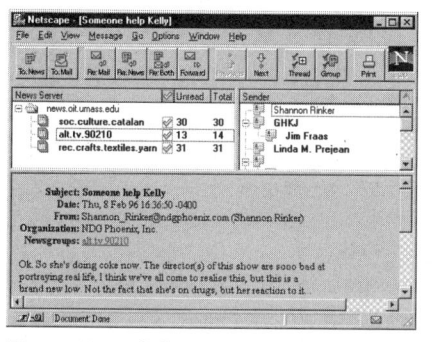

Figure 12.2 *Click a message in the right pane to display its contents in the lower pane.*

3. Use the scroll bars to view more of the message as necessary.

4. Navigate to read more messages *(see page 104)*.

✔ Tips

- Adjust the width of the panes to suit the task at hand **(Figure 12.3)**. For more information, see *Changing the size of the panes* on page 97.

- You can show additional information about a message, including the route it took to get to you (which is sometimes useful for exposing fraudulent messages), by choosing Show All Headers in the Options menu.

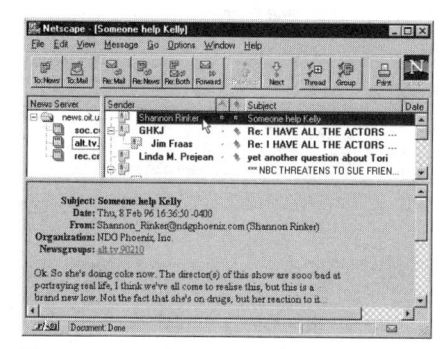

Figure 12.3 *When you're reading messages, make the right pane wider so that you can see the title of each message more clearly.*

Chapter 12

Posting a message to a newsgroup

With e-mail, you can only send messages to people you already know, or at least have the address of. In a newsgroup, you can post a message that may be seen by thousands of people you've never met. The one restriction about posting messages to a newsgroup is the topic. You should restrict your subject matter to that which is usually discussed in that newsgroup. Check the FAQ if you're not sure *(see page 133)*.

To post a message to a newsgroup:

1. In the News window, select the newsgroup—or a message in that group—where you want to post a message **(Figure 12.4)**.

2. Choose New News Message in the File menu or click the To: News button **(Figure 12.5)**. A fresh Message Composition window appears. The selected newsgroup is automatically filled in in the Newsgroups field **(Figure 12.6)**.

3. Type the subject of the message in the Subject field **(Figure 12.7)**. The subject is important: as the most visible part of the message, it can mean the difference between people reading your message or ignoring it.

4. Type the contents of the message in the area at the bottom of the window.

5. Choose Send Now (or Send Later) in the File menu or click the Send button to send the message **(Figure 12.8)**.

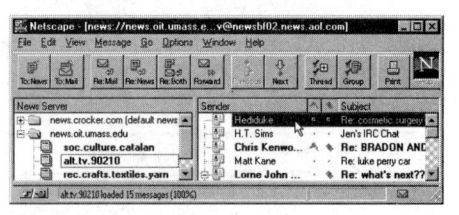

Figure 12.4 *In the News window, select the newsgroup—or a posting in that group—to which you wish to post a message.*

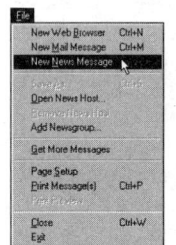

Figure 12.5 *Choose New News Message in the File menu (left) or click the To: News button on the toolbar (right).*

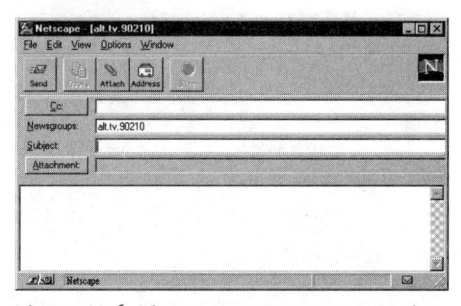

Figure 12.6 *The Message Composition window appears with the name of the newsgroup automatically entered in the Newsgroups field.*

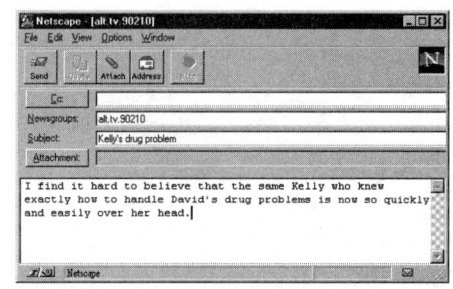

Figure 12.7 *Type the subject in the Subject field and the contents of the posting in the lower area.*

146

Reading and Posting News

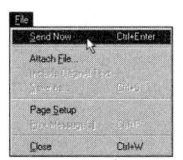

Figure 12.8 *Choose Send Now (or Send Later) in the File menu.*

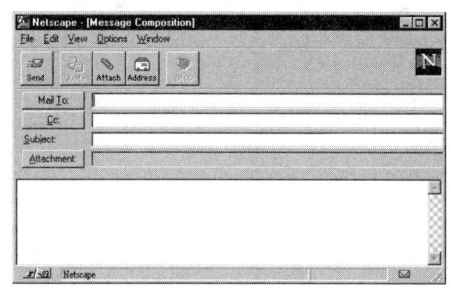

Figure 12.9 *If the Newsgroups field does not appear, you probably didn't choose a newsgroup first.*

Figure 12.10 *Simply choose Newsgroups in the View menu to make the Newsgroups field appear in the Message Composition window.*

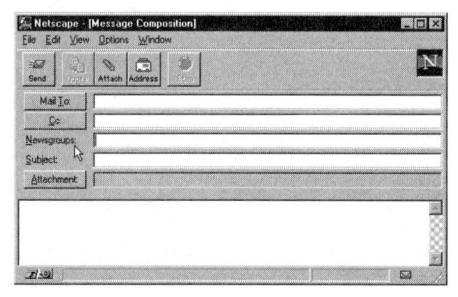

Figure 12.11 *The Newsgroups field appears. Now you can type the name of the newsgroup and post the message.*

✓ Tips

- Posting a message is virtually the same as sending e-mail. The only difference is that an e-mail message requires use of the Mail To field, while a news posting uses the Newsgroups field.

- Click the Address button (or any of the Mail To, Cc, etc. buttons) to make the Address Book appear.

- By default, your messages are posted immediately—although it may take a little while before they appear in the newsgroup. For information on deferred posting, consult *Composing postings offline* on page 149.

- If the Newsgroups field doesn't appear, you probably didn't select the newsgroup before opening the Message Composition window **(Figure 12.9)**. Choose Newsgroups in the View menu **(Figure 12.10)** to make the field appear **(Figure 12.11)** and type in the newsgroup's name. For more information on message parts, consult *Viewing or hiding the parts of a message* on page 106.

- You can post a message to several newsgroups at once. Separate each additional newsgroup name with a comma.

- You attach a URL or file to a news message in exactly the same way as you attach one to an e-mail message. For more information, consult *Attaching files to a message* on page 116 or *Attaching a URL to a message* on page 117.

147

Chapter 12

Replying to a newsgroup post

There are three ways to respond to a message in a newsgroup. If you want everyone in the newsgroup to see your reply, post the response to the newsgroup. If you only want the original sender to receive the reply, e-mail him or her directly. Finally, you can simultaneously post and mail a message to cover all your bases.

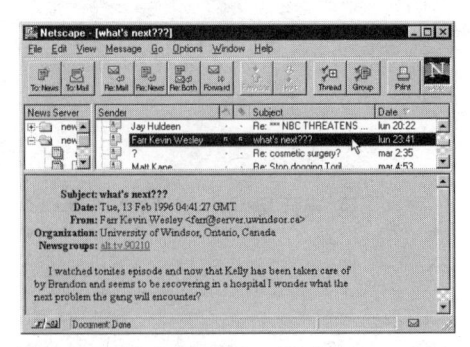

Figure 12.12 *Select the posting that you want to reply to in the right pane of the News window.*

To reply to a newsgroup post:

1. Select the message that you wish to reply to in the upper right pane of the News window **(Figure 12.12)**.

2. In the Message menu, choose Post Reply to have your reply appear in the newsgroup **(Fig. 12.13)**. Choose Send Reply to e-mail your reply only to the writer of the original message **(Fig. 12.14)**. Choose Post and Send Reply to do both things **(Fig. 12.15)**.

3. The Message Composition window appears, with the appropriate fields automatically filled in. The Newsgroups field only appears in postings, the Mail To field only appears in mail.

4. Choose Send Now (or Send Later) in the File menu.

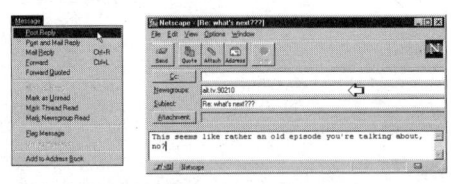

Figure 12.13 *Choose Post Reply in the Message menu (left) to publish the posting in the newsgroup. Notice that the Newsgroups field appears but the Mail To field does not (right).*

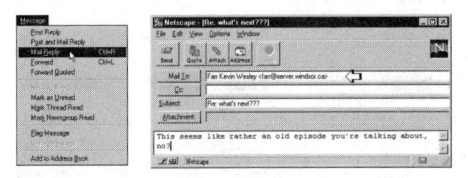

Figure 12.14 *Choose Mail Reply in the Message menu (left) to mail the posting to the original sender. Notice that the Mail To field appears but the Newsgroups field does not (right).*

✓ Tips

■ Generally, you are supposed to try and limit your postings to information that will interest the entire newsgroup. Mail a response when it applies only to the particular recipient.

■ Sometimes, people post messages and then don't check to see if they have any responses. You can post and mail a message to make sure that both the newsgroup members and the recipient receive (and see) a copy.

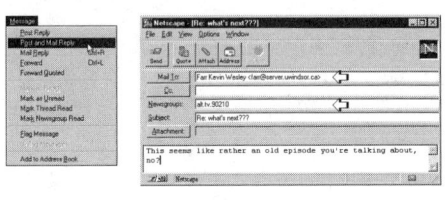

Figure 12.15 *Choose Post and Mail Reply in the Message menu (left) to publish the posting in the newsgroup and send a copy to the original sender. Notice that both the Newsgroups and Mail To fields appear (right).*

Replying to a newsgroup post

148

Reading and Posting News

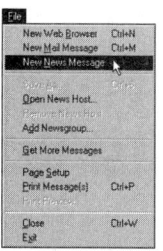

Figure 12.16 *Choose New News Message in the File menu (left) or click the To: News button on the toolbar (right).*

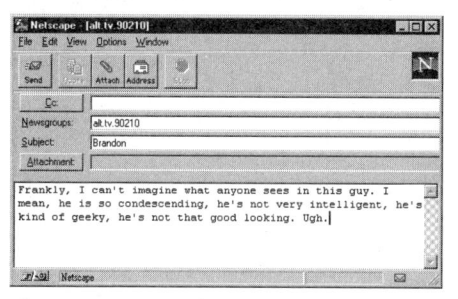

Figure 12.17 *Type the message in the Message Composition window.*

Figure 12.18 *Choose Deferred Delivery in the Options menu.*

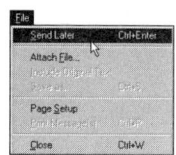

Figure 12.19 *Choose Send Later in the File menu (left) or click the Send button (right) on the toolbar.*

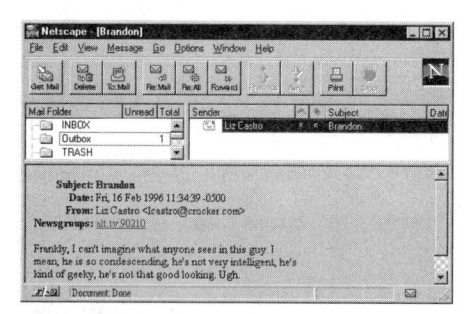

Figure 12.20 *Go to the Mail window and click the Outbox to see the outgoing posting.*

Composing postings offline

When you receive an e-mail message, Netscape downloads it to your hard disk, making it easy to reply to later, even if you're not connected to your Internet account. However, when you read a news posting, the message is not downloaded to your hard disk. So even though you can compose a new posting or a reply offline, you can't browse the existing messages and respond to them directly.

To compose postings offline:

1. Disconnect from the Internet without quitting Netscape (or launch Netscape without connecting to the Internet).

2. Choose New News Message in the File menu **(Figure 12.16)**. The Message Composition window appears.

3. Compose the posting as usual *(see pages 146 and 148)* **(Figure 12.17)**. If you are replying to a posting, type **Re: subject** in the Subject field where *subject* is the original topic.

4. In the Message Composition window's Options menu, choose Deferred Delivery **(Figure 12.18)**.

5. Choose Send Later in the File menu or click the Send button in the Message Composition window **(Fig. 12.19)**. The message is stored in the Outbox in the Mail window **(Figure 12.20)**.

6. When you're ready to send the posting(s) consult *Sending the messages in the Outbox* on page 109.

✔ Tip

- Leave the newsgroup open before disconnecting and make the window as large as possible so that you can at least see all the postings' subject lines.

149

Chapter 12

Sending mail from the News window

Reading a posting in the News window may motivate you to write someone. Perhaps it will just spark your imagination, perhaps you'll want to tell them about something you've read or offer a link to a newsgroup. At any rate, the process is virtually identical to sending e-mail from the Mail window.

To send mail from the News window:

1. Choose New Mail Message in the File menu or click To: Mail on the toolbar **(Fig. 12.21)**. The Message Composition window appears **(Figure 12.22)**.

2. Compose the message as usual *(see page 105)*.

3. If desired, add a link to the newsgroup that inspired you by typing **news:name.newsgroup** in the message area where *name.newsgroup* is the complete name of the newsgroup **(Figure 12.23)**. If the recipient reads the message with Netscape 2, the newsgroup will appear as a link, and a click on it will open the newsgroup for him or her **(Figure 12.24)**.

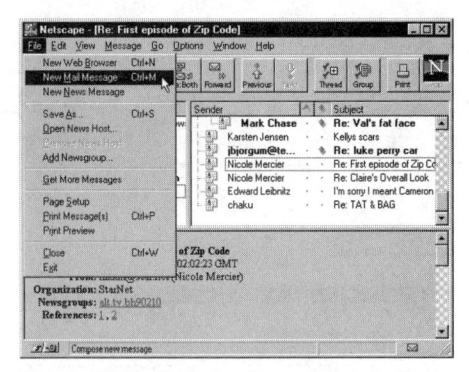

Figure 12.21 *From the News window itself, choose New Mail Message in the File menu.*

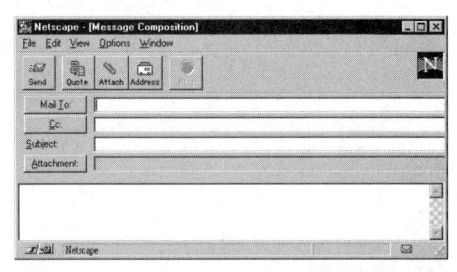

Figure 12.22 *An empty Message Composition window appears.*

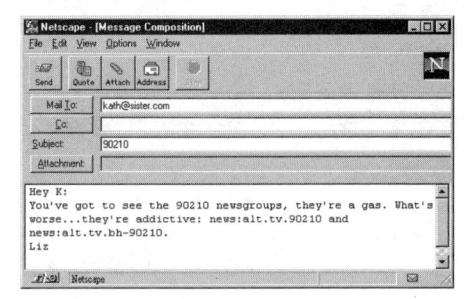

Figure 12.23 *Compose your messages as usual.*

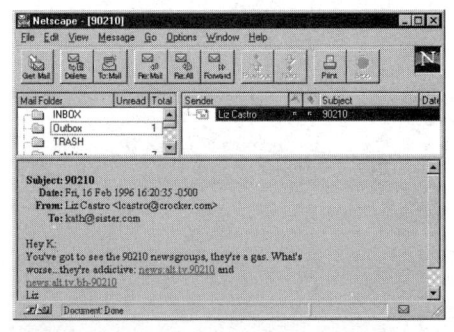

Figure 12.24 *Go to the Mail window and click the Outbox to see the outgoing message.*

150

Part II:
Netscape Navigator Gold
Creating your own Web pages

The Editor Window

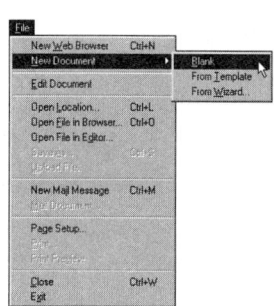

Figure 13.1 *Choose New Document in the File menu and then choose Blank in the submenu.*

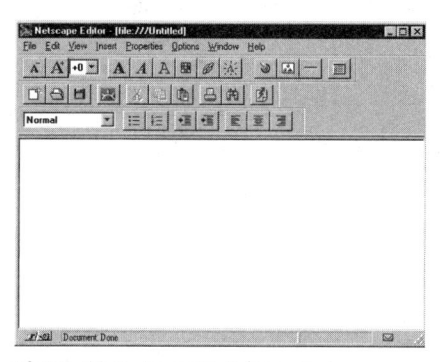

Figure 13.2 *An empty Editor window*

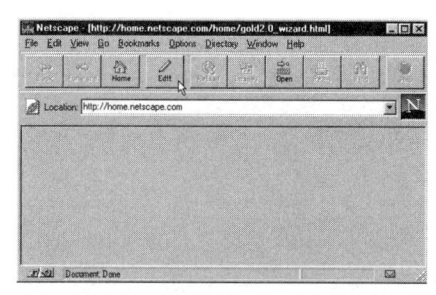

Figure 13.3 *Or, with a blank page in the browser showing, click the Edit button on the toolbar.*

The Editor window is where you create new Web pages and modify existing ones. The Editor window has three unique toolbars and some special menu commands.

There are several ways to open the Editor window, depending on whether you wish to start a new page or modify existing ones.

Opening a blank Editor window

If you wish to start a Web page completely from scratch, you should open a blank Editor window. Then you will be able to create a page using the instructions in this and subsequent chapters.

To open a blank Editor window:

1. Make sure you are in a browser, and not in the News or Mail windows.

2. Choose New Document in the File menu and Blank in the submenu that appears **(Figure 13.1)**. An empty Editor window appears **(Fig. 13.2)**.

✔ Tips

- You can also open a blank page by clicking the New Document button on the toolbar and choosing Blank Document in the dialog that appears.

- If you have specified a blank page as your home page *(see page 14)*, you can open a blank Editor window by clicking the Edit icon on the browser window's toolbar **(Figure 13.3)**.

- Close the Editor window by choosing Close in the File menu.

153

Chapter 13

Opening a new page with a template

Netscape Communications has developed a set of templates that you can use as a starting off point for your Web pages. There are templates for home pages and for small businesses, for resumes and job listings, for special interest groups and for special interest people.

Each template contains sample images, text and links that you should replace with your own elements. Beware that the links on the pages don't go anywhere; they're just designed to give you ideas.

To open a new page with a template:

1. Open your Internet connection.

2. From either the Editor window or the browser, choose New Document in the File menu and then choose From Template in the submenu **(Fig. 13.4)**. A browser will appear with the current collection of Netscape's templates **(Figure 13.5)**.

3. Navigate to the desired template and click its link. The template appears in the browser **(Figure 13.6)**.

4. Choose Edit Document in the File menu or click the Edit button on the toolbar. Since you must save a document before modifying it, the Save Remote Document dialog box appears **(Figure 13.7)**.

5. Check the Adjust links to assist in remote publishing option so that Netscape adapts the links in the page that you are browsing so that it works in a local setting (and you can test it).

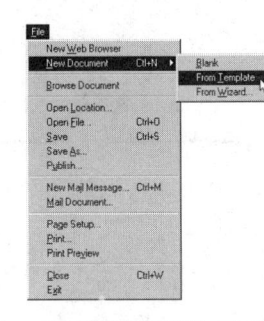

Figure 13.4 *Choose New Document in the File menu and then choose From Template in the submenu.*

Figure 13.5 *Click the desired template's link.*

Figure 13.6 *The template appears in the browser. A template may include images, text and links that you can replace with your own.*

154

The Editor Window

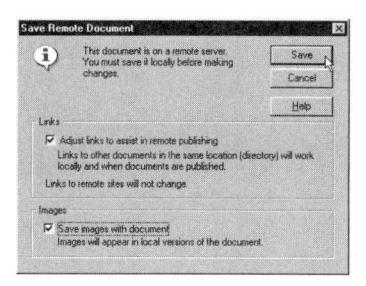

Figure 13.7 *The Save Remote Document appears whenever you try to edit a page from the Web that you have not yet saved. Generally, you should check both options and click Save.*

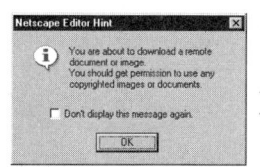

Figure 13.8 *You are not allowed to copy any images you find out on the Web for your page. Click OK.*

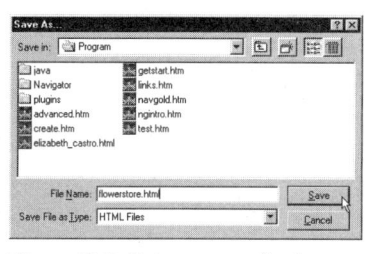

Figure 13.9 *Enter a name for the page and choose a location on your hard disk. Then click Save.*

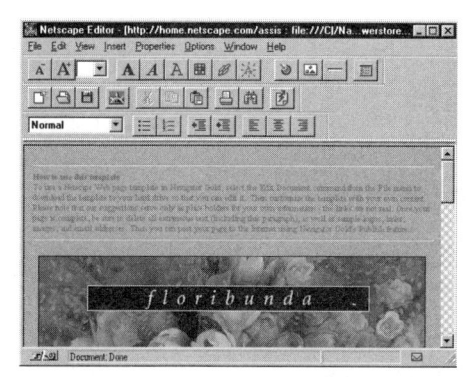

Figure 13.10 *The template is opened in the Editor window. Change the text, images and links to suit your needs.*

6. Check the Save images with document option. If you don't, Netscape only saves the text, that is, the HTML tags that make up the document.

7. Click Save.

8. A dialog box may appear warning you about copyright issues **(Fig. 13.8)**. You may not copy any images you find on the Web without permission. Click OK.

9. In the standard Save dialog box that appears **(Figure 13.9)**, choose a name and location for the page and click Save. The template will appear in the Editor window **(Figure 13.10)**.

✔ Tips

- You can also open a new page with a template by clicking the New Document button on the File/Edit Tools toolbar and then clicking From Template in the dialog box that appears.

- You must be connected to the Internet to be able to access Netscape's templates.

- You can create your own templates and then set up Netscape to open *them* when you choose New Document/From Template in the File menu *(see page 230)*.

Opening a new page with a template

155

Chapter 13

Opening a new page with the Page Wizard

Netscape has also set up a special script that takes information entered into a form and converts it into a Web page. You can then use the generated Web page as is or modify it further as desired.

To open a new page with the Page Wizard:

1. Open your Internet connection.

2. From the browser or Editor window, choose New Document from the File menu and then From Wizard in the submenu **(Figure 13.11)**. Netscape's Page Wizard is displayed in the browser **(Figure 13.12)**.

3. Fill in the form. Press Tab to move from one field to the next.

4. Click the Create Page button at the bottom of the Page Wizard to have Netscape create a page from the information you've entered. Click Clear Page to erase everything and start over. The generated page appears in the Editor window **(Figure 13.13)**.

5. Choose Edit Document in the File menu or click the Edit button to view the new page in the Editor window **(Figure 13.14)**.

6. The Save Remote Document will appear. Make sure both options are checked and click Save.

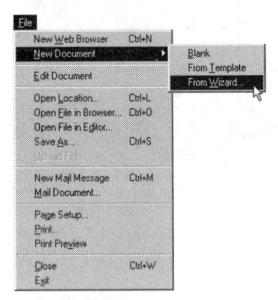

Figure 13.11 *Choose New Document in the File menu and then choose From Wizard in the submenu.*

Figure 13.12 *Netscape's Page Wizard is a long form. Fill out each of the boxes and choose various page elements and then click Create Page at the bottom of the page.*

156

The Editor Window

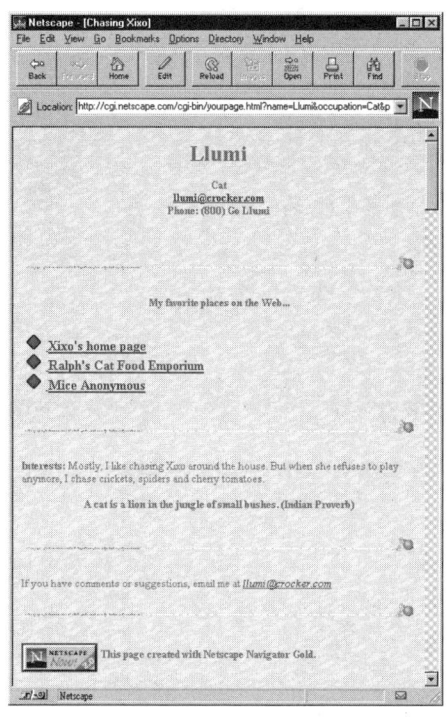

Figure 13.13 *Your page is generated from the responses given on the form. Notice the Netscape Gold logo at the bottom of the page.*

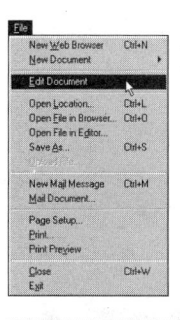

Figure 13.14 *Choose Edit Document in the File menu (or click the Edit button on the toolbar).*

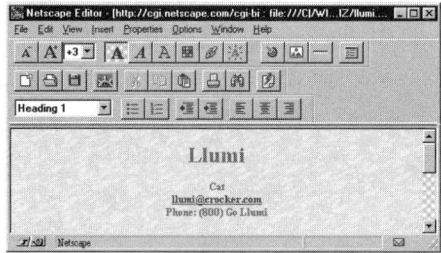

Figure 13.15 *You can polish the generated page in the Editor window.*

7. The Copyright warning dialog box may appear. Read it and click OK. The images in the generated page are not copyrighted.

8. In the Save dialog box that appears, give the page file a name and choose a location for it. Then click OK. The generated page appears in the Editor window **(Figure 13.15)**.

9. Edit the page as desired.

✓ Tips

- You can also jump to Netscape's Page Wizard by clicking the New Document button on the File/Edit Tools toolbar and then clicking From Page Wizard in the dialog box that appears.

- Be careful to choose a background pattern that contrasts enough with the text color so that people can read your page.

- If you don't like the way the page comes out, click the Back button, change the desired options (everything will be just as you left it) and click Create Page again.

- Netscape inserts its own logo at the bottom of every page created with the Page Wizard. If you don't feel like doing your part to advertise Netscape's stock, just erase it once you're in the Editor window.

- You have to be connected to the Internet to use the Page Wizard.

Chapter 13

Editing an existing page

You may save Web pages that you find on the Web and edit them to create new pages. This is a good way to learn different Web page construction techniques, although you should keep in mind that the images and text you find may be copyrighted, and at any rate, should not be used in your Web page without permission.

To edit an existing page:

1. Navigate to the page that you wish to edit **(Figure 13.16)**.

2. Choose Edit Document in the File menu or click the Edit button on the toolbar. The Save Remote Document dialog box appears **(Figure 13.17)**.

3. Check both options in the Save Remote Document dialog box and click Save.

4. The copyright warning dialog box appears. Read it and click OK.

5. In the Save As dialog box that appears, enter a name and choose a location for the file and then click Save **(Fig. 13.18)**. The page is displayed in the Editor window **(Figure 13.19)**.

✓ Tip

■ You shouldn't copy any text or images from another page without permission. Besides being against the law, it's pretty slimy. Instead, use other pages as a source of inspiration. Then write your own text and draw or scan your own pictures.

Figure 13.16 *Navigate to the desired page and click the Edit button on the toolbar.*

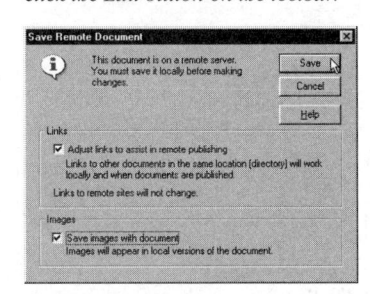

Figure 13.17 *You should generally check both options in the Save Remote Document dialog box.*

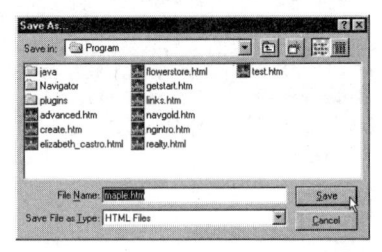

Figure 13.18 *Enter a name and choose a location for the file and then click Save.*

Figure 13.19 *The page viewed in the Editor window.*

158

The Editor Window

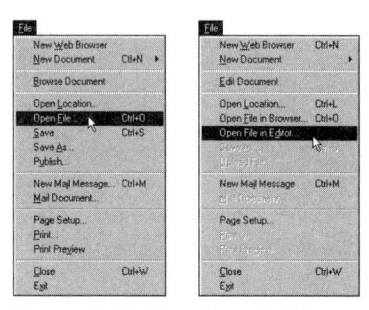

Figure 13.20 *If you have the Editor window active, choose Open File in the File menu (left). If a browser is active, the option will be Open File in Editor (right).*

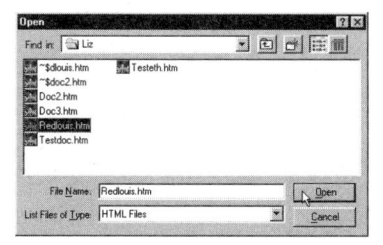

Figure 13.21 *Find the file on your hard disk that you wish to edit. You can open any text file, as long as it has the .htm or .html extension.*

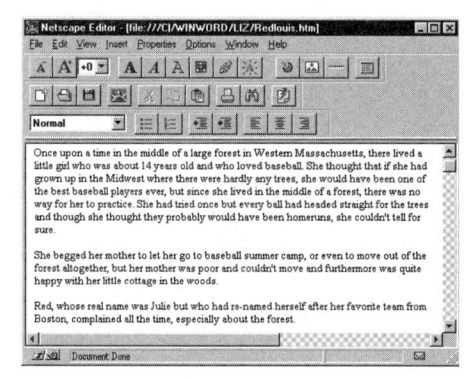

Figure 13.22 *Once the text file is in the Editor window, you can format it and add images and links.*

Editing a saved file

You don't have to go out on the Web to find a page to copy. You can open any HTML file that you have previously created or saved—indeed *any* text file—in the Editor window.

To edit a saved file:

1. Make sure the saved file is either an HTML or text only document. In both cases, it must carry either the .htm or .html extension.

2. If you're in the Editor window, choose Open File in the File menu. With a browser active, choose Open File in Editor in the File menu **(Fig. 13.20)**. The Open dialog box appears.

3. Navigate to the desired file and click Open **(Fig. 13.21)**. The file appears in the Editor window **(Figure 13.22)**.

✓ Tips

- If you want to convert an existing document into a Web page, first save it in Text only format with the .htm extension. Then open it in the Editor window.

- You are not limited to documents created with Netscape. Any text document will do.

159

Chapter 13

Adding a title and keywords

The title and keywords of a page, and in lesser degree, the author, description and classification, are used by search services to categorize Web pages. By creating a descriptive title and inserting specific keywords, you make it easier for people to find your page.

To add a title and keywords:

1. With the Editor window active, choose Document in the Properties menu. The Document Properties dialog box appears.

2. Enter a title for your page. Make it short (less than 60 characters) and descriptive.

3. If desired, enter your name in the Author field, and a short description in the Description field.

4. In the Keywords field, type three or four important words that appear on your page or that your page is about.

5. If desired, type a category in the Classification field.

6. Click OK to save the changes.

✔ Tip

■ You can set the Author name in the Editor Preferences dialog box *(see page 230)* so that you don't have to type it in each time.

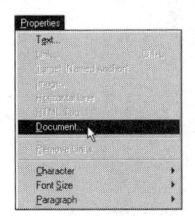

Figure 13.23 *Choose Document in the Properties menu.*

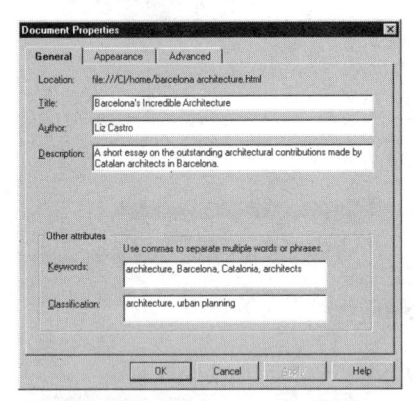

Figure 13.24 *In the Document Properties dialog box, fill in the fields and then click OK.*

Figure 13.25 *The new title appears in the title bar, in front of the page's file name.*

The Editor Window

Saving your Web page

It's important to save your Web pages frequently while creating them.

To save your Web page:

1. With the Editor window active, choose Save in the File menu **(Figure 13.26)**.

2. If you have not saved the file before, the Save As dialog box will appear. Enter a name and location for the document and make sure that HTML Files appears in the Save File as Type pop-up menu **(Figure 13.27)**.

3. Click Save. The document is saved and the new file name appears in the title bar **(Figure 13.28)**.

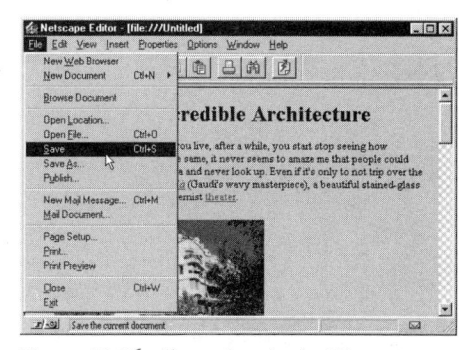

Figure 13.26 *Choose Save in the File menu.*

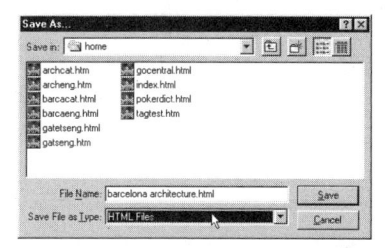

Figure 13.27 *Give the file a name, choose a location, make sure the format is HTML Files, and then click Save.*

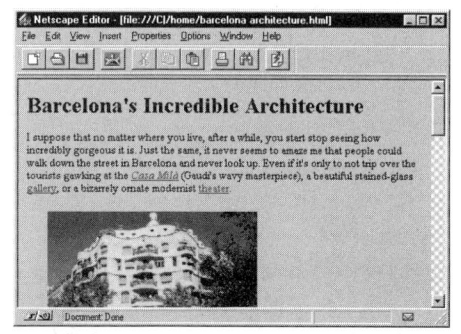

Figure 13.28 *The new file name appears in the title bar.*

✔ Tips

- After you've saved the document once, choose Save to save additional changes and Save As to save the document with a new name or location.

- You can also save a Web page by clicking the Save Document button on the File/Edit Tools toolbar.

- The first time you create a link or insert an image on a page, Netscape will automatically make you save the page on your hard disk.

- If you try and close a page without saving the changes, Netscape will give you a chance to save the page.

Chapter 13

The Editor window's toolbars

The Editor window has three toolbars: File/Edit Tools **(Figure 13.29)**, Paragraph Properties **(Figure 13.30)** and Character Properties **(Figure 13.31)**. The buttons on the toolbars are simply shortcuts to menu commands.

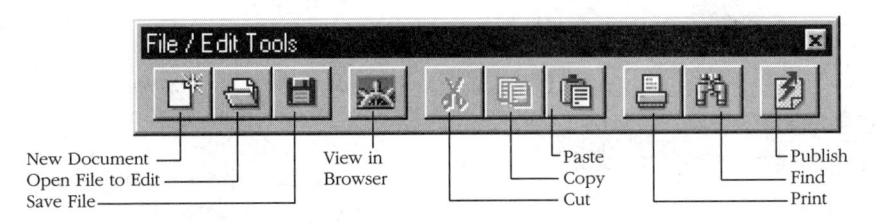

Figure 13.29 *The File/Edit Tools toolbar contains many of the commands available in the File and Edit menus.*

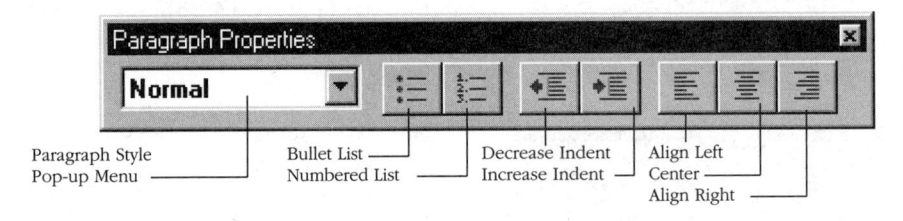

Figure 13.30 *The Paragraph Properties contains formatting commands that affect the entire paragraph (not just a few words).*

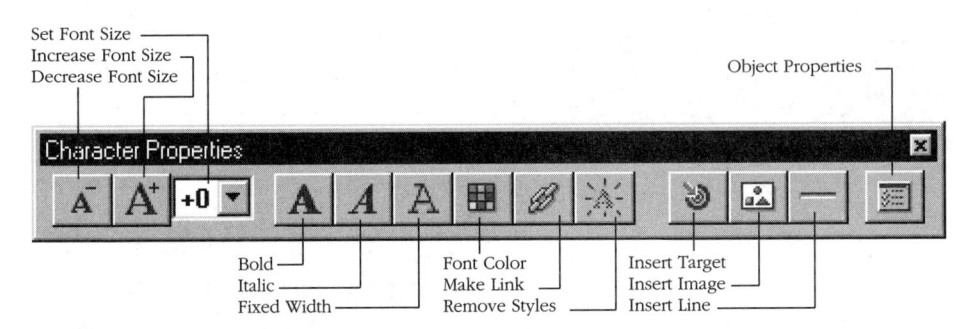

Figure 13.31 *The Character Properties toolbar contains formatting commands that affect individual characters or words, as well as the Insert commands.*

162

The Editor Window

Repositioning the toolbars

The Editor window's toolbars are very flexible. You can move them from side to side, or from row to row in the toolbar area, or you can drag them out of the toolbar area altogether, converting them into floating palettes.

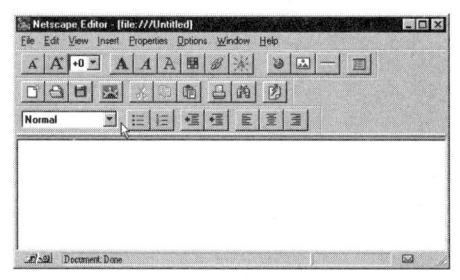

Figure 13.32 *Each time you open a new Editor window, the three toolbars appear aligned to the left at the top of the window in individual rows.*

To move a toolbar from one row to another:

Drag the toolbar from the current row to the desired location in the top or bottom toolbar area **(Figure 13.33)**. You can also shift toolbars horizontally **(Figure 13.34)**.

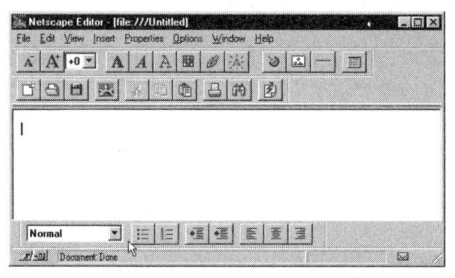

Figure 13.33 *You can drag any toolbar to any other row, or even to the bottom of the window, as shown here.*

To convert a toolbar into a floating palette:

Drag the desired toolbar outside the toolbar area. The toolbar changes into a floating palette and acquires a close box **(Figure 13.35)**. Drag it back to the top or bottom toolbar area to convert it back into a fixed toolbar.

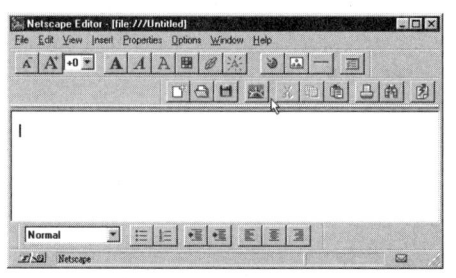

Figure 13.34 *You can also drag the toolbars horizontally.*

✓ Tips

- The configuration of one Editor window's toolbars does not affect the other Editor windows' toolbars.

- Return the toolbars to their original positions by opening a new Editor window.

- You can tell if a toolbar is going to be turned into a palette by the size of the shadow as you drag it. A smaller shadow means it will stay a toolbar. A larger shadow means it will be a palette.

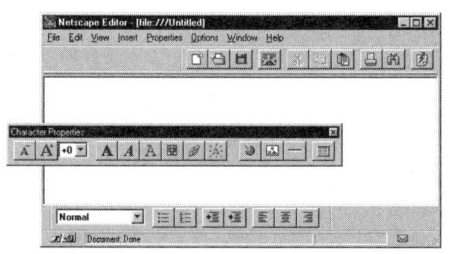

Figure 13.35 *If you drag the toolbar outside of the toolbar areas (top or bottom) it becomes a floating palette.*

163

Chapter 13

Hiding or showing the toolbars

You can hide the toolbars altogether, to give yourself more room for editing a Web page.

To hide or show the toolbars:

In the Options menu, choose Show File/Edit Toolbar, Show Character Format Toolbar, or Show Paragraph Format Toolbar **(Figure 13.36)**. When a checkmark appears, the toolbar is visible. Choose the command again to toggle it.

✔ Tip

- When the toolbars are in palette form, hide them by clicking their close boxes **(Figure 13.37)**. Reveal them by choosing the appropriate option in the Options menu.

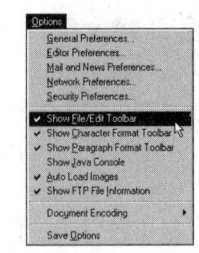

Figure 13.36 *Hide or reveal a toolbar (or palette) by choosing the corresponding command in the Options menu. A checkmark means that the toolbar is visible.*

Click the close box to hide a floating palette.

Figure 13.37 *You can also hide a toolbar in the form of a floating palette by clicking its close box.*

164

Formatting a Web Page

A Web page is not just a regular word processing document. Its formatting is added with special tags that enable you to save the page in text only format. This means that the document can be read by practically any computer in existence. Although you could write the tags, called HTML, with any word processor, even NotePad or WordPad, the Editor window in Netscape Gold has one important advantage: instead of showing the tags, it shows you the actual formatting.

HTML was designed to be a universal language, equally intelligible from a PC as from a Mac, or even a UNIX computer. For that reason, not all formats are available in the Editor window. For example, you can't choose a font for the page. Although this might be frustrating for font aficionados, it's a blessing for the rest of us who may have a more limited supply.

Chapter 14

Adding basic character formatting

As in word processors and page layout software, character formatting means any style that can be added to a single character or word. *Basic* character formatting means bold, italic, fixed width, strikethrough, superscript, subscript and blinking **(Figure 14.1)**.

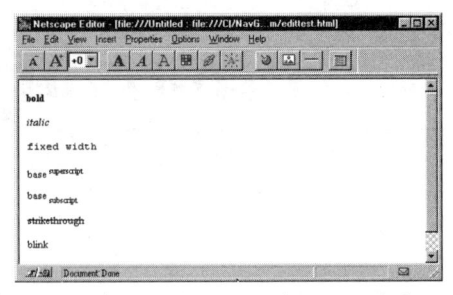

Figure 14.1 *All character styles except* Blink *are displayed properly in the Editor window. Of course, it would be hard to show you Blink in a book even if it* were *blinking.*

To add basic character formatting:

1. Select the character(s) you wish to modify **(Figure 14.2)**.

2. Choose Character in the Properties menu and then choose the desired style in the submenu **(Figure 14.3)**. The changes are applied to the text immediately **(Figure 14.4)**.

✔ Tips

- If you don't select anything before applying styles, the formatting will be applied to the next thing you type.

- You can also apply character formatting by checking an option in the Style section of the Character Properties dialog box *(see page 169)*.

- Apply bold, italic and fixed width formatting by clicking the corresponding button on the Character Properties toolbar: A, *A* or A, respectively.

- Unfortunately, Netscape Gold only uses *physical* formatting like bold and italic. To apply *logical* formatting like emphasis or strong, you must add the HTML tag manually. For more information, consult *Adding HTML tags manually* on page 206.

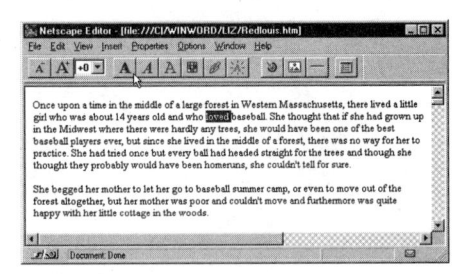

Figure 14.2 *Select the letters or words that you wish to format.*

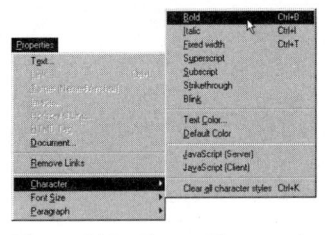

Figure 14.3 *Choose Character in the Properties menu and then choose the desired style in the submenu.*

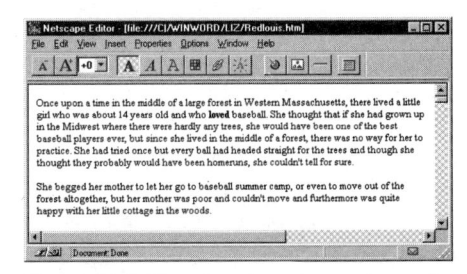

Figure 14.4 *The selected word now appears in* Bold *formatting.*

Changing the size of text

You may change the size of certain words to give them emphasis **(Figure 14.5)**. Unfortunately, the font size is not a standard HTML tag and may not be recognized by other Web browsers besides Netscape. For more information, consult *Standard HTML* on page 204.

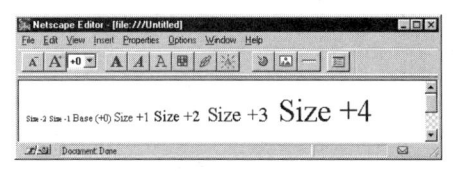

Figure 14.5 *There are seven possible sizes, two smaller than the base size and four larger.*

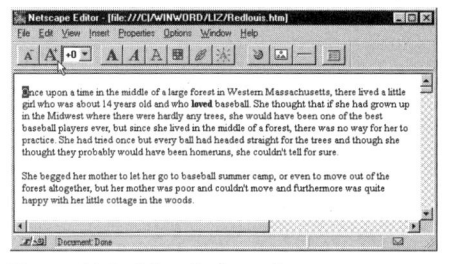

Figure 14.6 *Select the letter that you want to change. Here, only the initial O is selected.*

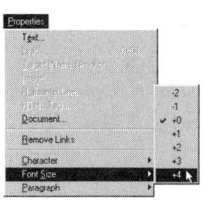

Figure 14.7 *Choose the desired size in the Font Size submenu in the Properties menu.*

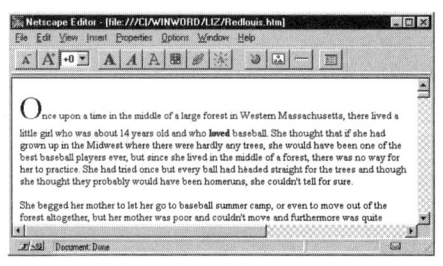

Figure 14.8 *The initial O is now several sizes larger than the rest of the text.*

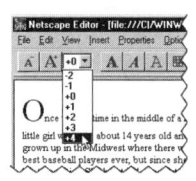

Figure 14.9 *You can also apply a new size by choosing it from the Font Size pop-up menu on the Paragraph Properties toolbar.*

To change the size of text:

1. Select the character(s) that you wish to make larger or smaller **(Fig. 14.6)**.

2. Choose Font Size in the Properties menu and then a relative size in the submenu that appears **(Figure 14.7)**. The text is changed **(Fig. 14.8)**.

✔ **Tips**

- You can't choose an absolute size for text; each paragraph has a size, and you can modify individual characters with respect to that size. In addition, the sizes you choose all depend on the font that your reader has chosen to view your page with *(see page 16)*.

- You can also click the Decrease Font Size icon A in the Character Properties toolbar to make text one unit smaller. Click the Increase Font Size icon A to make text one unit larger.

- Use the Font Size pop-up menu to choose a particular (relative) size **(Figure 14.9)**.

- As illustrated in the example, changing the size of an individual letter may change the spacing (leading) of the entire line. There's no simple solution. (The hard solution is to insert an *image* of the opening letter and wrap the text around it—see page 184.)

Chapter 14

Changing the color of text

You should be a little careful about changing the color of the text on your Web page. First of all, some colors already have standard uses, like blue for links and purple for visited links. Secondly, the colors should have good contrast with the background color or image. Finally, realize that not all of your readers will have color screens (or may choose to view pages with their own colors) and may not benefit from your efforts.

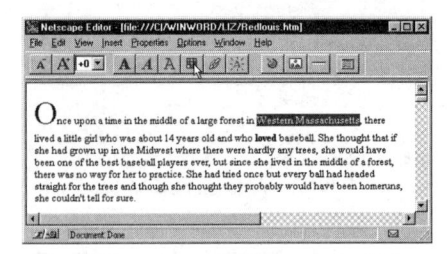

Figure 14.10 *Select the letters or words that you wish to change.*

To change the color of text:

1. Select the character(s) that you wish to change the color of **(Figure 14.10)**.

2. Choose Character in the Properties menu and then Text Color in the submenu that appears **(Figure 14.11)**. The Color dialog box appears.

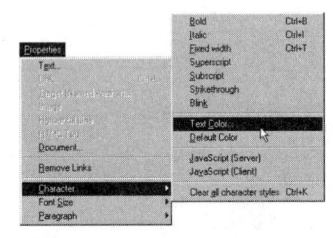

Figure 14.11 *Choose Character in the Properties menu and then Text Color in the submenu.*

3. Click the desired color for the text and click OK **(Figure 14.12)**. The text changes color **(Figure 14.13)**.

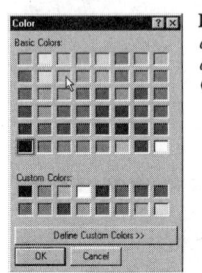

Figure 14.12 *Click the desired color in the Color dialog box and then click OK.*

✓ Tips

- You can also change the color of text by clicking the Font Color button on the Character Properties toolbar.

- Change text back to its default color by selecting the text and choosing Default Color in the Character submenu under Properties. The default colors are specified in the Editor window dialog box. Typically, regular text is black, links are blue, visited links are purple and active links are red.

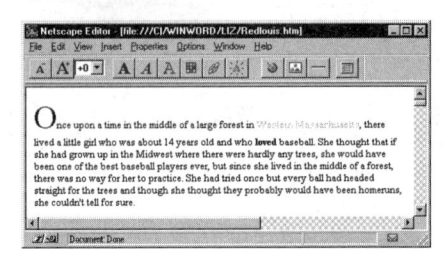

Figure 14.13 *The text is changed to the selected color.*

168

Formatting a Web Page

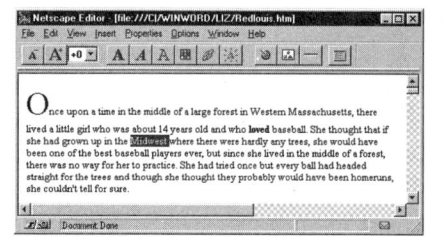

Figure 14.14 *Select the text you wish to change.*

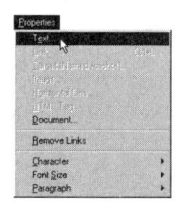

Figure 14.15 *Choose Text in the Properties menu.*

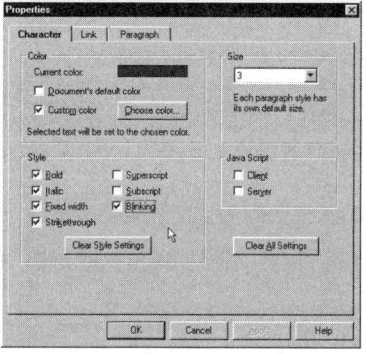

Figure 14.16 *Choose the desired character styles in the Character Properties dialog box and then click Apply or OK.*

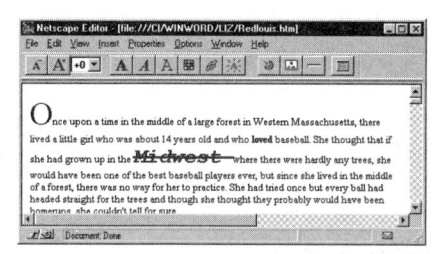

Figure 14.17 *All the chosen styles are applied to the selected text.*

Applying many character styles at once

Although there are about twelve ways to apply character formatting (OK, maybe four), one of the nicest is through the Character Properties dialog box, since you can apply several styles at once, see the changes without closing the dialog box, modify the options, and try again and again until you're satisfied with the results.

To apply many character styles at once:

1. Select the character(s) that you wish to modify **(Figure 14.14)**.

2. Choose Text in the Properties menu **(Figure 14.15)**. The Properties dialog box appears.

3. Click the Character tab to see the Character properties.

4. Check the desired character styles, select a size and choose a color for the text **(Figure 14.16)**.

5. If desired, click Apply to apply the changes without closing the dialog box. You may then check or uncheck the desired options, and click Apply again until you are satisfied.

6. Click OK (or Close if you've already applied the changes) to close the Character Properties dialog box. All the changes are applied **(Fig. 14.17)**.

✓ Tip

■ You can make the Character Properties box appear by right clicking the text selection and selecting Character Properties in the submenu that appears.

169

Chapter 14

Clearing character styles

Sometimes it's easy to go overboard with character formatting. Luckily, it's easy to get rid of. Netscape has two commands for clearing character styles. One eliminates only the basic character styles like bold and italic while the other eliminates all possible character styling, including size, color, and JavaScript coding.

To clear character styles:

1. Select the desired text and choose Text in the Properties menu **(Figure 14.18)**.

2. Click the Character tab to see the Character properties.

3. To eliminate basic style settings click Clear Style Settings. To eliminate all character formatting, click Clear All Settings **(Figure 14.19)**.

4. Click Apply to apply the changes without closing the dialog box.

5. Click OK (or Close if you've already applied the changes) to close the dialog box. The formatting is removed **(Figure 14.20)**.

✔ Tips

- Another way to "deformat" text is by clicking the Clear All Styles button on the Character Properties toolbar or selecting Clear all character styles in the Properties menu under Character **(Figure 14.21)**.

- You can open the Character Properties box by right clicking the text and choosing Character Properties in the submenu that appears.

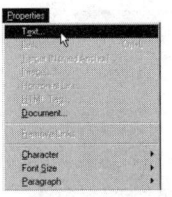

Figure 14.18 *Choose Text in the Properties menu.*

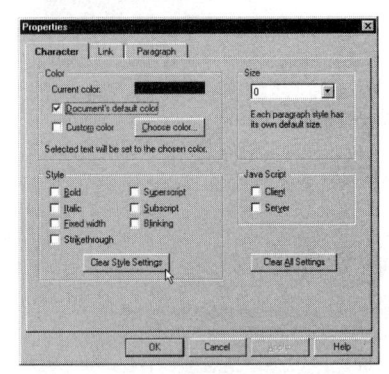

Figure 14.19 *Click Clear Style Settings (left with the arrow) to remove all the basic character styles. Click Clear All Settings to reset all the styles in this dialog box to their defaults. Then click Apply or OK.*

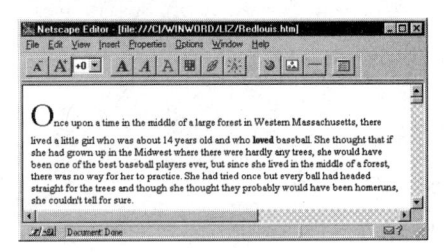

Figure 14.20 *All of the formatting is removed from the selected text.*

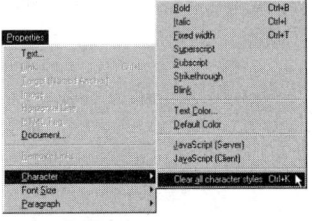

Figure 14.21 *Another way to remove all of the character formatting is by choosing Character in the Properties menu and then Clear all character styles in the submenu.*

170

Formatting a Web Page

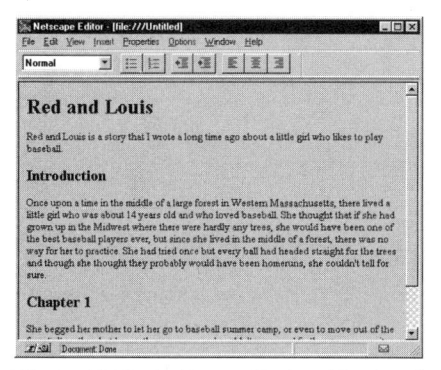

Figure 14.22 *In this page,* Red and Louis *is formatted with Heading 1,* Introduction *and* Chapter 1 *are formatted with Heading 2. The rest of the text is Normal.*

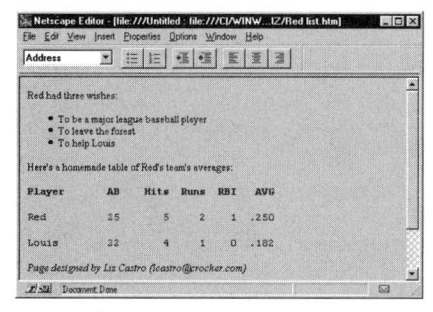

Figure 14.23 *Here we have an unordered list, with round bullets, and a table made from formatted text (that is, fixed width text). At the bottom of the page is the author's name, formatted with Address.*

Using paragraph styles

Paragraph styles, by definition, affect an entire paragraph. In Netscape Gold, and indeed in HTML in general, the styles are already defined and each browser on each platform interprets them in its own way. This way, you can distinguish one paragraph from another and organize your information without restricting your page to a particular platform.

To use paragraph styles:

1. Decide how you want to organize your information. Divide your page into sections, with descriptive headings. Apply the Heading styles to section heads **(Figure 14.22)**.

2. Use the List Item for lists. There are several kinds: Numbered, Unnumbered (unordered), Directory, Menu and Description **(Fig. 14.23)**. These are described more fully on page 173.

3. The Formatted style (known as Preformatted in regular HTML lingo) is for fixed width text like handmade tables **(Figure 14.23)** or ASCII images. All spaces are maintained and the text is displayed in a fixed width font like Courier.

4. Use the Address style to format your name and e-mail address as a signature at the bottom of the page **(Figure 14.23)**.

5. Use Description Title and Description Text to format the pairs of entries in Description lists.

Using paragraph styles

171

Chapter 14

Applying paragraph styles

Once you've figured out which paragraph styles to use, applying them is quite easy.

To apply paragraph styles:

1. Click anywhere in the paragraph that you wish to modify **(Figure 14.24)**. You don't need to select the whole paragraph.

2. Select Paragraph in the Properties menu and then choose the desired paragraph style in the submenu that appears **(Figure 14.25)**. The entire paragraph is affected **(Figure 14.26)**.

✓ Tips

- You can also apply paragraph styles by choosing the desired option in the Paragraph style pop-up menu on the Paragraph Properties toolbar **(Figure 14.27)**.

- One more way to apply paragraph styles is with the Paragraph Properties dialog box *(see page 178)*.

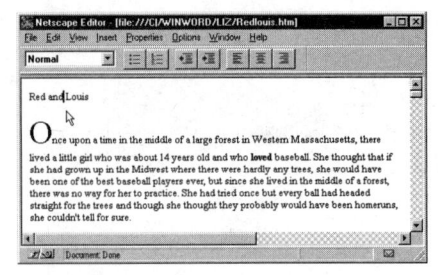

Figure 14.24 *Click in the paragraph you want to format.*

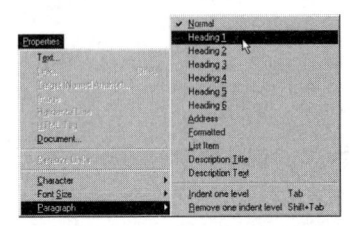

Figure 14.25 *Choose Paragraph in the Properties menu and then choose the desired style in the submenu.*

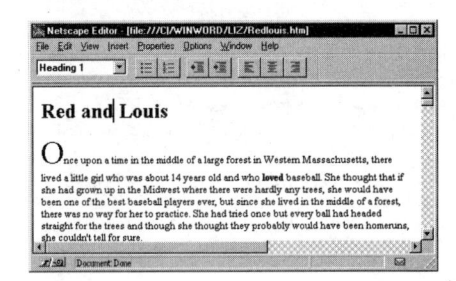

Figure 14.26 *The whole paragraph is formatted.*

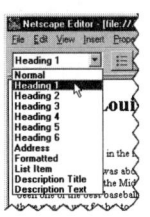

Figure 14.27 *You can also choose styles in the Style pop-up menu on the Paragraph Properties toolbar.*

172

Formatting a Web Page

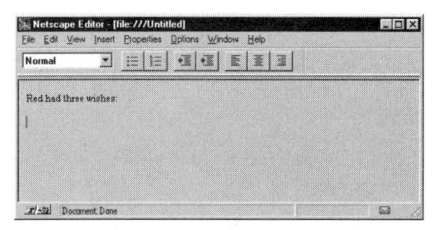

Figure 14.28 *Click in the paragraph where you want to create a list. You needn't type anything.*

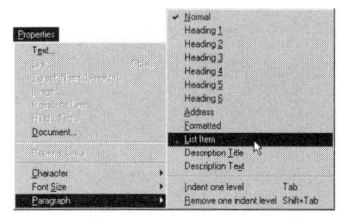

Figure 14.29 *Choose Paragraph in the Properties menu. Then choose List Item in the submenu.*

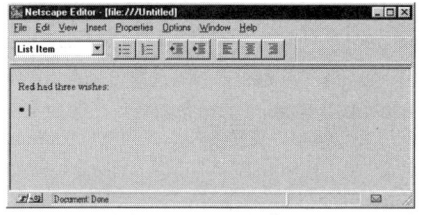

Figure 14.30 *You can tell by the bullet that the paragraph is formatted as a list.*

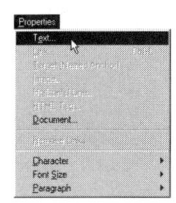

Figure 14.31 *Choose Text in the Properties menu.*

Creating lists

While applying other paragraph styles is a one step process as described on page 172, creating a list has two parts: applying a list style and choosing what kind of list you want it to be.

To create a list:

1. Place the cursor in the paragraph that you want to convert into a list item **(Figure 14.28)**. There doesn't have to be text in it yet.

2. Select Paragraph in the Properties menu and then choose List Item in the submenu that appears **(Fig. 14.29)**. The selected paragraph is converted into a list item in an unnumbered list (*unordered*, in HTML lingo) and the bullet of the first line appears **(Figure 14.30)**.

3. If you want to choose a different kind of list, select Text in the Properties menu **(Figure 14.31)**. The Properties dialog box appears.

4. Click the Paragraph tab to see the Paragraph Properties. The Paragraph style will already show List Item. Choose List in the Additional style pop-up menu if it's not already selected.

5. In the List section, which is now active, choose the kind of list you want to create **(Figure 14.32)**.

6. For unnumbered lists, you can select what kinds of bullets should be used in the Bullet Style pop-up menu. If you've chosen the Numbered list style, you can decide what kind of numbering to use with the Number Style pop-up menu. Then choose an initial number for the list in the Starting number text box.

173

Chapter 14

7. If desired, click Apply to apply the changes without closing the dialog box. Make additional changes and apply them until you are satisfied.

8. Click OK (or Close if you've previously applied the changes) to close the dialog box. The changes will be evident **(Figure 14.33)**.

9. Type the contents of the list if you haven't done so already, adding a return after each list item **(Fig. 14.34)**.

✔ Tips

- Use the Bullet List button or the Numbered List button on the Paragraph Properties toolbar to change a list from one format to the other.

- If you have any characters selected in a list item line before using the unnumbered or numbered list buttons on the toolbar, the changes affect the selected line and the one preceding it. With the cursor in the list item but with nothing selected, the changes affect all the lines in the list, both above and below the current one.

- After you're finished typing a list and you choose Normal style to add some more body text, Netscape doesn't quite make the paragraph normal, but instead makes it *indented* normal. To make it really normal, click the Remove one indent level button on the Paragraph Properties toolbar.

- The numbers in a numbered list do not appear until you browse the page **(Figure 14.35)**. Until then, they are shown as ##. All initial letters appear as lowercase *a*.

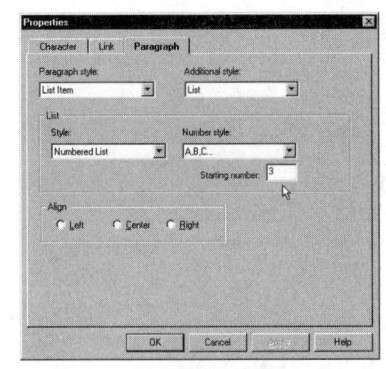

Figure 14.32 *Choose List in Additional Style and select the type of list in the Style menu. Then choose a bullet or number style. Finally, click OK.*

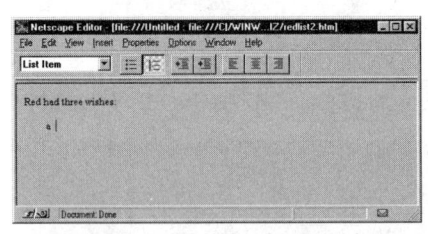

Figure 14.33 *In the Editor window, Numbered lists with letters are shown with a lower case* a.

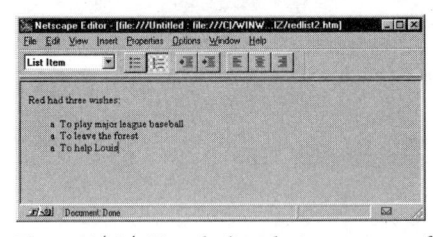

Figure 14.34 *Type the list, placing a return after each item. You could just as easily type the list at the beginning and then format it using the same steps.*

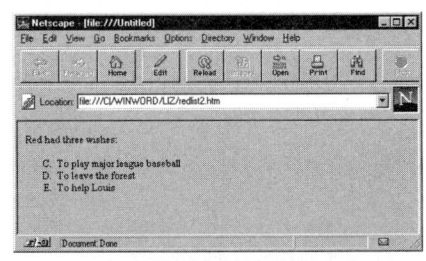

Figure 14.35 *When you view the page with a browser, the letters appear as they should: capital, sequential, starting with C (see Figure 14.32) and with a period after each initial letter.*

174

Formatting a Web Page

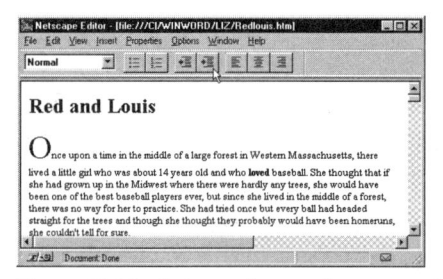

Figure 14.36 *Click anywhere in the paragraph that you want to indent.*

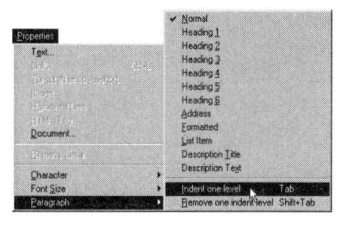

Figure 14.37 *Choose Paragraph in the Properties menu and then Indent one Level in the submenu.*

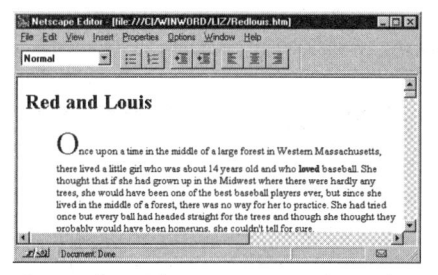

Figure 14.38 *The entire paragraph is indented.*

Indenting a paragraph

HTML does not accept multiple spaces or returns. If you try and type two spaces, the program will simply ignore you. However, Netscape Gold lets you indent an entire paragraph, with a device that approximates a tab.

To indent a paragraph:

1. Place the cursor anywhere in the paragraph that you want to indent **(Figure 14.36)**. You don't have to select anything.

2. Choose Paragraph in the Properties menu and choose Indent one level in the submenu **(Figure 14.37)**. The paragraph is indented toward the right **(Figure 14.38)**.

When you remove an indent from a paragraph, the whole paragraph is shifted back toward the left.

To remove an indent:

1. Place the cursor anywhere in an indented paragraph.

2. Choose Paragraph in the Properties menu and then choose Remove one indent level in the submenu that appears. The indent disappears and the paragraph is moved to the left.

✓ Tips

- You can also add an indent with the Tab key and remove one using Shift+Tab. It's strange, but it even works in the middle or end of a line.

- Or use the Increase Indent button or the Decrease Indent button on the Paragraph Properties toolbar.

175

Chapter 14

Aligning text

You can align the text on your page to the left or to the right, or you can center it. By default, all paragraphs are aligned to the left.

To align text:

1. Click anywhere in the paragraph you wish to align **(Figure 14.39)**. You don't have to select anything.

2. Choose Text in the Properties menu. The Properties dialog box appears.

3. Click the Paragraph tab to see the Paragraph Properties.

4. Click the desired alignment option at the bottom of the dialog box **(Figure 14.40)**.

5. If desired, click Apply to apply the changes without closing the dialog box. Change the options and click Apply again until you are satisfied with the results.

6. Click OK (or Close if you've applied the changes) to close the dialog box. The text is aligned as specified **(Figure 14.41)**.

✔ Tip

■ You can also align text by choosing the Align Left, Center or Align Right buttons on the Paragraph Properties toolbar.

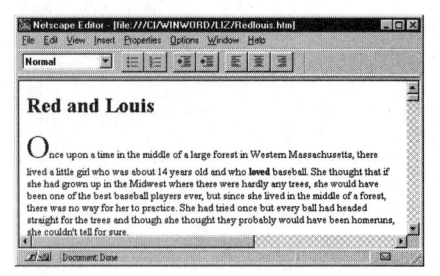

Figure 14.39 *Click anywhere in the paragraph whose alignment you want to change.*

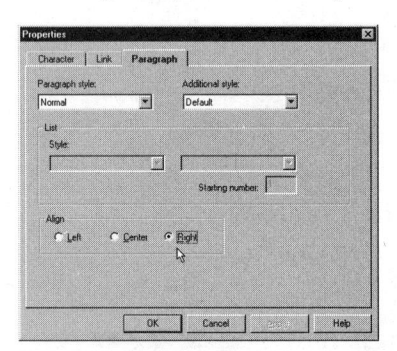

Figure 14.40 *Choose the desired alignment option and click Apply or OK.*

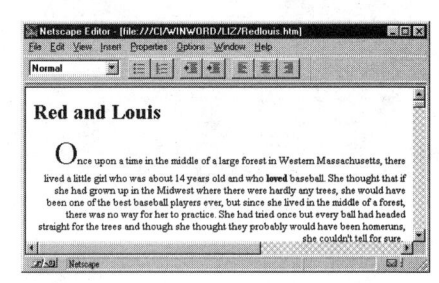

Figure 14.41 *The paragraph is aligned to the right.*

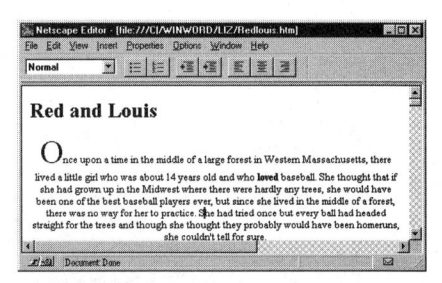

Figure 14.42 *On this page, the paragraph has been centered.*

176

Formatting a Web Page

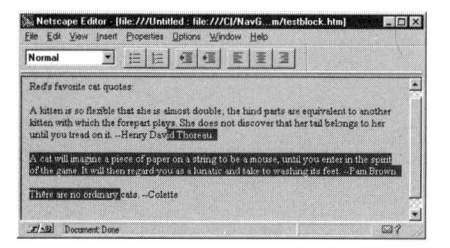

Figure 14.43 *Select the paragraph(s) that you wish to convert to block quotes. (You don't have to select the entire paragraph.)*

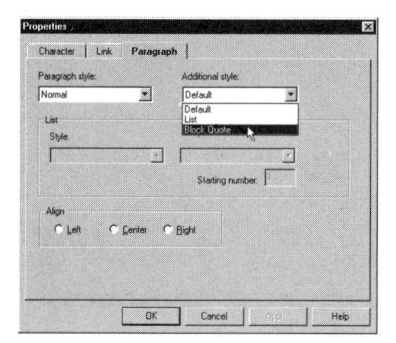

Figure 14.44 *Choose any style you want in the Paragraph style pop-up menu. Then choose Block Quote in the Additional style pop-up menu.*

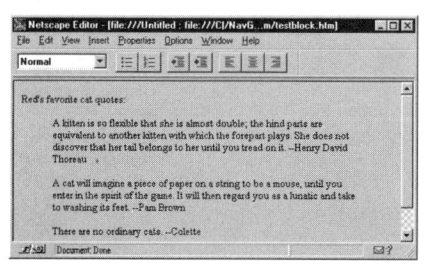

Figure 14.45 *The block quotes are indented on both sides.*

Creating a block quote

A block quote is a special device used on Web pages to call attention to a short paragraph. In Netscape, block quotes are formatted in the proportional font and are indented from both margins.

To create a block quote:

1. Click anywhere in the paragraph that you wish to make into a block quote **(Figure 14.43)**. It doesn't matter if the paragraph has any text in it yet.

2. Choose Text in the Properties menu. The Properties dialog box appears.

3. Click Paragraph to see the Paragraph Properties.

4. Choose the desired style in the Paragraph style pop-up menu.

5. Then choose Block Quote in the Additional style pop-up menu **(Figure 14.44)**.

6. If desired, choose an alignment option.

7. Click Apply to apply the changes without closing the dialog box. Change the options and click Apply again until you're satisfied.

8. Click OK (or Close if you've already applied the changes) to close the dialog box. The selected paragraph is changed to block quotes **(Fig. 14.45)**.

✓ Tips

■ You can combine block quotes with any other principal paragraph style.

■ In many browsers, block quotes are displayed in a fixed width font at a smaller size.

177

Chapter 14

Applying many paragraph features at once

Although it's a bit easier to select the desired paragraph styles from the toolbar or the menu, the Paragraph Properties dialog box lets you apply several paragraph characteristics at once.

To apply several paragraph features at a time:

1. Place the cursor in the paragraph that you wish to modify. You don't need to select anything.

2. Choose Text in the Properties menu **(Figure 14.46)** to view the Properties dialog box.

3. Click the Paragraph tab to see the Paragraph Properties.

4. Choose the desired paragraph style, additional style, list styles, as well as an alignment **(Figure 14.47)**.

5. Click Apply to apply the changes without closing the dialog box. Make changes in the selections and click Apply again until you are satisfied.

6. Click OK (or Close if you've already applied the changes) to close the dialog box. The styles are applied.

✔ Tips

- You can also make the Paragraph Properties appear by right clicking a paragraph and choosing Paragraph/List properties in the submenu that appears **(Figure 14.48)**.

- How do you eliminate styles? Since all paragraphs must have some style, simply apply a different one.

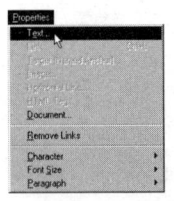

Figure 14.46 *Choose Text in the Properties menu.*

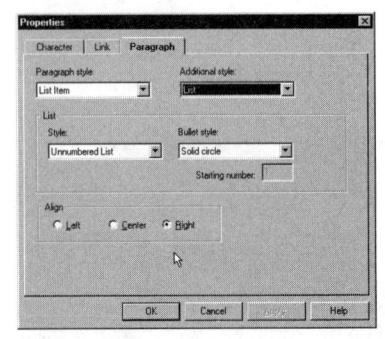

Figure 14.47 *Select the desired styles and click Apply or OK.*

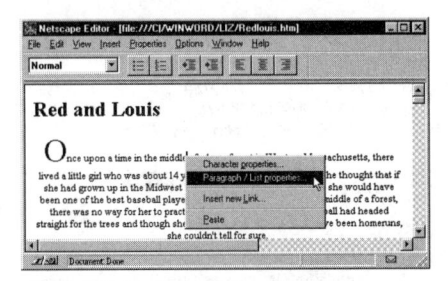

Figure 14.48 *Right click anywhere in a paragraph to make the pop-up menu appear. Then choose Paragraph properties.*

Adding Images to a Page

Perhaps the greatest appeal of the World Wide Web and of HTML documents in particular is that they can contain colorful images. You can insert a photo of your cat on your personal home page, or a representation of your company's logo on your business page. And you can add images to link definitions, making buttons that take your reader to their next destination.

Image formats

Because the Web is accessed by all different kinds of computers, the graphics you use in your Web page must be in a format that each of these operating systems can recognize. The two most widely used formats are JPEG and GIF.

GIF, or Graphics Interchange Format, was developed by CompuServe. LZW, the compression it uses, reduces the size of images with large blocks of the same color—common in computer generated art. In addition, LZW is *lossless* compression. You can compress, uncompress and recompress the image without any loss in quality.

The JPEG compression scheme is ideal for photographs and other "natural" color images. JPEG compressed images may have millions of colors, and their file size is determined primarily by their image size, not their number of colors.

However, JPEG is *lossy* compression—deciding that the eye cannot distinguish as many colors as are in your original image, it may eliminate them permanently to save space. Uncompressing the image will not restore the lost data.

Chapter 15

Inserting an image

Images add interest to your pages. They also make it slower to view. If you add too many images, readers will get frustrated with the download time. If you add too few, they may be bored. Balance is key.

To insert an image:

1. Click in the Editor window where you wish to insert the image **(Fig. 15.1)**.

2. Choose Image in the Insert menu **(Figure 15.2)**. The Image Properties dialog box appears.

3. Next to Image file name, click Browse **(Figure 15.3)**.

4. Locate the image that you wish to insert. Click Open. The image's file name appears in the Image Properties dialog box **(Figure 15.4)**.

5. Netscape will copy the image to the same directory that contains the page you are working on. If you don't want Netscape to do that, deselect the Copy image to the document's location checkbox at the bottom left corner of the dialog box.

6. Click OK. The image appears in the Editor window **(Figure 15.5)**.

✔ Tips

- You can also click the Insert image button on the Character Properties toolbar to make the Image Properties dialog box appear.

- You can quickly open an image in your preferred image editing software by clicking Edit image in the Image Properties dialog box. To choose the program, see page 230.

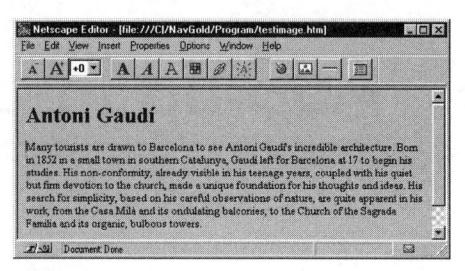

Figure 15.1 *Click in the Editor window where you wish the image to appear.*

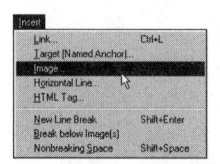

Figure 15.2 *Choose Image in the Insert menu.*

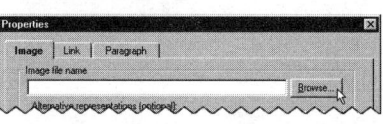

Figure 15.3 *Click Browse next to the Image file name text box. (Or enter the name manually.)*

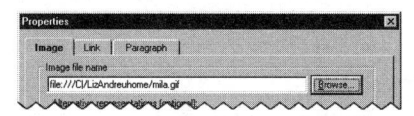

Figure 15.4 *The file name appears in the Image Properties dialog box. Click Close to exit.*

Figure 15.5 *The image appears in the Editor window at the insertion point, displacing text as necessary.*

180

Adding Images to a Page

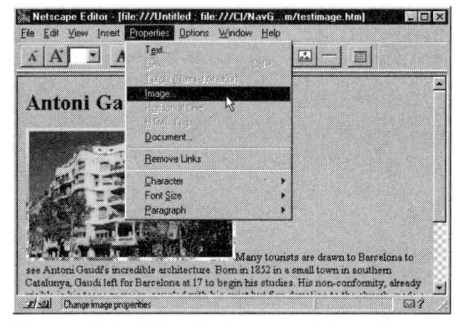

Figure 15.6 *Select the image and then choose Image in the Properties menu.*

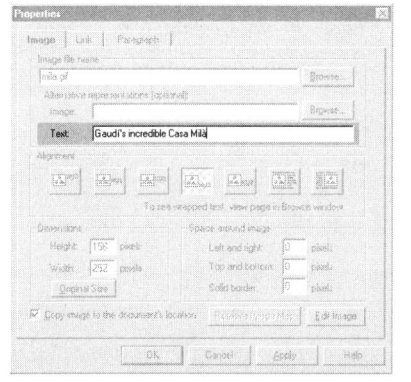

Figure 15.7 *Type the alternative text in the Text box under Alternative representations.*

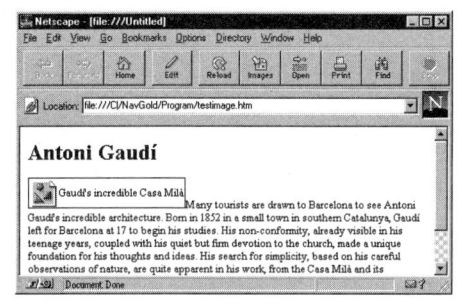

Figure 15.8 *Netscape users who have deactivated the Auto Load Images option and users of non-graphical browsers won't see the images, but will see the alternative text instead.*

Using alternative text

It's important to remember that not everyone who browses the World Wide Web uses Netscape to do it. Unix users, for example, typically use a program called Lynx, that does not show images at all. Users with a slow modem or computer may disable image viewing to speed up their browsing. In order to communicate what the images contain to those users who can't see them on the page, you can use alternative text which appears when the images don't.

To use alternative text:

1. If you are inserting a new image, follow steps 1–4 on page 180. For an existing image, select the image and choose Image in the Properties menu **(Figure 15.6)**. The Image Properties dialog box appears.

2. In the Image Properties dialog box, under Alternate representations, type the alternative text in the Text text box **(Figure 15.7)**.

3. Click OK to close the Image Properties dialog box. The effect is not readily seen in Netscape's browser until you deselect the Auto Load Images option **(Figure 15.8)**.

✓ **Tips**

- Users who disable automatic image loading to save time can be enticed into loading your images if you use *descriptive* alternative text.

- If you use images as navigational buttons, it is essential to use alternative text. Otherwise, the user who doesn't view images will be unable to navigate on your page.

181

Using low resolution images to speed viewing

Low resolution images load faster than high resolution images. You can specify a low resolution version of your image to load immediately while the high resolution is coming in slowly. This way, your reader gets instant feedback.

To use a low resolution image:

1. If you are inserting a new image, follow steps 1–4 on page 180. For an existing image, select the image and choose Image in the Properties menu. The Image Properties dialog box appears.

2. In the Image text box under Alternative representations, type the path and file name of the low resolution version of the image, or click Browse to locate it on your hard disk **(Figure 15.9)**.

3. Click OK to close the Image Properties dialog box.

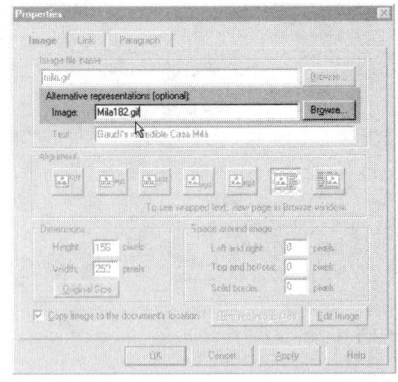

Figure 15.9 *In the Image text box under Alternative representations, type the file name and path of the low resolution version of your image. Or click Browse to locate the file on your hard disk.*

Adding Images to a Page

Image size

If you've wandered a bit around the Internet, you are sure to have experienced The Page From Hell. The designer was so anxious to show you every image he's every created, that he placed them all on the same page. And no small images either—these are 24 bit color images. You're still on a 14.4 modem, but that's no excuse to make you wait this long to see the page. After a minute or two staring at the progress indicator at the bottom of the browser, you bag, and surf to a friendlier page.

When you construct *your* page, make sure you keep your entire page to under 30K—including images. It will take your users with 14.4 modems, not to mention those who are still on 9600s, about a second to load each K of data, for a total of 30 seconds. That's about how long you can expect anyone to wait.

If you want to include larger images, you have several options. First, you can use a miniature version, or icon, of the image on your page that links the user—if they so choose—to the full image. Next, you can create a low resolution version of the image that loads almost immediately and allows the user to browse the text areas of your page while the high resolution image is loading *(see page 182)*. Finally, you can interlace the image which also lets the user browse almost immediately as the image gradually comes into focus. If your pages are still interminably slow, try dividing your images among several pages.

Why the resolution is not so important

Since most monitors display everything at 72 or 96 dpi, there is no reason to save your images with a higher resolution, unless you want your users to be able to download and print your images at the other end. Generally, that's not necessary, and the higher resolution only guarantees longer download times.

Why the number of colors *is* so important

Although many Macintoshes and some higher-end monitors for PCs can show thousands or even millions of colors on the screen at once, the vast majority of users are limited to 256 colors. This means that if you create several images and each uses its own set of 256 colors, the images will not appear correctly. Therefore, if you plan to include several images on a single page, you need to be careful to either limit each image to 50 or so colors, or to use the same set of colors for all the images.

Chapter 15

Wrapping text around images

Thanks to Netscape and its extensions, you can wrap text around images, making for a more visually interesting page. Beware, many other browsers do not support text wrap.

To wrap text around images:

1. If you are inserting a new image, follow steps 1–4 on page 180. For an existing image, select the image and choose Image in the Properties menu. The Image Properties dialog box appears.

2. Netscape considers text wrap a kind of alignment. Click the desired text wrap option (either to the right of the image or to the left of the image) in the Alignment section of the Image Properties dialog box **(Figure 15.10)**.

3. Click OK to close the dialog box. Text wrap is not shown in the Editor window **(Figure 15.11)**.

4. To view the results, choose Browse window in the File menu or click the View in Browser button. In the browser, the text is wrapped around the image **(Figure 15.12)**.

✓ Tips

- Insert an image *before* the text you want to wrap around it.

- You can also regulate the amount of space between the image and the text. For more information, consult *Adding space around an image* on page 186.

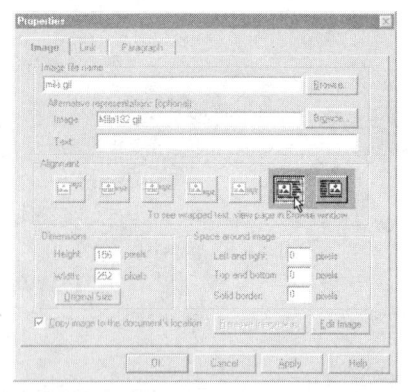

Figure 15.10 *Choose one of the two text wrap options in the Alignment area of the Image Properties dialog box.*

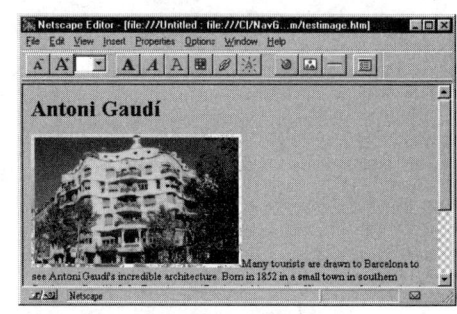

Figure 15.11 *Text wrap is not shown in the Editor window.*

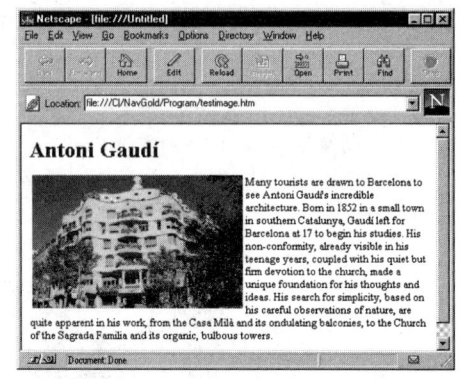

Figure 15.12 *Choose Browse Document in the File menu to view the page in the browser where the text wrap is visible.*

Adding Images to a Page

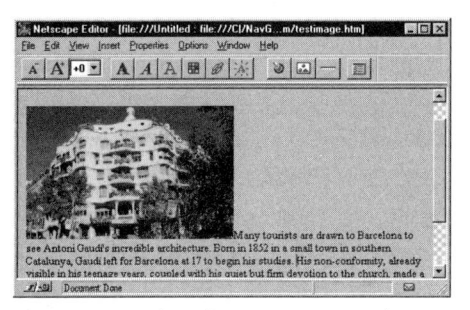

Figure 15.13 *Place the insertion point where you want to stop the text from wrapping.*

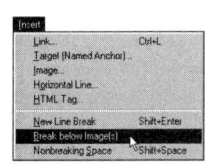

Figure 15.14 *Choose Break below Image(s) in the Insert menu.*

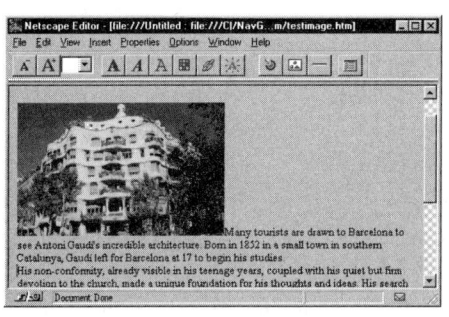

Figure 15.15 *Since text wrap is not visible in the Editor window, it's hard to see how the break affects the final look of the page.*

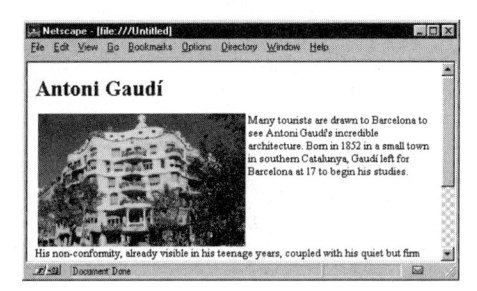

Figure 15.16 *In the browser, the break makes the text stop flowing until it reaches the end of the image.*

Stopping text wrap

Once you tell Netscape to wrap text around an image, it does so until it runs out of text—or encounters a break. You can insert a manual break, as needed.

To stop text wrap:

1. Place the insertion point where you want the text to stop wrapping **(Figure 15.13)**.

2. Choose Break below Image(s) in the Insert menu **(Figure 15.14)**. In the Editor window, you will see a line break **(Figure 15.15)**. In the browser, the text will stop flowing and won't begin again until below the image **(Figure 15.16)**.

185

Chapter 15

Adding space around an image

When you wrap text around images, the image is sometimes squashed or crowded by the text. You can remedy this effect by adding extra space around the image.

To add space around an image:

1. If you are inserting a new image, follow steps 1-4 on page 180. For an existing image, select the image and choose Image in the Properties menu. The Image Properties dialog box appears.

2. Enter the amount of space, in pixels, that you wish to leave around the image in the Left and right and Top and bottom text boxes in the Space around image section **(Figure 15.18)**.

3. Click OK to close the Image Properties dialog box. Although the added space is theoretically visible in the Editor window, you can get a better picture in the browser where the text is wrapped as well.

4. Choose Browse Document in the File window or click the View in Browser button on the File/Edit Tools toolbar. You may be asked to save the page. Click OK to do so. The page is shown as it will appear on the Web **(Figure 15.19)**.

✔ **Tip**

■ Unfortunately, in Netscape Gold (or indeed in HTML), there's no way to add space on just one side of an image (e.g., the text side). One solution is to add the space in Photoshop, and then make it transparent.

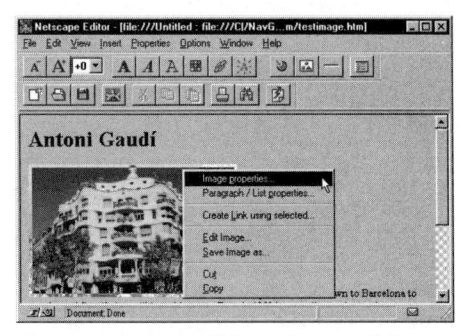

Figure 15.17 *Right click an image and choose Image Properties to make the Image Properties dialog box appear.*

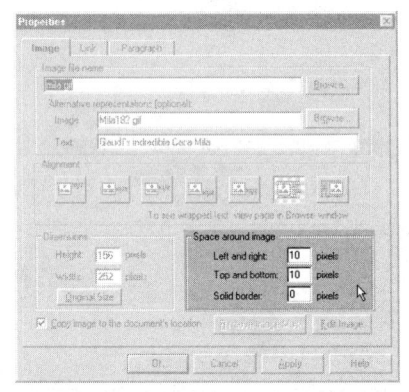

Figure 15.18 *Enter the amount of space—in pixels—that you want to create around the image.*

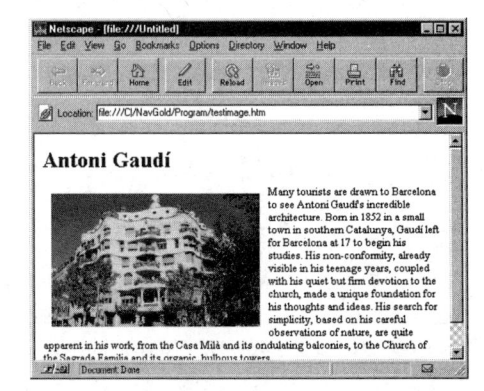

Figure 15.19 *Now the image is not jammed up next to the text. Notice also how space has been added to all sides of the image.*

186

Adding Images to a Page

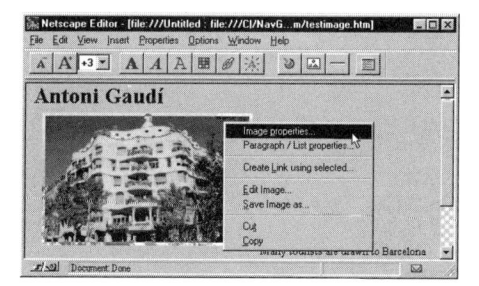

Figure 15.20 *Right click an image and choose Image Properties in the pop-up menu.*

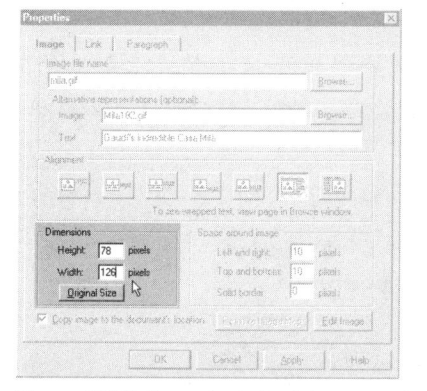

Figure 15.21 *Enter the desired size, in pixels, for the image in the Dimensions area.*

Figure 15.22 *In this example, the image has been reduced to half its size.*

Figure 15.23 *You can distort an image by entering non-proportional dimensions.*

Changing the display size of an image

One of Netscape Gold's advantages is that it automatically includes the size of the image in your Web page, according to the image's real dimensions. This allows the browser to allocate the necessary space for the image as it is downloaded and to display the surrounding text immediately. You can also use the size coordinates to change the display of the image on the page.

To change the display size of an image:

1. If you are inserting a new image, follow steps 1–4 on page 180. For an existing image, select the image and choose Image in the Properties menu. The Image Properties dialog box appears.

2. Enter the desired size for the image in the Dimensions area **(Figure 15.21)**.

3. If desired, click Apply to apply the changes without closing the dialog box. Adjust the dimensions and click Apply again until you are satisfied.

4. Click OK (or close if you've already applied the changes) to close the Image Properties dialog box. The changes are shown immediately in the Editor window **(Figure 15.22)**.

✓ Tips

- To return an image to its original size, click Original Size in the Dimensions area of the Image Properties box.

- You can distort an image by entering non-proportional dimensions **(Figure 15.23)**.

187

Chapter 15

Creating a border around an image

To set off an image from the surrounding elements on the page, you can create a border around it.

To create a border around an image:

1. If you are inserting a new image, follow steps 1–4 on page 180. For an existing image, select the image and choose Image in the Properties menu. The Image Properties dialog box appears.

2. Enter the width of the border, in pixels, in the Solid border text box in the Space around image area **(Figure 15.24)**.

3. If desired, click Apply to apply the changes without closing the dialog box. Adjust the width and click Apply again until you are satisfied with the results.

4. Click OK (or close if you've already applied the changes) to close the Image Properties dialog box. The border is shown immediately in the Editor window **(Figure 15.25)**.

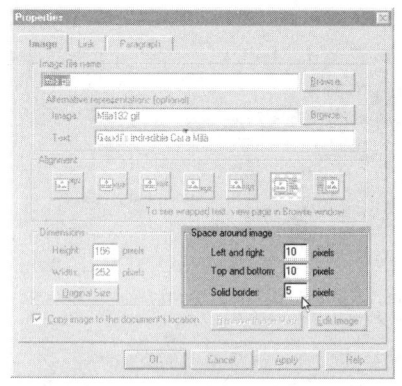

Figure 15.24 *Enter the border thickness in pixels.*

Figure 15.25 *The image appears with a 5-pixel wide border.*

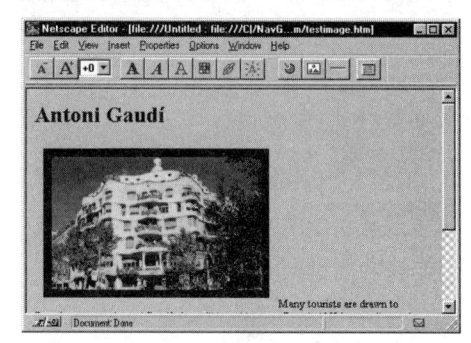

Figure 15.26 *This is a 10-pixel wide border.*

Adding Images to a Page

Aligning images

Images can be aligned in several different ways, depending on what effect you're trying to create. The only thing you can't do is align an image and wrap text around it at the same time.

To align an image:

1. If you are inserting a new image, follow steps 1–4 on page 180. For an existing image, select the image and choose Image in the Properties menu. The Image Properties dialog box appears.

2. Choose one of the first five options in the Alignment area **(Figure 15.27)**. (The last two are for text wrap; see page 184.)

3. If desired, click Apply to apply the changes without closing the dialog box. Choose a different alignment option and click Apply again until you are satisfied with the results.

4. Click OK (or Close if you've already applied the changes) to close the Image Properties dialog box. The image is immediately aligned in the Editor window **(Figure 15.28)**.

✔ **Tips**

■ The alignment option you choose only affects the first line of text.

■ If you have several images on the same line, you can align them in different ways.

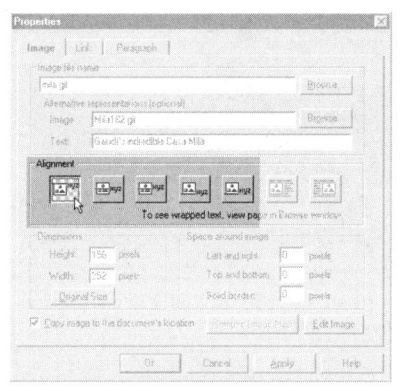

Figure 15.27 *Select an alignment option (one of the first five icons in the Alignment section) in the Image Properties dialog box.*

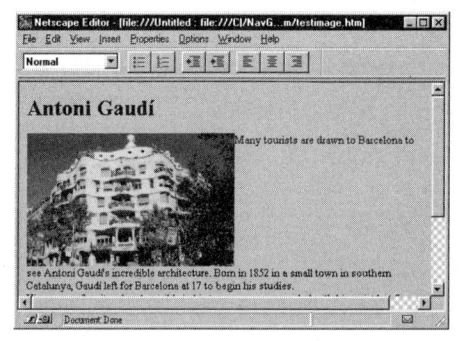

Figure 15.28 *This image is aligned with the top line of text (the first Alignment option, as shown in Figure 15.27). Notice that only the first line of text is affected.*

Figure 15.29 *The middle of this image is aligned with the middle of the first line of text (which is the second Alignment option).*

189

Chapter 15

Adding a horizontal line

Horizontal lines are amazingly useful for dividing Web pages into intelligible chunks of information. Netscape lets you control the size, width and shading of a horizontal lines, but most other browsers don't recognize these fancy additions.

To add a horizontal line:

1. Click in the Editor window where you wish to insert the horizontal line **(Figure 15.30)**.

2. Choose Horizontal Line in the Insert menu **(Figure 15.31)**. The default style line is inserted **(Figure 15.32)**.

3. If desired, change the line as described on page 191.

✔ Tips

- You can also insert a new horizontal line by clicking the Insert Horizontal Line button on the Character Properties toolbar.

- Eliminate a horizontal line by selecting it and pressing Backspace.

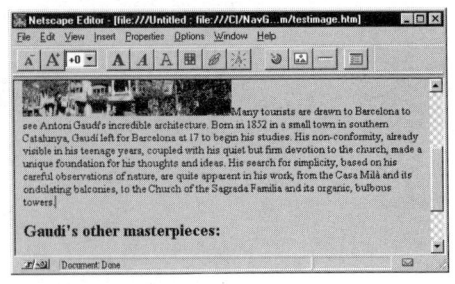

Figure 15.30 *Click in the Editor window where you wish the line to appear.*

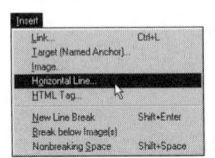

Figure 15.31 *Choose Horizontal line in the Insert menu.*

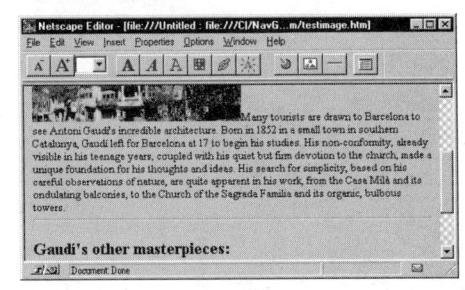

Figure 15.32 *The default horizontal line is 2 pixels high, as wide as the window, and uses 3D shading (at least in Netscape's browser).*

190

Adding Images to a Page

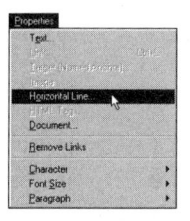

Figure 15.33 *Choose Horizontal Line in the Properties menu.*

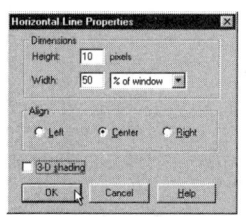

Figure 15.34 *Choose the desired options for the horizontal line and click OK.*

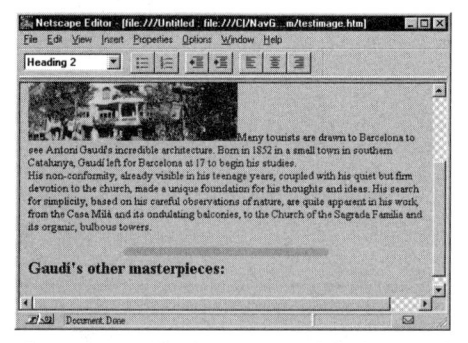

Figure 15.35 *This line is 10 pixels high, 50% of the width of the window, and centered. It does not use 3D shading.*

Changing a horizontal line

Netscape has added several options to its horizontal lines. You can adjust a line's thickness (height), width—both as a percentage of the window width and in absolute pixels—alignment, and shading.

To change a horizontal line:

1. Select the line and choose Horizontal Line in the Properties menu **(Figure 15.33)**. The Horizontal Line Properties dialog box appears.

2. Choose a height, or thickness, in pixels, for the line **(Figure 15.34)**.

3. Enter a number for the width of the line, either as a percentage of the total window size, or in absolute terms, in pixels.

4. If you've chosen a line width that is narrower than the window width, choose an alignment.

5. Finally, you can choose to add 3D shading for the line or to leave it in black and white.

6. Click OK to save the changes. The results are shown in the Editor window **(Figure 15.35)**.

✓ Tips

- Right click a line and choose Horizontal Line Properties in the pop-up menu to access the Horizontal Line Properties dialog box.

- Selecting a line and clicking the Horizontal Line button ▢ on the toolbar *should* make the Horizontal Line Properties dialog box appear. It doesn't; it simply inserts a new line.

191

Chapter 15

Choosing colors and/or a background image

You can set your own default colors for text, new links, active links, and visited links. You can also choose a color or an image for the background. Although it's rather in vogue to use garish colors on the Web, it also makes the page hard to read.

To choose a page's colors (and/or background image):

1. Choose Document in the Properties menu (**Figure 15.36**). The Document Properties dialog box appears.

2. In the Custom Colors section, click the element whose color you wish to change. The Color dialog box appears. Choose a color and click OK.

3. In the Background section, either click Solid color, and then click Choose color to pick one color for the background or click Image file and then Browse to choose a background image (**Figure 15.37**).

4. Click OK to close the Document Properties dialog box.

✔ Tips

- Netscape includes a series of "color schemes" in the Color Schemes pop-up menu. You can choose one of these color schemes and then modify it as desired.

- A preview of your choices is always shown at the right of the Custom Colors section in the dialog box.

- If the image is smaller than the page, it will be tiled to fill the background.

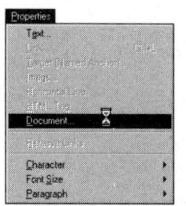

Figure 15.36 *Choose Document in the Properties menu.*

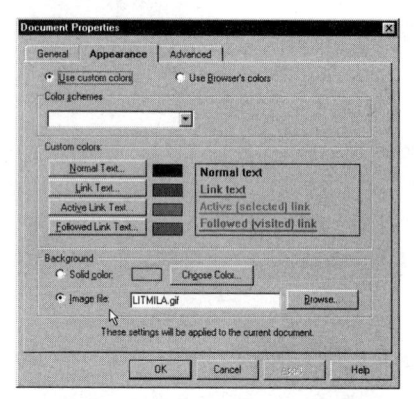

Figure 15.37 *Choose colors for the different elements. Choose between a color and an image for the background. Then click OK to save the changes.*

Figure 15.38 *If the image is smaller than the page, it will be tiled to cover the background.*

Creating Links in a Page   16

As discussed in Chapter 2, *Surfing the Web*, a Web page can contain dynamic connections with other Web pages, enabling users to jump from one page to another in search of information. These connections are called *links*.

A link can bring the user to the top of a new Web page or to a specific section of that page, to an FTP or Gopher site, and even to an e-mail address. The Web page designer decides where the link will go.

Links and URLs

Links are made out of URLs, or *Uniform Resource Locators*. The URL is an address that gives the exact location on the Internet of a link's destination. A URL is comprised of a protocol, a server name and a file name, including the path **(Fig. 16.1)**. The protocol defines what kind of connection will be made (Web, FTP, Gopher, Mail, etc.). The server name is the official name, or IP address, of the server that contains the desired file. The file name is the exact name, including the path indicating its location on the server, of the desired file.

Every single piece of information on the Internet—every page, every image, every file—has a unique URL. Thus, when a user clicks a link, Netscape knows exactly where to go to find the information and display it.

In addition to the URL, a link has *display text*, that is, the text that will be underlined and in blue (in most cases) and that indicates the content of the link to the user.

Figure 16.1 *Place the pointer over a link and its URL becomes visible in the status bar at the bottom of the window. If the Location bar is visible, it will display the URL of the page you're currently viewing.*

http://www.ntplx.net/~senft/nields.nwaudiog.html
Protocol — Server address — File name (including path)

Chapter 16

Copying a link from another source

The pages you find on the Web already contain many interesting links, to other pages, FTP and Gopher sites, e-mail addresses and newsgroups. You may also find good links in e-mail you receive or in news postings. Or you may wish to include links from your Bookmarks collection. You can copy any link you find and insert it on your own page.

To copy a link from another source:

1. Open the page you are designing in the Editor window and place the cursor where you want the link to appear **(Figure 16.2)**.

2. Open the browser, Mail, News or Bookmark window and the document that contains the link you wish to copy **(Figure 16.3)**.

3. Organize the two windows on your screen so that the link is visible on the browser window and a piece of the Editor window is also visible.

4. Click the link and drag it to the Editor window. The browser window becomes active. When the icon is over the Editor window and gains a plus sign, let go **(Figure 16.4)**.

5. Click the Editor window to make it active. The link is added at the insertion point. The display text is the same as it was on the original page **(Figure 16.5)**.

6. If desired, select the display text and change it to something more descriptive or specific **(Figure 16.6)**.

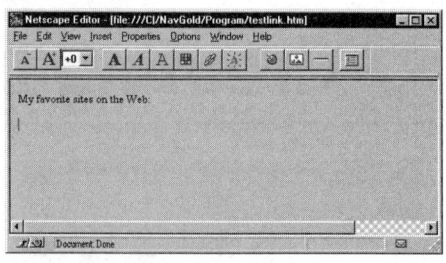

Figure 16.2 *Click in the Editor window where you wish the link to appear.*

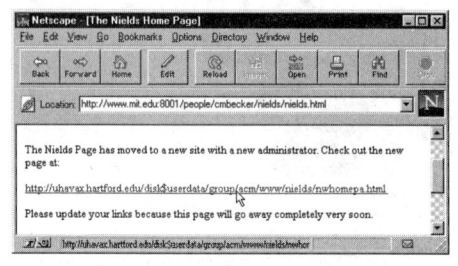

Figure 16.3 *In the browser, navigate to the page that has the link you want to copy.*

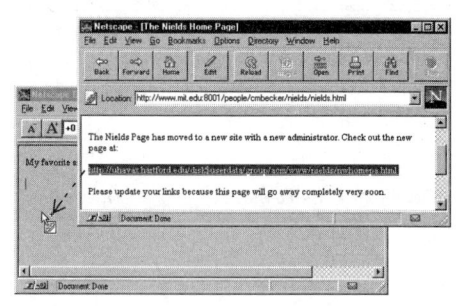

Figure 16.4 *Drag the link from the browser to the Editor window. When the cursor shows the link icon and a plus sign, let go of the mouse button.*

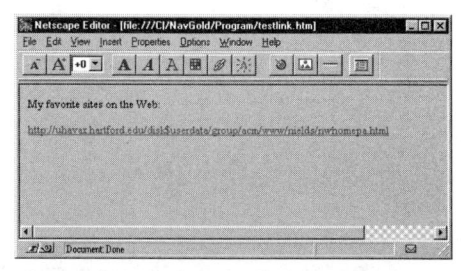

Figure 16.5 *The link is added to the page in the Editor window, with the same display text it had on the original page.*

194

Creating Links in a Page

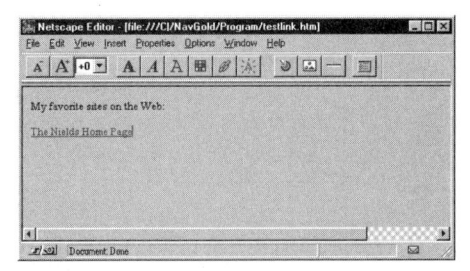

Figure 16.6 *Select the link and type over it to change the display text to something slightly more intelligible, if necessary.*

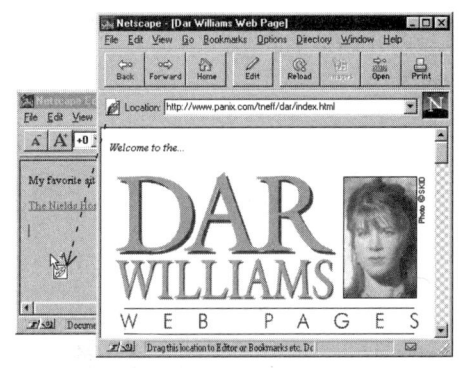

Figure 16.7 *To copy a link of the page you're currently* browsing *and not a link it contains, drag the Link icon (at the left of the Location text box) to the Editor window.*

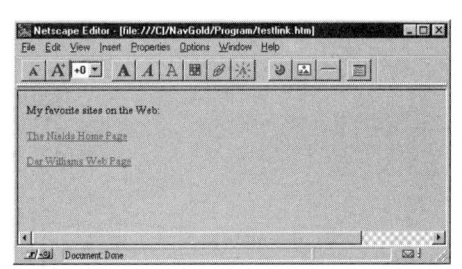

Figure 16.8 *When you use the Link icon, the title of the page you're browsing is used as display text for the link.*

✔ Tips

- To insert a link to the *current* page showing in the browser, whether it be a remote page on another server or a local file on your hard disk, drag the Current Page Link button at the left of the Location text box to the desired spot in the Editor window **(Figure 16.7 and Figure 16.8)**.

- If you prefer, double click the Current Page Link icon to copy the page's URL to the clipboard and then paste it in the Link Properties dialog box manually *(see page 196)*. If you don't see the Current Page Link icon or the Location text box, you'll have to make them visible *(see page 15)*.

- If the Editor window isn't hidden by the document that contains the link, you'll be able to see the insertion point and choose where you want to "drop" the copied link.

- If you try to drag a *folder* from the Bookmarks window, the URL of the first item is copied to the Editor window in text form instead of as a link.

- You can't drag an address from the Address Book to create an e-mail link. Instead, either open the Address Book as a Web page *(see page 130)* and drag links from there or enter the address manually *(see page 196)*.

Copying a link from another source

195

Creating a link manually

If the link doesn't already exist on another page or if you want to create a link without browsing the page (perhaps you don't want to open your Internet connection), you can type the link's URL manually.

To create a link manually:

1. Click in the Editor window where you want the link to appear.

2. Choose Link in the Insert menu **(Figure 16.9)**. The Insert Link dialog box appears.

3. Type the display text in the Link source text box **(Figure 16.10)**.

4. Type or copy the URL for the link in the Link to box. If the link will be to a local page on your hard disk, click Browse File and find the desired page.

5. Click OK. The link appears in the Editor window **(Figure 16.11)**.

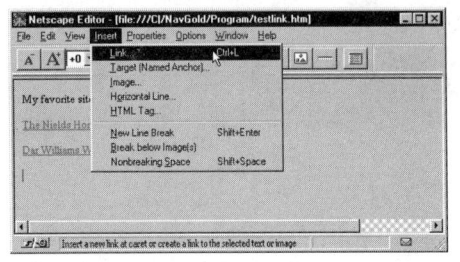

Figure 16.9 *Click in the Editor window where you want the link to appear and then choose Link in the Insert menu.*

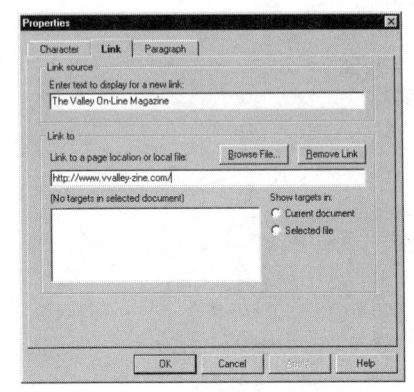

Figure 16.10 *Type the display text in the Link source text box and the URL for the link in the Link to text box. Then click OK.*

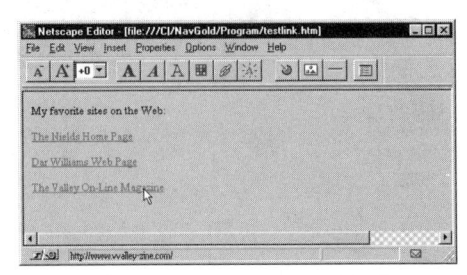

Figure 16.11 *The link appears in the Editor window as defined.*

Creating Links in a Page

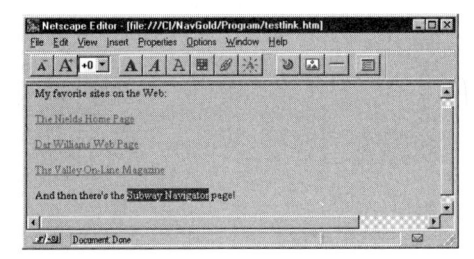

Figure 16.12 *Select the text that you wish to make into a link.*

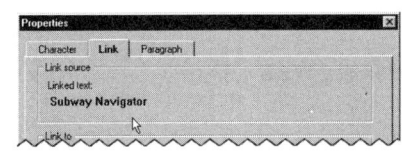

Figure 16.13 *The selected text is automatically entered as display text.*

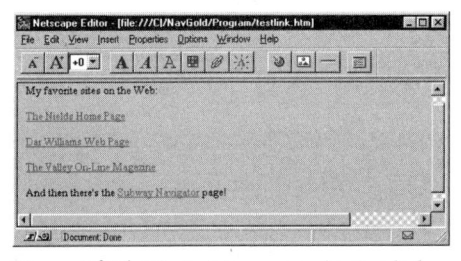

Figure 16.14 *The text is converted into a link.*

If the display text already exists and you simply want to add a link to it, there is an easier way.

To create a link manually from existing text:

1. Select the text that you want to make a link out of **(Figure 16.12)**.

2. Choose Link in the Insert menu. The Link Properties dialog box appears with the display text automatically inserted **(Figure 16.13)**.

3. Type the URL for the link or click Browse if the link is to a local file on your hard disk.

4. Click OK. The selected text is now a link **(Figure 16.14)**.

✔ Tips

- You can insert any kind of URL in the Link to a page location text box, including URLs for Web pages, FTP or Gopher sites, e-mail addresses and newsgroups or newsgroup postings. Links to Web sites should be in the form: **http://www.site.com/path/page.htm**. Links to FTP sites should resemble **ftp://ftp.site.com/path/**. Links to Gopher sites should look like **gopher://gophersite.edu/path/**. The format for links to e-mail addresses is **mailto:name@site.com**. The format for links to newsgroups is **news:newsgroup.name**.

- You can also right click a selection (or insertion point) in the Editor window and then choose Create Link using selected (or Insert new Link if you had nothing selected). The Link Properties dialog box appears and you continue as described above.

197

Chapter 16

Creating a target

The simplest kind of link brings the user to the *top* of a Web page. If you want a link to bring the user to a *specific part* of the page, you have to create a target and then set the link to that target.

To create a target:

1. Select the text in the Editor window that you want to appear at the top of the browser window when the user clicks the link **(Figure 16.15)**. This is the target.

2. Choose Target (Named Anchor) in the Insert menu **(Figure 16.16)**. The Target Properties dialog box appears.

3. The text box automatically contains the text you selected in step 1. Either accept that word or type another that identifies this section of the Web page you are designing and click OK **(Figure 16.17)**.

4. A small target icon appears next to the selected text **(Figure 16.18)**. You can now create a link that connects to this target.

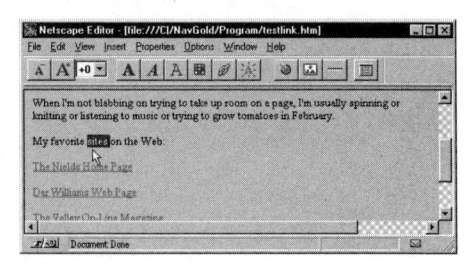

Figure 16.15 *Click in the area that should appear at the top of the page when the user clicks the targeted link.*

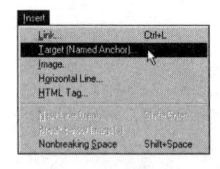

Figure 16.16 *Choose Target (Named Anchor) in the Insert menu.*

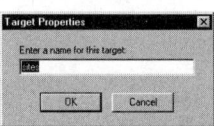

Figure 16.17 *Type a name for the target. Any text selected at the beginning is automatically entered here.*

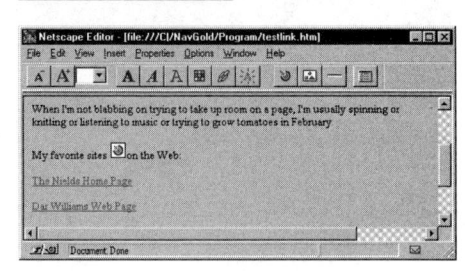

Figure 16.18 *A target icon is inserted next to the selected text.*

✔ Tips

- To create a link that points to the target, consult *Creating a link to a target on the same page* on page 199 or consult *Linking to a target on a different page* on page 200.

- The target icon does not appear on the page in the browser.

- You can also insert a target by clicking the Insert Target (Named Anchor) button on the File/Edit Tools toolbar.

198

Creating Links in a Page

Creating a link to a target on the same page

If you have a particularly long Web page, you can create a kind of table of contents at the top of the page. Then set up each entry as a link to the section farther down on the page with targets.

To create a link to a target on the same page:

1. Click in the Editor window where you want to create the link. If desired, select the text you want to convert into display text for the link (**Fig. 16.19**).

2. Choose Link in the Insert menu. The Link Properties dialog box appears.

3. If necessary, type the display text at the top of the dialog box.

4. Choose the desired target in the scroll list in the Link to area. The target name appears in the Link to text box (**Figure 16.20**).

5. Click OK. The link appears in the Editor window (**Figure 16.21**).

✓ Tips

- You can also access the Link Properties dialog box by right clicking with the mouse and then choosing Insert new Link in the submenu. Or, click the Make Link button on the Character Properties toolbar.

- If you select text before choosing the Link command, the selected text is automatically entered as display text.

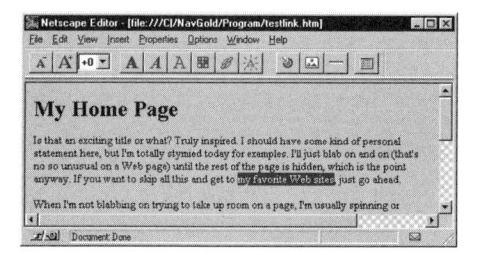

Figure 16.19 *Select the text that you want to convert into a link (or click where you wish to insert a link).*

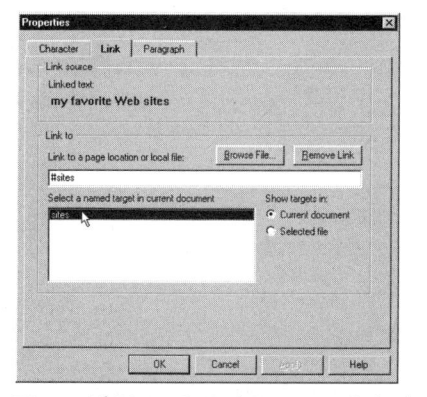

Figure 16.20 *In the Link Properties dialog box, click Current Document and then select the desired target for the link in the list.*

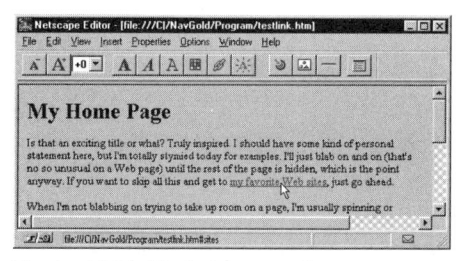

Figure 16.21 *The link is created.*

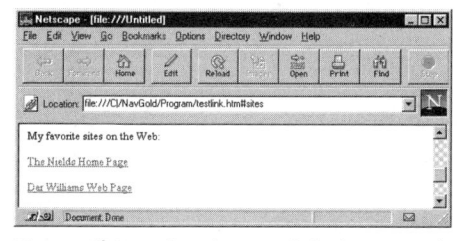

Figure 16.22 *When the user clicks the targeted link, the corresponding section of the page is displayed at the top of the browser.*

199

Chapter 16

Linking to a target on a different page

Once you've created a target in one of your Web pages, you can create a link to it. The link can be on the same page (as in a table of contents) or from another page. Since you can't create targets in e-mail addresses, FTP or Gopher sites, or newsgroups or postings, a link to a target must be to a Web page.

To create a link to a target on a different page:

1. Create a link to the remote page *(see pages 194 and 196)*.

2. Right click the link and select Link Properties in the pop-up menu or click the Make Link button on the toolbar **(Figure 16.23)**. The Link Properties box appears with the display text and URL already entered.

3. Under Show targets in, choose Selected File **(Figure 16.24)**.

4. Choose the desired target in the list. It is automatically appended to the URL, separated by a number symbol (#) **(Figure 16.25)**.

5. Click OK to save the changes.

✔ Tips

- If you accidentally click Current Document in step 3 and then try to go back to Selected file, the targets don't always appear. Just click Cancel and start over. That's a bug.

- You can create the link at the same time you select the target, by entering all the information manually, but it's not as easy.

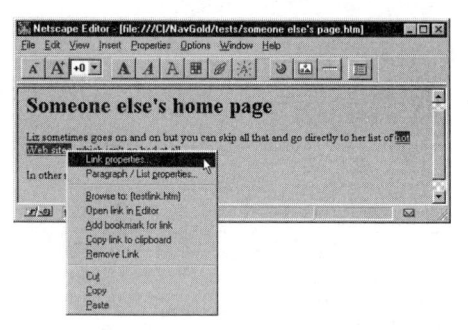

Figure 16.23 *Right click the link and select Link Properties in the pop-up menu.*

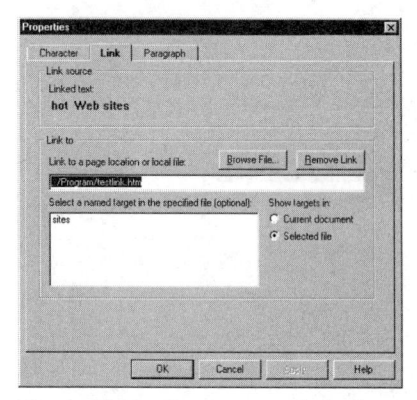

Figure 16.24 *When you open the Link Properties dialog box, the URL appears in the Link to text box while a list of possible targets appears.*

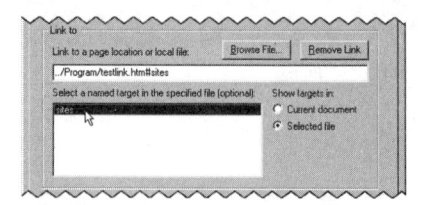

Figure 16.25 *When you choose a target, its name is appended to the URL, separated by a # sign.*

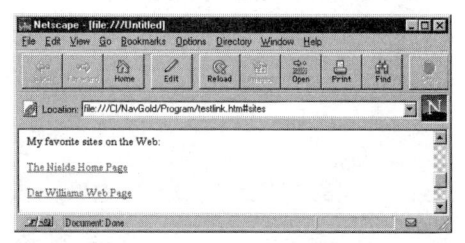

Figure 16.26 *When the user clicks the targeted link, the corresponding section of the page is displayed.*

200

Creating Links in a Page

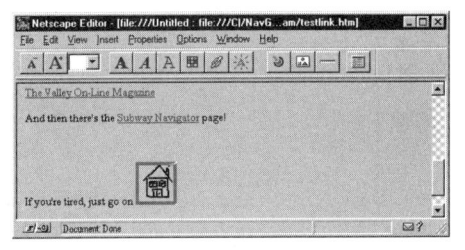

Figure 16.27 *Add the image to the page and select it.*

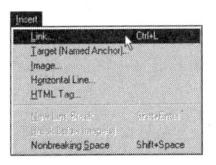

Figure 16.28 *Choose Link in the Insert menu.*

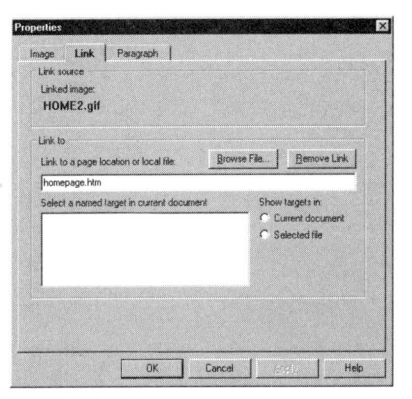

Figure 16.29 *Type or copy the URL in the Link to text area. Choose a target if desired.*

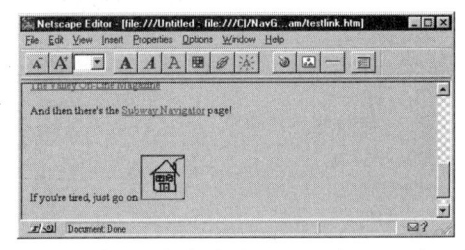

Figure 16.30 *The linked image is shown with a blue frame.*

Creating a link to an image

To add navigational buttons to your page, you have to first insert an image and then make it into a link.

To create a link to an image:

1. Add the image to the page in the Editor window *(see page 180)* and select it **(Figure 16.27)**.

2. Choose Link in the Insert menu **(Figure 16.28)**. The Link Properties dialog box appears with the image's file name in the Link source area.

3. Type the URL for the link in the Link to text box, or click Browse if the link is to a local file on your hard disk **(Figure 16.29)**.

4. Select a target for the link, if desired *(see page 199)*.

5. Click OK to close the Link Properties dialog box. The image now appears with a blue border to show that it is a link **(Figure 16.30)**.

✔ **Tips**

- You can also right click the image and then choose Create Link using selected in the pop-up menu to make the Link Properties dialog box appear for the image.

- Or, you can select the image and then click the Make Link button on the Character Properties toolbar to open the Link Properties dialog box for the image.

201

Chapter 16

Changing or removing a link

As you design a Web page, you will find that every so often you need to update a link or add a target to it—or get rid of it.

To change or delete a link:

1. Select the link you want to change **(Figure 16.31)**.

2. Choose Link in the Properties menu **(Figure 16.32)**. The Link Properties dialog box appears **(Figure 16.33)**.

3. Change the URL or target *(see pages 196 and 198)* or click Remove Link to make the link into regular text.

4. Click OK to save the changes.

✓ Tips

- To change a link's display text, simply select the text and type something else.

- Another way to eliminate the link properties from text is by selecting the link and choosing Remove Links in the Properties menu. Or right click a link and choose Remove Link in the pop-up menu. The display text remains.

- To eliminate a link *and* its display text, select it and press Backspace.

- You can also make the Link Properties dialog box appear by right clicking the link and choosing Link properties in the pop-up menu **(Figure 16.34)** or by selecting the link and clicking the Make Link button.

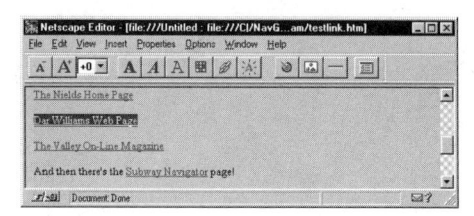

Figure 16.31 *Select the link you want to change.*

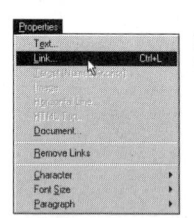

Figure 16.32 *Choose Link in the Properties menu.*

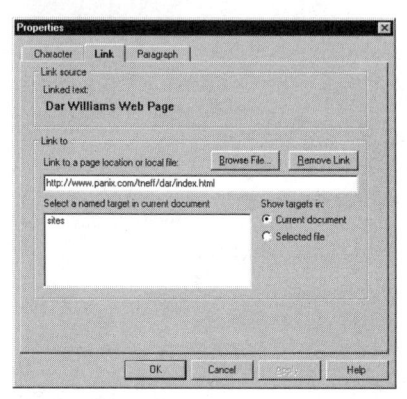

Figure 16.33 *Make any necessary changes to the URL or to the target. Or click Remove Link to remove the link information from the text. Click OK to save the changes.*

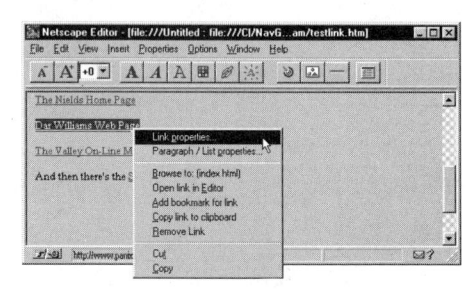

Figure 16.34 *Right click the link and choose Link properties in the pop-up menu to make the Link Properties dialog box (Figure 16.33) appear.*

Advanced Page Design

Advanced is a relative term, of course. While the topics discussed in this chapter may be advanced for those new to Netscape Gold and to designing Web pages in general, seasoned HTML writers would be hard pressed to agree.

HTML, or Hypertext Markup Language, is the stuff that pages are made of. It looks a little bit like WordPerfect formatting in the early days of computers: to make something bold you had to add <B> in front of the word. On screen it looked terrible, but once printed, it *almost* made the tags worthwhile.

Netscape Gold is great for simple page design. It makes inserting images and adding special attributes to them (like alignment or size) very simple. It is much more careful about its end brackets than any human could ever be. However, it has certain limitations that can be overcome with a little manual editing.

For example, in Netscape Gold, you cannot apply logical formatting such as emphasis or strong. You cannot create tables or frames. And, Netscape inserts information about its own company on every page you create, which you may decide not to include.

If you'd like to learn more about HTML, you might try my other book: *HTML for the World Wide Web: Visual QuickStart Guide*, published by Peachpit Press.

Chapter 17

Standard HTML

In the fight between universality and features, Netscape stands squarely behind the latter. In fact, there are a certain set of HTML tags, known as *Netscape extensions* that generally, can only be viewed with Netscape. Other browsers, such as Mosaic and Microsoft's Internet Explorer may be able to interpret some of the extensions, but not all.

When designing your page, you have to decide between standard HTML, which, by definition, can be viewed properly in all Web browsers, and Netscape's extensions, which may make your page more attractive—at least to those who can view it correctly. Generally, the answer is somewhere between there and here. The trick is to view your finished page from more than one browser so that you can see which effects are totally lost on non-Netscape browsers, and which information needs to be reworked.

One last solution is to create several versions of your pages, one that uses Netscape's extensions freely and another that presents the information in a way all browsers can understand—using standard HTML.

Advanced Page Design

Adding nonbreaking spaces

HTML doesn't allow you to add extra spaces between words. Netscape's nonbreaking space not only lets you put more than one space between words, but it also holds those words together like glue. They can't be separated by a line break.

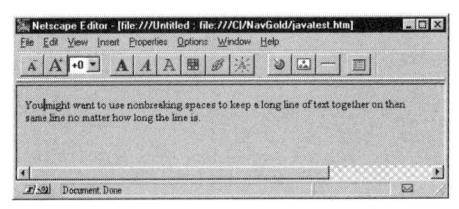

Figure 17.1 *Click where you want to insert a nonbreaking space (or select a space you want to convert in a nonbreaking space as shown here.)*

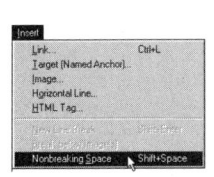

Figure 17.2 *Choose Nonbreaking Space in the Insert menu.*

To add a nonbreaking space:

1. Click in the Editor window where you wish to enter the nonbreaking space **(Figure 17.1)**.

2. Choose Nonbreaking Space in the Insert menu **(Figure 17.2)**. The space is inserted **(Figure 17.3)**.

✔ Tips

- You can also insert a nonbreaking space by pressing Shift+Space.

- Many browsers do not recognize nonbreaking spaces. They will divide words and eliminate the spaces as always **(Figure 17.4)**.

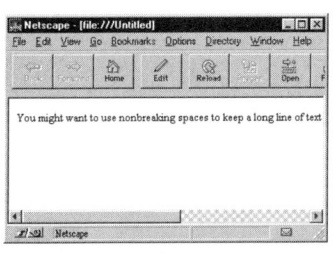

Figure 17.3 *With nonbreaking spaces between each word, no matter how narrow the user makes the window, the line won't break.*

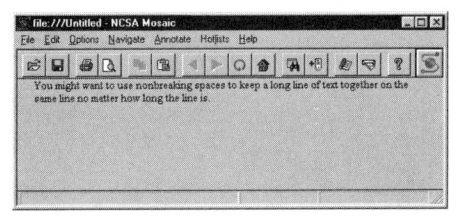

Figure 17.4 *In other browsers like Mosaic, the nonbreaking spaces are shown as regular ones.*

205

Chapter 17

Adding HTML tags manually

Thankfully, you are not limited to the tags that Netscape can insert through its commands and buttons. You can add any HTML tag manually.

To add an HTML tag manually:

1. Place the cursor where you wish to insert the opening HTML tag **(Figure 17.5)**.

2. Choose HTML Tag in the Insert menu **(Figure 17.6)**. The Insert HTML Tag dialog box appears.

3. Type a single HTML tag in the text area **(Figure 17.7)**. Netscape automatically checks to see if you have typed an end bracket (>) and that you have enclosed all attributes in quotation marks.

4. If desired, click Verify to have Netscape check if your HTML tag is standard HTML. (That's ironic!)

5. Click OK to insert the tag. It appears as a big, yellow tag in the Editor window **(Figure 17.8)**.

6. If necessary, click where you wish to insert the closing HTML tag and repeat steps 2–5 **(Figure 17.9, Figure 17.10, and Figure 17.11)**.

7. Browse the page to view the effects of the HTML tag **(Figure 17.12)**.

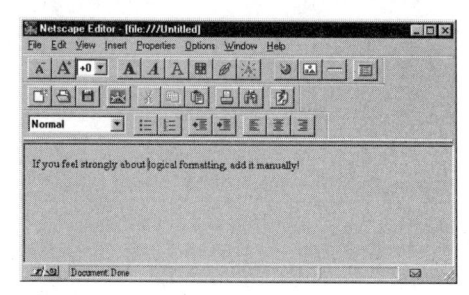

Figure 17.5 *Click where you want to insert the HTML tag manually.*

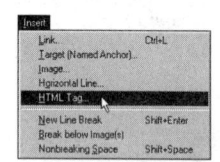

Figure 17.6 *Choose HTML Tag in the Insert menu.*

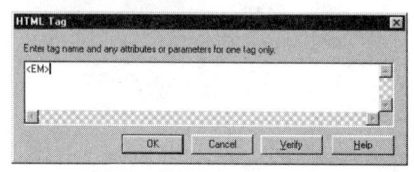

Figure 17.7 *Type one single tag in the HTML Tag dialog box. Click OK to close the dialog box.*

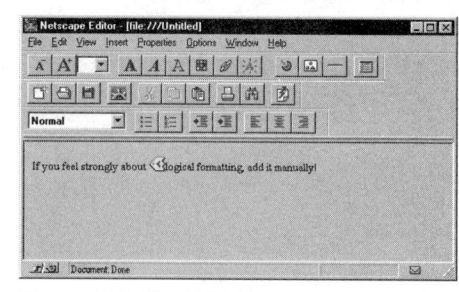

Figure 17.8 *The HTML Tag is shown with a big, yellow tag.*

206

Advanced Page Design

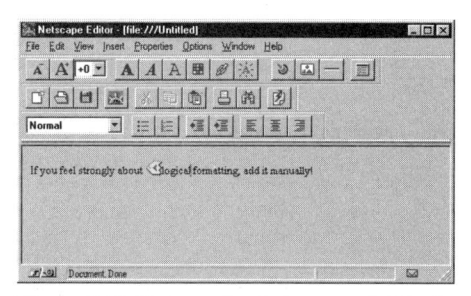

Figure 17.9 *To insert the closing tag, click in the Editor window where you wish to put it.*

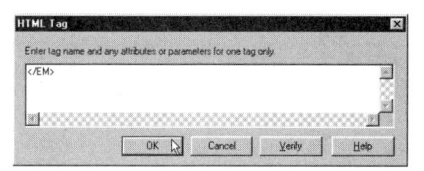

Figure 17.10 *Type the closing tag in the HTML Tag dialog box and click OK.*

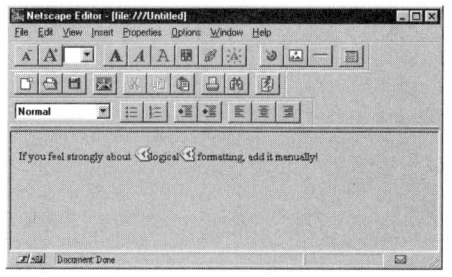

Figure 17.11 *The closing tag looks just like the first. It's* not *pointed the other way.*

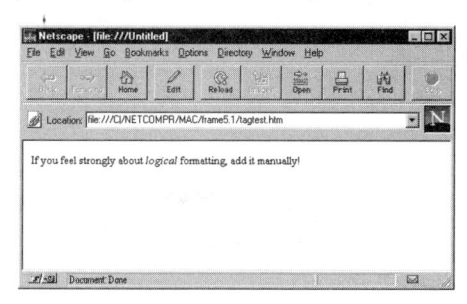

Figure 17.12 *The browser knows how to interpret the HTML tag correctly.*

✔ Tips

- I wouldn't try adding tables or frames to your page with Netscape Gold. Besides the fact that the program has a hard time dealing with those features and bombs a lot, it's just not worth the hassle. Use a text editor.

- You can only insert one tag at a time. For tags that have opening and closing versions, you'll have to insert the opening tag, type the affected text and then insert the closing tag.

Adding HTML tags manually

207

Chapter 17

Editing HTML tags manually

You can look at the HTML tags on your page by opening the page with any text editor. Once in the text editor, you can remove Netscape's annoying, automatic self-identification tags and add features that Netscape Gold does not support.

To edit HTML tags manually:

1. From the Editor window, choose Edit Document Source in the View menu **(Figure 17.13)**. Netscape launches the program you've specified for editing HTML *(see page 209)* and opens the page **(Figure 17.14)**.

2. Make any desired changes.

3. Choose Save As in the File menu of the text editor **(Figure 17.15)**.

4. Choose Text Only for the format and give the file either the .htm or .html extension. Otherwise, browsers won't recognize the file **(Figure 17.16)**.

✔ Tips

- Of course, you don't even have to open Netscape to edit your HTML tags manually. Simply open the text editor (Notepad or Wordpad will do fine, though you can use Word or WordPerfect if you prefer) and then open the HTML document.

- When you choose Edit Document Source, Netscape launches a new instance of the text editor even if there's one already open. To reduce clutter, open the document manually.

- If you use Microsoft Word, be sure to convert the page from Text Only (and not from HTML) when it opens. This way, you'll see the actual tags.

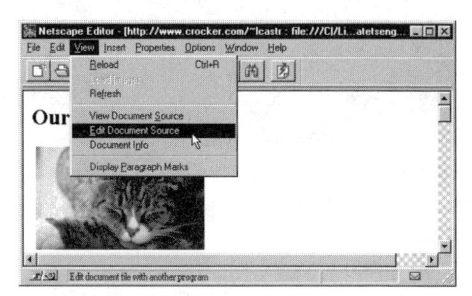

Figure 17.13 *With the page in the Editor window, choose Edit Document Source in the Edit menu.*

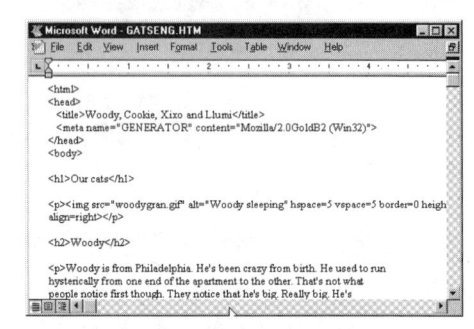

Figure 17.14 *The page is opened with the selected text editor. Now you can see and edit the HTML tags.*

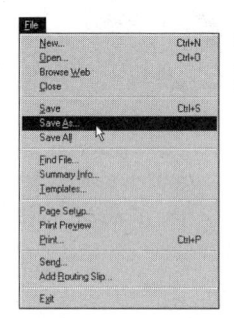

Figure 17.15 *Choose Save As in the text editor's File menu.*

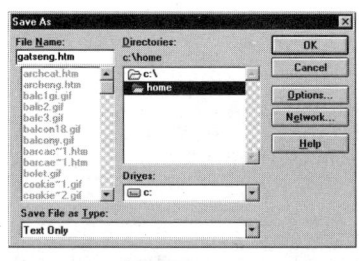

Figure 17.16 *Make sure you save the file in Text Only format with the .htm or .html extension.*

208

Advanced Page Design

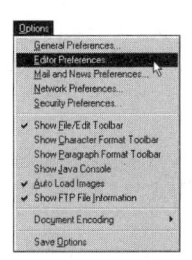

Figure 17.17 *Choose Editor Preferences in the Options menu.*

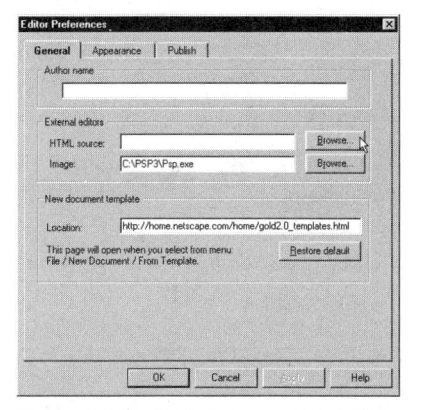

Figure 17.18 *Click Browse next to HTML source in the External editors section.*

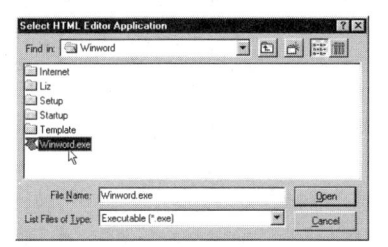

Figure 17.19 *Find the text editor that you want to use and click Open.*

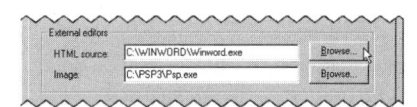

Figure 17.20 *The path to the text editor now appears in the HTML source text box.*

Specifying a program for editing HTML tags

Since HTML documents are always saved in Text Only or ASCII format, you can use virtually any word processor—from WordPad to WordPerfect—to edit HTML tags. You can specify which program you'd like to use, and Netscape will launch it automatically when you decide to edit the tags manually *(see page 208)*.

To specify a program for editing HTML tags:

1. Choose Editor Preferences in the Options menu **(Figure 17.17)**.

2. Click the General tab to see the general Editor preferences.

3. In the External editors section, click Browse next to HTML source **(Figure 17.18)**. The Open dialog box appears.

4. Locate the desired text editor on your hard disk and click Open **(Figure 17.19)**. The path to the program now appears next to HTML source in the Editor Preferences dialog box **(Figure 17.20)**.

5. Click OK to close the dialog box.

Chapter 17

Adding JavaScript to your page

Java is a unique language, developed by Sun Microsystems, that lets you add little applications to your pages. JavaScript is a special version of Java that runs with Netscape 2. There are entire books that explain how to program with Java. Here you'll learn how to insert the code into your page.

To add JavaScript to your page:

1. In the Editor window, type the code that you wish to insert and select it **(Figure 17.21)**.

2. Choose Character in the Properties menu and then JavaScript (Client) or JavaScript (Server) in the submenu **(Figure 17.22)**. JavaScript client text is shown in red while JavaScript server text is shown in blue. Both are shown in fixed width text **(Figure 17.23)**.

3. Choose Browse Document to see the JavaScript code in action **(Fig. 17.24)**.

✓ Tips

■ You can also convert text into JavaScript code by selecting Text in the Properties menu, clicking the Character tab and selecting the desired JavaScript option.

■ For more information about Java and JavaScript, go to *http://home.netscape.com/eng/mozilla/2.0/handbook/javascript/index.html*.

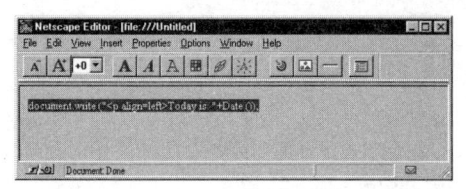

Figure 17.21 *Type your JavaScript code and then select it.*

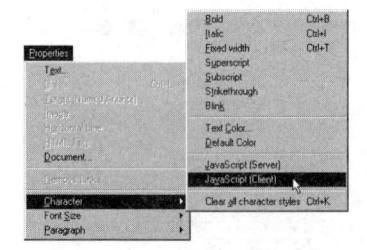

Figure 17.22 *Choose Character in the Properties menu and then JavaScript (Client) or JavaScript (Server) in the submenu.*

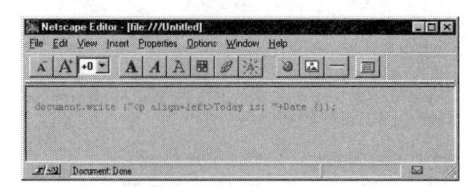

Figure 17.23 *The JavaScript client text is shown in red in a fixed width font.*

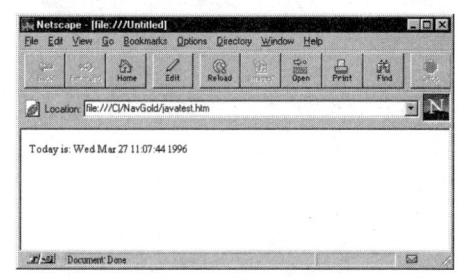

Figure 17.24 *In the browser, the JavaScript is interpreted.*

Publishing a Page 18

Once you've finished designing your page, you have to make it accessible to your public. First you should test your page and make sure all your images appear as they should, that your text is formatted properly, and that your links lead where you intended.

Then you're ready to transfer the files to your server. Netscape Gold boasts a one-step publishing command that copies a page and its associated images to a given location on a remote server.

Once your page is up and running, you'll want to put out the word so that people know how to find it.

Chapter 18

Testing your page

You should always test your Web pages in at least one browser, if not more. It is not necessary to connect to the server to test your pages. Instead, use the Open Local or Open File command to open the pages from your local computer.

To test your pages:

1. Make the browser active and choose Open File in Browser in the File menu **(Figure 18.1)**.

2. In the Open dialog box that appears, locate and select the file that you wish to test and click Open **(Figure 18.2)**. The page appears in the browser.

3. Go through the whole page and make sure it looks exactly the way you want it to **(Figure 18.3)**. For example:

   Is the formatting like you wanted?

   Does each of your links lead to the correct destination?

   Are your images aligned properly?

   Have you included your name and e-mail address (preferably in a link, and/or formatted with Address) so that your users can contact you with comments and suggestions?

4. Choose Edit Document in Netscape's File menu or click the Edit button on the toolbar to switch to editing mode **(Figure 18.4)**.

5. The page appears in the Editor window **(Figure 18.5)**. Make any necessary changes.

6. Choose Save in the File menu to save the changes **(Figure 18.6)**.

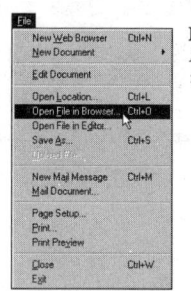

Figure 18.1 *Choose Open File in Browser in the File menu.*

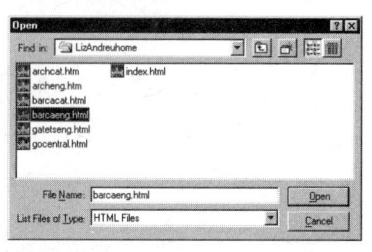

Figure 18.2 *Choose the page on your hard disk that you wish to test.*

Figure 18.3 *Read the page over, checking for spelling and formatting errors. Do the images appear as desired? Do the links go where they should?*

212

Publishing a Page

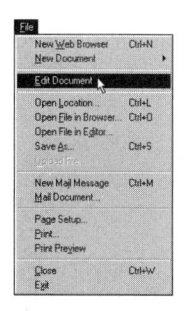

Figure 18.4 *Choose Edit Document in the File menu.*

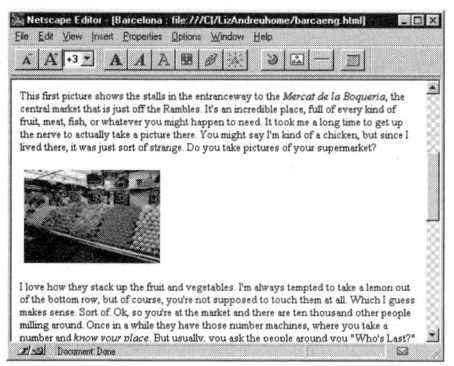

Figure 18.5 *In the Editor window, make any necessary corrections.*

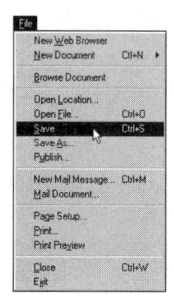

Figure 18.6 *Choose Save in the File menu to save the corrections made to your Web page.*

7. Choose Browse Document in the File menu or click the View in Browser icon to view the changes.

8. Repeat steps 1–5 until you are satisfied with your pages. Don't get discouraged if it takes several tries.

9. View your page with other browsers to make sure your page will be attractive no matter what browser your readers use.

10. Transfer the files to the server, if you haven't done so already *(see page 214).*

11. Test all your links again to make sure that they work correctly from the server.

✔ **Tips**

■ Use several browsers (Mosaic, Cello, Lynx, etc.) to test your pages. You never know what browser your user is going to view your pages with.

■ You can test the links locally by clicking them as long as the destination documents are in the same relative position on your computer. In other words, if the files will be in the same directory on the server, they should be in the same directory on your hard disk.

Testing your page

213

Chapter 18

Publishing your page

Netscape Gold has a special publishing option that automatically transfers all of the files in your Web site to your server so that your public has access to them.

To publish your page:

1. Choose Publish in the File menu **(Figure 18.7)**. The Publish Files dialog box appears.

2. If you are publishing one page (with its images), next to Include files check Images in the document. If you are publishing more than one page, next to Include files check All files in document's folder **(Figure 18.8)**.

3. The images from the current document (or all the images in the current page's folder) appear in the scroll list. Click the files that you want to copy to the server, using the Select None and Select All buttons as necessary. Your readers will only be able to see the images on a page if you copy them to the server.

4. Enter the location where the files should be copied on the server **(Figure 18.9)**. If you're not sure what to type here, ask your Internet service provider. Typically, it will be the FTP address of your Web site on the server.

5. Enter your user name and password. If desired, click Save password so that you don't have to enter it each time you publish a page.

6. Open a connection to the Internet if you're not already connected.

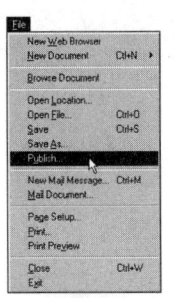

Figure 18.7 *With the Editor window active, choose Publish in the File menu.*

Figure 18.8 *In the Local files section, choose the files you wish to copy to the server.*

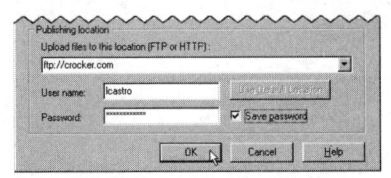

Figure 18.9 *In the Publishing Location area, enter the FTP or Web address where you wish to publish your page. Enter a name and password if necessary.*

214

Publishing a Page

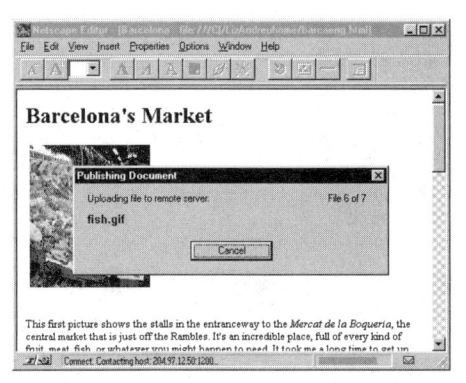

Figure 18.10 *As the files are published, a dialog box gives you a progress report.*

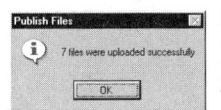

Figure 18.11 *An alert appears when Netscape has finished publishing your files.*

7. Click OK to send the files to the server. As the selected HTML page and the additional files listed in the scroll box are copied, a dialog box keeps you apprised of the progress **(Figure 18.10)**. An alert assures you that you have successfully published the page **(Figure 18.11)**.

✔ **Tips**

- The default publishing location on the server should appear in the pop-up menu. However, you can type any location that you wish. The addresses that you use will be recorded, and you can choose them from the pop-up menu during future publishing sessions. You can always go back to the default location by clicking Use Default Location. For more information, consult *Setting up a default publishing location* on page 216.

- The name of the file you are about to publish appears at the top of the Publish Files dialog box. If this is not the file you want to publish, click Cancel and start again. The page to be published is always the one active in the Editor window when you chose Publish in the File menu.

- If you are wary of automatic gadgets, you can publish your pages manually with FTP. For more information, consult *Uploading a file with FTP* on page 43.

Publishing your page

215

Setting up a default publishing location

Generally, one always publishes to the same location on the server. You can define that location so that you don't have to enter it manually during each publishing session.

To set up a default publishing location:

1. Choose Editor Preferences in the Options menu **(Figure 18.12)**.

2. Click the Publish tab to see the Publish preferences.

3. In the Default publishing location section, enter an FTP or Web address where you want to publish your pages **(Figure 18.13)**. If you're not sure what address to use, contact your Internet service provider.

4. If desired, enter your user name and password at the bottom of the dialog box. Click Save password so that Netscape doesn't ask you for your password each time you publish a page.

5. Click OK to save the changes.

✓ Tip

- If you don't enter your user name and password in the Editor Preferences dialog box, Netscape will ask you for it when you publish your page. If you *do* enter it, anyone with access to your computer will be able to publish files to your FTP or Web site.

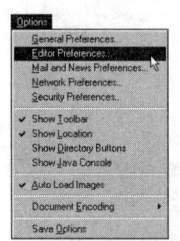

Figure 18.12 *Choose Editor Preferences in the Options menu.*

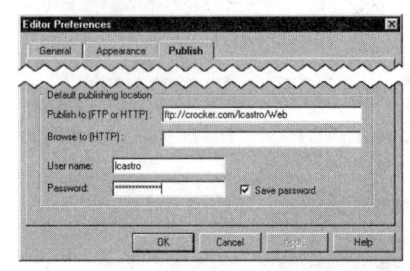

Figure 18.13 *Enter the location where you publish most of your pages in the Publish to text box. If desired, enter a user name and password.*

Publishing a Page

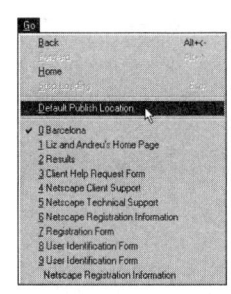

Figure 18.14 *Choose Default Publish Location in the Go menu.*

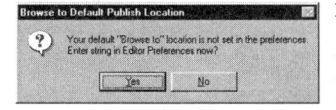

Figure 18.15 *Click OK to enter the default location.*

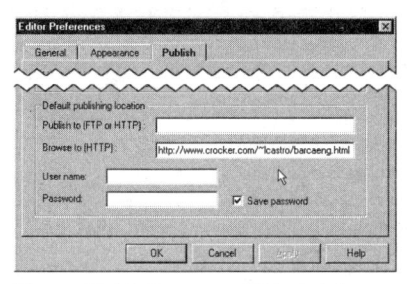

Figure 18.16 *Enter your Web site's home page, or other page that you view regularly, in the Browse to text box.*

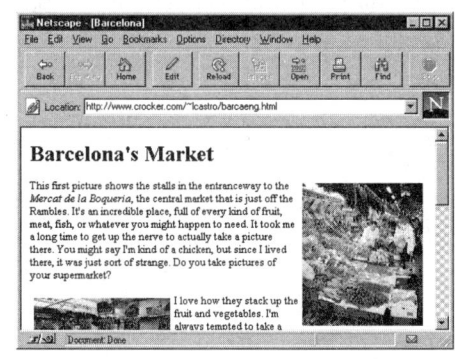

Figure 18.17 *The desired page on the server is shown in the browser.*

Viewing your published page

Once you've published your page, you should connect to your server and check that it looks the way it's supposed to.

To view your published page:

1. Open your connection to the Internet, if it isn't already.

2. Choose Default Publishing Location in the Go menu **(Figure 18.14)**.

3. If you haven't yet entered the location of your Web page, you can do that now. Click OK in the alert box **(Figure 18.15)**.

4. In the Editor Preferences dialog box that appears, type the URL of the page you would like to view in the Browse to text box **(Figure 18.16)**. Click OK to close the dialog box.

5. Your published page is shown in the browser **(Figure 18.17)**. Notice the URL in the Location field; it is *not* local.

✓ Tips

- A good choice for the Browse to text box is your Web site's home page. That way you can quickly jump to your own base and test all of your published pages.

- You can always get back to the Editor Preferences dialog box by choosing Editor Preferences in the Options dialog box, and then clicking the Publish tab *(see page 232)*.

Viewing your published page

217

Chapter 18

Advertising your site

With the growing popularity of the Web, there has come an explosion in services for both Web page publishers (that's you!) and browsers. There are many ways to get the word out about your page. Here are some starters.

To advertise your site:

1. Use the What's New fill in forms at free Web indexing services like Yahoo! **(Fig. 18.18)**, NCSA Mosaic and Global Network Navigator **(Fig. 18.19)**.

   Yahoo!: *http://add.yahoo.com/bin/add?*

   NCSA Mosaic: *http://www.ncsa.uiuc.edu/SDG/Software/Mosaic/Docs/whats-new-form.html*

   Global Network Navigator: *http://gnn.com/gnn/netizens/addform.html*

   (There are no spaces in any of these URLs. The hyphens are *not* optional.)

2. Pay a company to advertise your page for you.

3. Post a note in the moderated newsgroup *comp.infosystems.www.announce* or the unmoderated *comp.internet.net-happenings* or in newsgroups that have similar interests as your Web site.

4. Send e-mail to your associates and friends. You can include the URL for your site in all your correspondence in a signature *(see page 120)*.

5. Send e-mail to the creators of other sites with similar interests or topics.

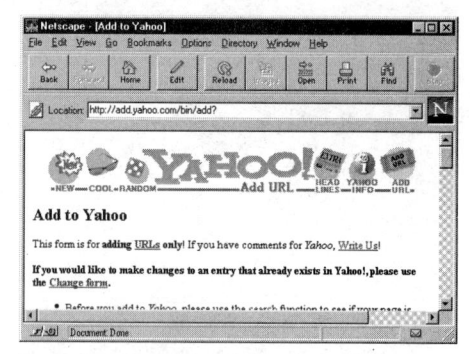

Figure 18.18 *Fill in Yahoo's form to add your page to their index.*

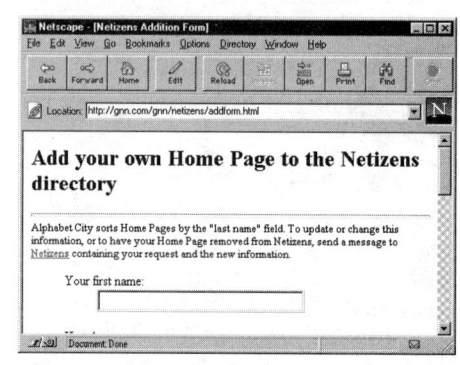

Figure 18.19 *The Netizens directory is especially designed for personal home pages.*

Part III: Preferences
Personalizing Netscape Navigator

General Preferences

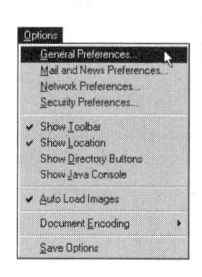

Figure 19.1 *Choose General Preferences in the Options menu to view the General Preferences dialog box.*

The settings in the General Preferences dialog box control many different aspects of Netscape. To access the General Preferences box, choose General Preferences in the Options menu **(Figure 19.1)**.

The General Preferences dialog box is divided into seven sections called *tabs*. Click a tab's name to make it active and access its settings. Each tab is described in detail in the following pages.

Once you've made the desired changes to the settings, click OK to save the changes, or Cancel to leave the dialog box without saving them. Click Help to access Netscape's Help file.

Chapter 19

Appearance

Click the Appearance tab in the General Preferences dialog box to display the Appearance preferences. Use the Appearance preferences to control the appearance of the toolbar, the initial window (and page) that Netscape shows upon launch, and links.

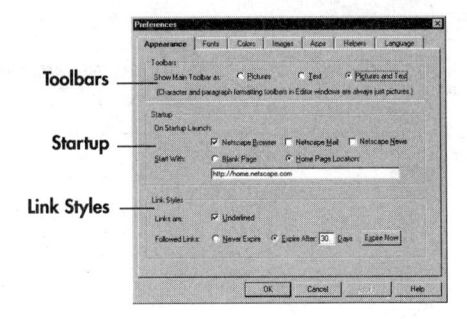

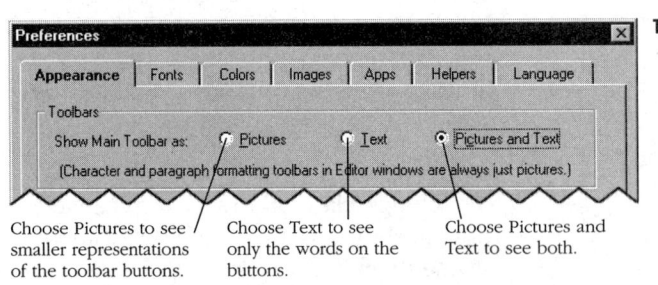

Toolbars

Startup

Link Styles

Toolbars

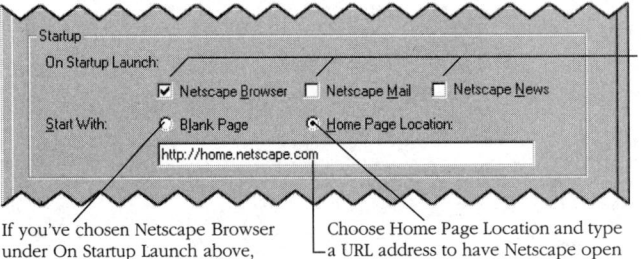

Choose Pictures to see smaller representations of the toolbar buttons.

Choose Text to see only the words on the buttons.

Choose Pictures and Text to see both.

Startup

Click Netscape Browser so that the first window you see when entering Netscape is the Web Browser. Click Netscape Mail to start with the Mail window (and automatically check your mail). Click Netscape News to start with the News window.

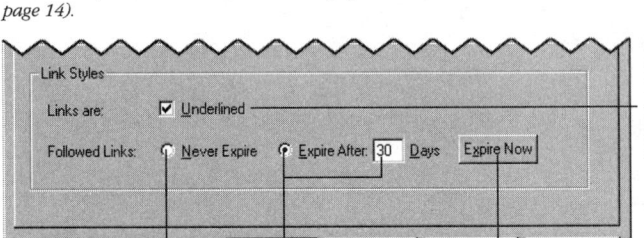

If you've chosen Netscape Browser under On Startup Launch above, choose Blank page to open Netscape with a clean, blank window (see page 14).

Choose Home Page Location and type a URL address to have Netscape open a particular page upon launch (see page 14).

Link Styles

Click Underlined to display the hypertext links in your Web pages with an underline (see page 21). Uncheck it to hide the line.

Links change color when you click them. Choose Never Expire to keep the "visited" color forever.

Choose Expire After xx days (and type a number of days) to have the links return to their original color after a certain number of days.

Click Expire Now to immediately return all links to their unclicked color.

General Preferences

Fonts

Click the Fonts tab in the General Preferences dialog box to display the Fonts preferences. Use the Fonts preferences to choose the default font encoding for the documents you browse, as well as the particular fonts that should be used.

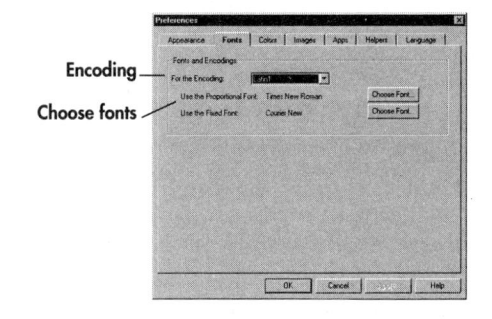

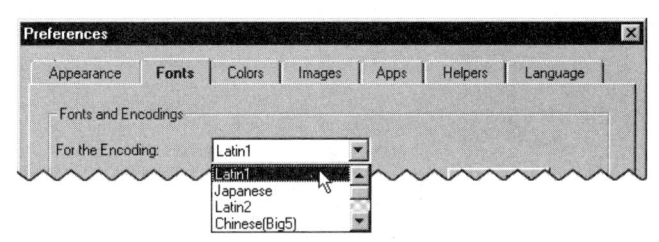

Encoding
Choose an encoding that matches the alphabet of the documents you will read. An encoding describes the relationship between characters and their hexadecimal representations.

Choose Fonts
Click one of the Choose Font buttons to designate the desired fonts.

Most of the text you see in a document will be displayed with a proportional font like Times or Helvetica.

The text displayed in entry forms and sometimes in block quotes or other special parts of a page is displayed with a fixed font like Courier.

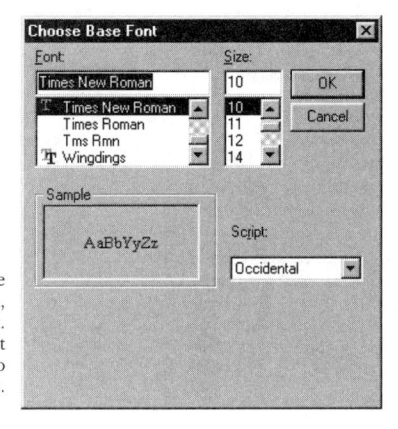

When you click the Choose Font button, you'll see this dialog box. Select a font and a font size and then click OK to save the changes.

223

Chapter 19

Colors

You have some control over the colors used on the pages you browse. You can choose a different color for new and visited links and for regular text. For the background, choose either a color or an image. Finally, you can make these choices override the options used in any individual Web page.

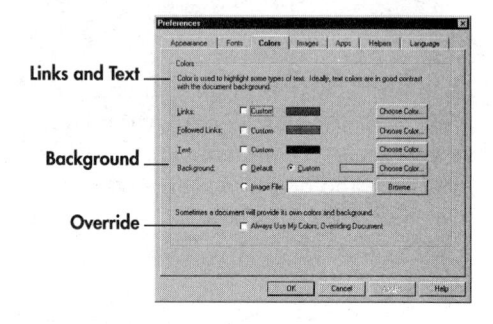

Links and Text

Background

Override

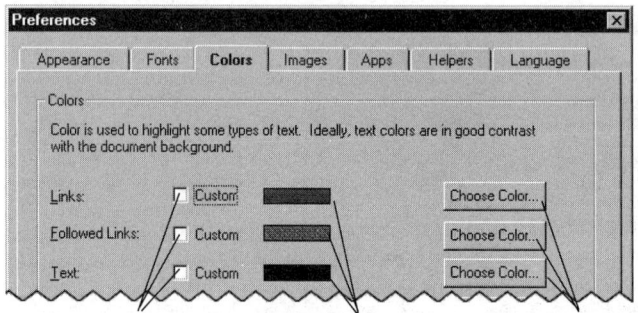

To change a color, first click the Custom button.

The current color is shown in the swatch.

After clicking Custom, click the Choose Color button.

Links and Text
You can choose your own colors for links you haven't visited (Links), links you have visited (Followed Links) and for regular text (Text). Simply click Custom and then click Choose Color. Choose a color in the dialog box that appears and click OK. The new color will be shown in the swatch.

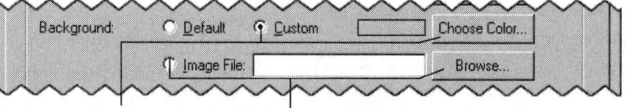

To choose a background color, click Custom and then click Choose Color.

To choose an image, click Image file, then click Browse and locate the desired file (GIF or JPEG format) on your hard disk.

Background
You may choose a special color or even an image for the background of all the pages you browse.

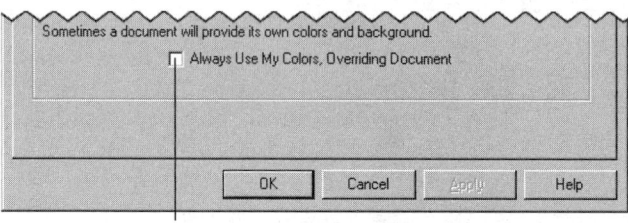

Override
Some Web page designers define their own colors for text, links, and background. You can choose to override their choices.

Click Always Use My Colors, Overriding Document if you want your colors (chosen above) to take precedence over a particular Web page designer's fancy. For example, if you're having trouble reading a page because the Web designer chose rotten colors, you can go back to normal colors by using this option.

224

General Preferences

Images

Click the Images tab in the General Preferences dialog box to display the Images preferences. You can choose the method in which extra colors should be displayed and how images should be loaded onto the page.

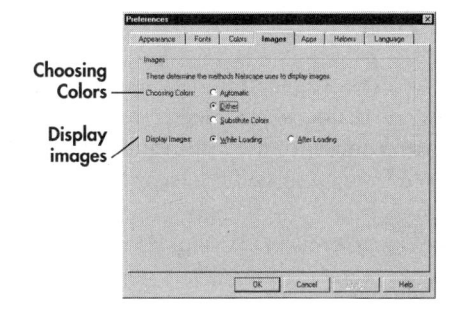

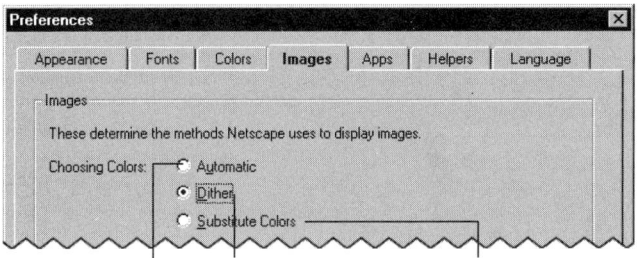

Choosing Colors

Display images

Choose Automatic to let Netscape decide how to best deal with the colors.

Click Dither to approximate the image's colors by using a combination of the available ones. Dithering gives the best results but may be slow.

Use Substitute colors to use the existing colors in place of missing ones. Substitute is faster but gives poorer results.

Choose While Loading if you want to see the images as they load.

Choose After Loading to display the images all at once, after all the data has been received. On a fast network, this may be slightly faster.

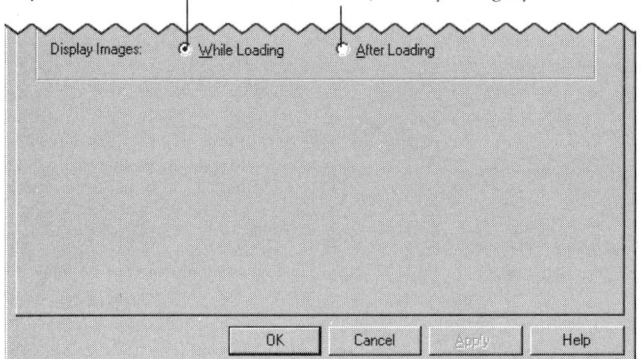

Choosing Colors
Many monitors can only view 256 colors at once. If you try to load several images that contain more than the allowed number of colors, Netscape has to fudge the results: either by dithering or substituting colors.

Display images
If you have chosen Auto Load Images in the Options menu, Netscape will load images as it loads each page. With the preferences in this section, you can choose to display the images incrementally while loading, or display them all at once, when all the information has been received.

225

Chapter 19

Apps

Click the Apps tab in the General Preferences dialog box to see the application preferences for the applications you use in conjunction with Netscape. You can also choose the program that you wish to use to view HTML tags *(see page 208)* and the folder where temporary files should be stored.

Telnet applications
View Source
Temporary Directory

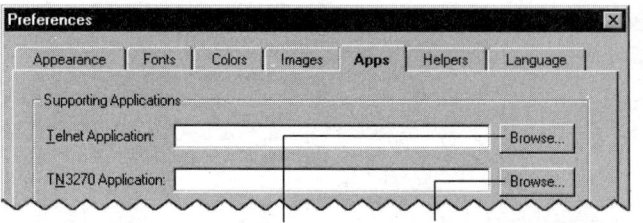

Telnet applications
You can designate a Telnet or TN3270 application of your choice for connecting to another computer via Telnet through Netscape.

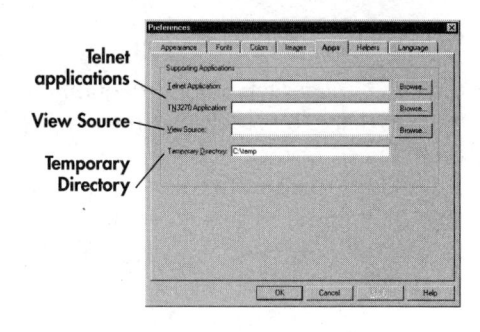

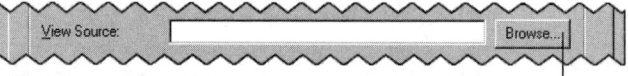

Click Browse and locate the Telnet application that you wish to use. Telnetting means connecting to a remote computer as if you were there in person.

A TN3270 application is for telnetting to an IBM mainframe. Click Browse to locate the desired TN3270 application on your hard disk.

View Source
You can designate which program to launch when viewing HTML tags.

Click Browse to locate the desired program with which to view a page's HTML tags, when you select Document Source in the View menu. For example, you might choose to view HTML tags with Microsoft Word or Word Perfect.

Type the path of the directory where temporary files should be stored.

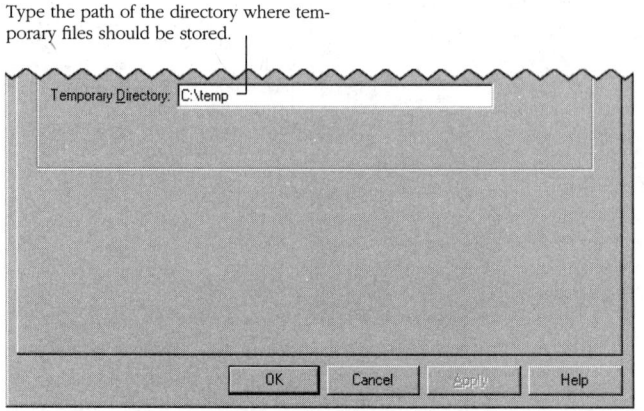

Temporary directory
When Netscape encounters a file it cannot display by itself, it downloads the file and launches a helper application to deal with it. Once the file has been viewed, it is deleted. You can choose where these temporary files should be kept on your hard disk.

226

General Preferences

Helpers

Click the Helpers tab in the General Preferences dialog box to see the Helpers preferences. You can choose which helper applications should be launched according to which files Netscape encounters out on the Web, or if the files should simply be saved.

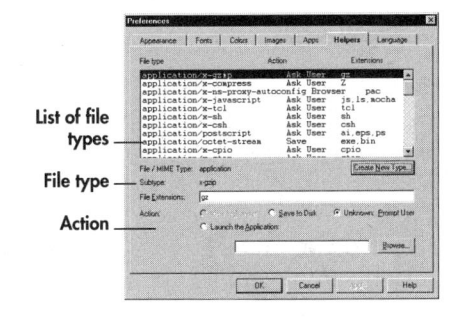

List of file types
File type
Action

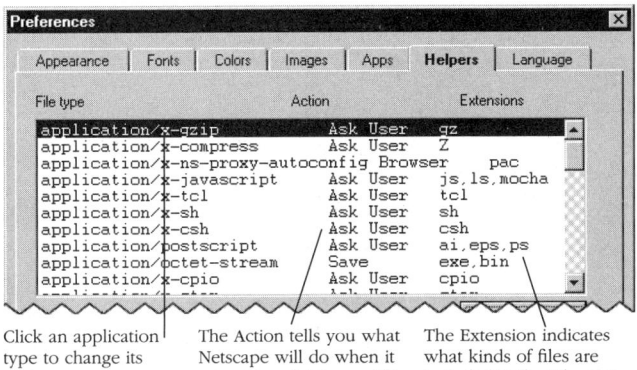

List of file types
Many different kinds of files are listed, along with the action that will take place when Netscape encounters them, and the extensions that define those kinds of files.

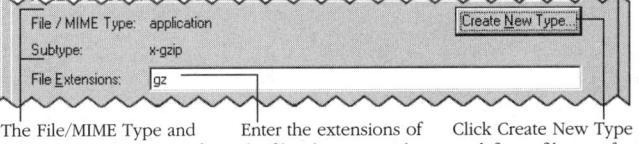

Click an application type to change its options.

The Action tells you what Netscape will do when it encounters this type of file.

The Extension indicates what kinds of files are included in the File type.

File type
This section defines the file type, lets you choose a new file type, and lets you see (or add) new extensions.

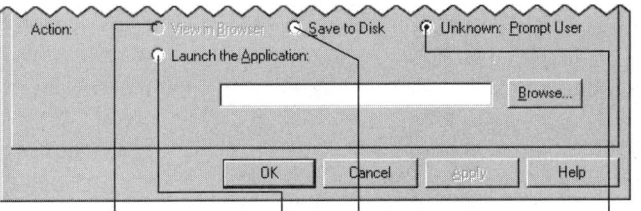

The File/MIME Type and Subtype give the same information as in the scroll list above, for the selected type.

Enter the extensions of the files that you wish to define as the selected File type.

Click Create New Type to define a file type for a kind of file not already in the list.

Action
You tell Netscape what you want it to do with each kind of file it finds. You can view the file directly (if Netscape can), save it, have it ask you, or launch a helper application that, in turn, opens the file.

Click View in Browser to view the file in Netscape, if possible.

Choose Save to Disk to have Netscape automatically save the files with this extension to your hard disk.

Click Unknown: Prompt User to have Netscape ask you what to do when it encounters a file type that it doesn't recognize.

Choose Launch the Application (and click Browse and find the application on your hard disk) to have Netscape automatically open a program that can open the files that have this extension.

227

Chapter 19

Language

Click the Language tab in the General Preferences dialog box to see the language preferences. When a page on the Web is available in more than one language, you can tell the server what language(s) you prefer to browse by creating an "accept list" of languages.

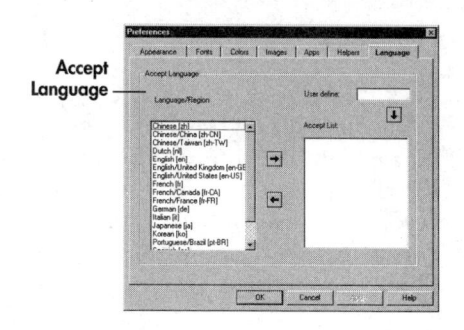

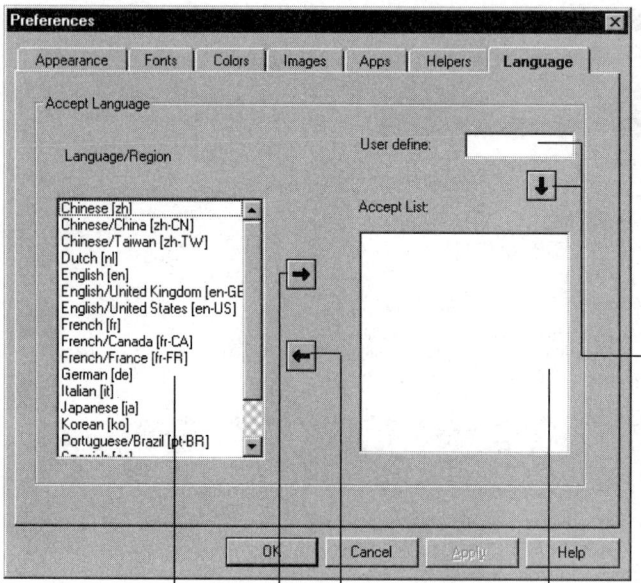

Accept Language ─

Accept Language
You can create a priority list of languages in which you prefer files to be downloaded or viewed through the Accept list. Then Netscape advises the server of the desired languages and if the server understands, it gives you access to the appropriate language version.

If the desired language or region does not appear in the left list, enter the non-standard language or region and then click the down arrow to add it to the accept list. The first tag should be a two letter ISSO 639 language abbreviation. The second two letters should be an ISO 3166 country tag.

Click a Language/Region in the left list to select it.

Click the right pointing arrow to add the new language to the accept list. Click the left pointing arrow to remove a language from the Accept list.

The acceptable languages are listed in the right list in order of preference.

228

Editor Preferences

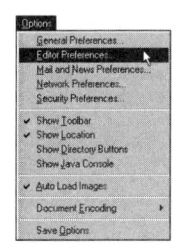

Figure 20.1 *Choose Editor Preferences in Netscape Gold's Options menu.*

The settings in the Editor Preferences dialog box control how documents are created, what colors they use and how they're published. To access the Editor Preferences box, choose Editor Preferences in the Options menu **(Figure 20.1)**. The Editor Preferences are only available in Netscape Gold.

The Editor Preferences dialog box is divided into three sections called *tabs*. Click a tab's name to make it active and access its settings. Each tab is described in detail in the following pages.

Once you've made the desired changes to the settings, click OK to save the changes, or Cancel to leave the dialog box without saving them. Click Help to access Netscape Gold's Help file.

Chapter 20

General

Click the General tab to change the default author's name, to choose external text and image editors, and to specify which pages you would like to use as a template when creating new Web pages of your own.

Author name — identifies the Editor Preferences dialog

External editors

New document template

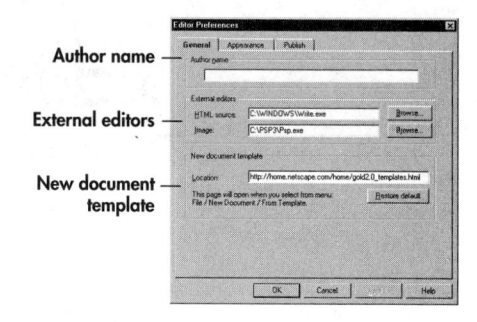

Author name
The Author name identifies the pages you create. The information does not appear on the Web page when viewed with a browser, but instead is inserted into the HTML tags and can be used by search services.

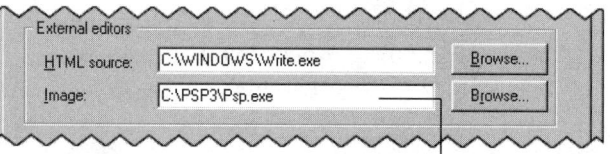

Type the name with which you wish to identify all the pages you create.

External editors
Netscape gives you a shortcut to the programs you use most often for editing HTML tags and images.

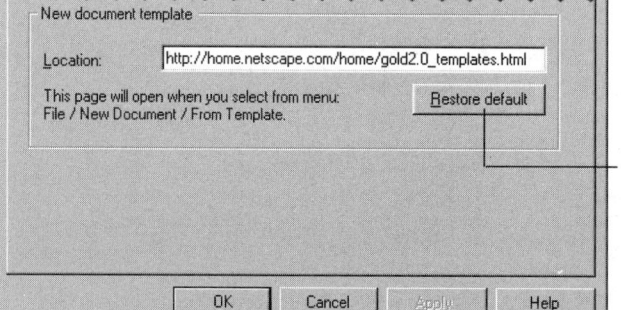

Type the path to a text editor that you would like to use, in addition to Netscape Gold, for viewing and modifying HTML tags. Or click Browse and locate the program on your hard disk.

Type the path to an image editor (like PaintShop Pro or Photoshop) that you would like to use for editing images. Or click Browse and locate the program on your hard disk.

New document template
When you choose New Document in the File menu and then From Template in the submenu, Netscape loads the page specified at left. You can create your own templates and type the path to them here.

Click Restore Default to use Netscape's default templates (at Netscape's Web site).

230

Editor Preferences

Appearance

Click the Appearance tab to change the colors and background of the Web pages you create. The options chosen here don't affect the current page. To change the colors or background of the current page, choose Document in the Properties menu and click the Appearance tab (which looks just like this one).

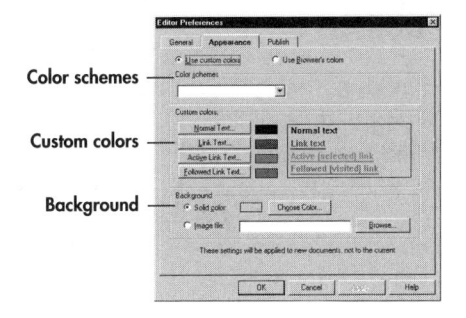

Color schemes

Custom colors

Background

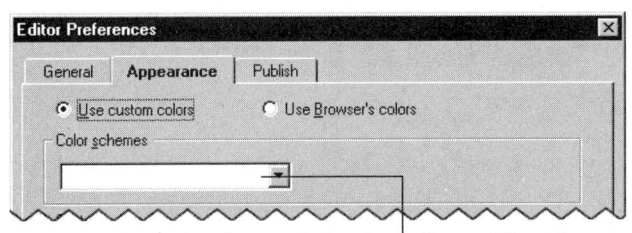

Netscape has designed a collection of color schemes that are different from the norm, but sill readable. Click in the pop-up menu to choose one.

Custom colors vs. Browser's colors and Color schemes
Click Use custom colors to use the options specified in the rest of this dialog box. Choose Use Browser's colors to use the colors specified in the Colors tab of the General Preferences dialog box.

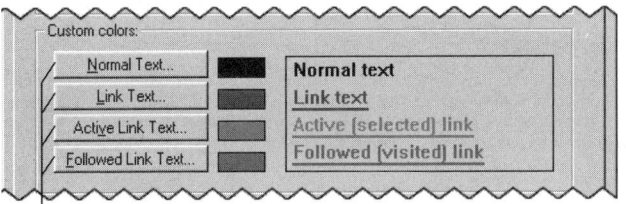

Custom colors
Choose which color to use for regular text, new links (Link Text), links being clicked on (Active Link Text) and visited links (Followed Link Text).

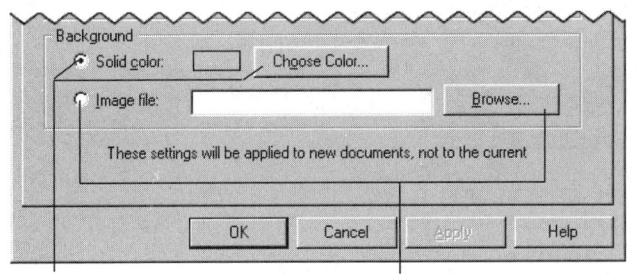

Click the text whose color you wish to change. In the Color dialog box that appears, choose the desired color and click OK. The new color will be shown next to the corresponding text type.

Background
Choose how the background of your Web pages should appear: either with a solid color or with an image.

Click Solid Color and then the Choose Color button. In the Color dialog box that appears, choose a color for the background.

Click Image file and then Browse to locate the desired image on your hard disk. If the image is smaller than the page, it will be tiled (repeated) to fit.

231

Chapter 20

Publish

Click the Publish tab to determine how Netscape treats links and images in the pages you create and edit, and to specify the location of the server where you wish your page and its associated images to be copied when you choose Publish in the File menu.

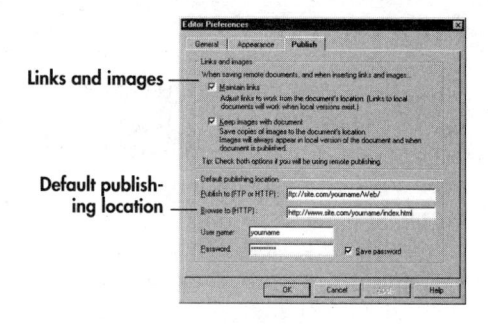

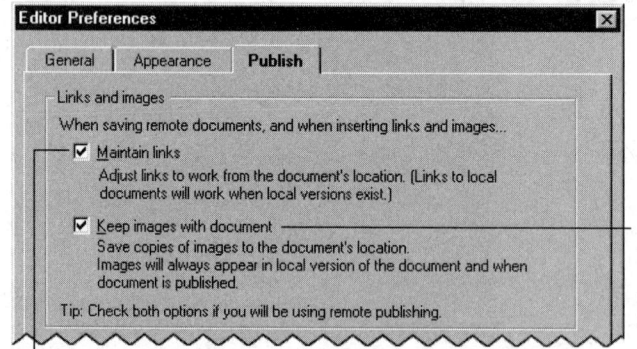

Links and images

Default publishing location

Links and images

Check Keep images with document if you want Netscape to copy all the images inserted on a page to the same directory on your hard disk that contains the Web page itself.

Choose Maintain Links to have Netscape convert absolute links into relative ones on the pages that you copy from the Web. This will enable the links to continue to work correctly when you open them locally (from your hard disk).

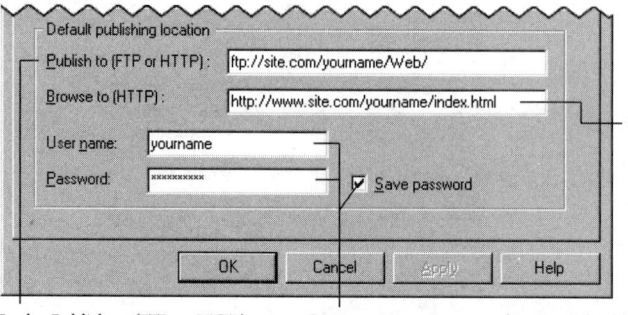

Default publishing location
Specify where your pages should be published when you choose Publish in the File menu.

Type a URL in the Browse to (HTTP) text box to determine where the Default Publish Location command in the Go menu takes you *(see page 217)*.

In the Publish to (FTP or HTTP) text box, type the URL of the FTP or Web site where you wish to publish your files. If you're not sure, ask your Internet service provider.

Enter your user name and password in the corresponding boxes and click Save password so that Netscape doesn't ask you for it each time. Of course, this lets anyone with access to your computer publish documents to your FTP site. If you prefer, enter just the user name and let Netscape ask you for your password manually.

Mail and News Prefs

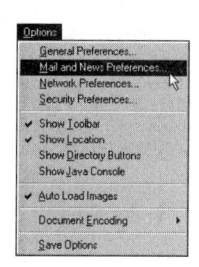

Figure 21.1 *Choose Mail and News Preferences in the Options menu to see the Mail and News Preferences dialog box.*

The settings in the Mail and News Preferences dialog box control many different aspects of the mail and news windows. To access the Mail and News Preferences dialog box, choose Mail and News Preferences in the Options menu **(Figure 21.1)**.

The Mail and News Preferences dialog box is divided into five sections called *tabs*. Click a tab's name to make it active and access its settings. Each tab is described in detail in the following pages.

Once you've made the desired changes to the settings, click OK to save the changes, or Cancel to leave the dialog box without saving them. Click Help to access Netscape's Help file.

233

Chapter 21

Appearance

Click the Appearance tab in the Mail and News Preferences dialog box to change the way messages appear in the Mail and News windows. You can choose the font that messages should be displayed in, as well as the style and size of quoted sections. In addition, you can choose not to use Netscape Mail at all!

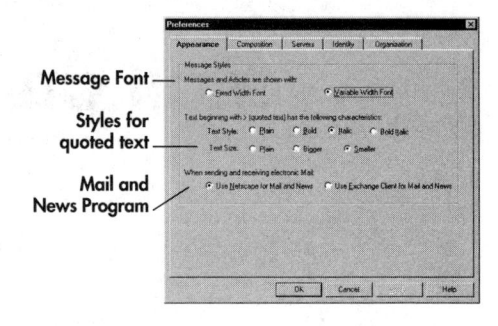

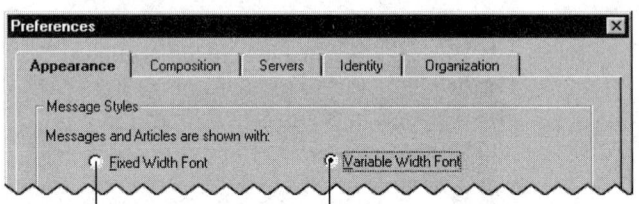

Message Font — points to the Message Styles section of the Preferences dialog.

Styles for quoted text — points to the Text Style/Size section.

Mail and News Program — points to the "When sending and receiving electronic Mail" section.

Message Font
In the General Preferences box *(see page 222)*, you chose a specific font for proportional text and another for fixed font text. Here, you can choose which of those fonts should be used for displaying messages in the Mail and News windows. (Unfortunately, the Message Composition window is not affected.)

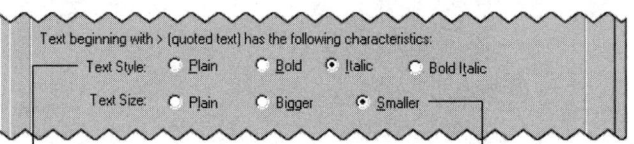

Click Fixed Width Font to use the font defined next to "Use the Fixed Font" in the Fonts section of the General Preferences dialog box.

Click Variable Width Font to use the font defined next to "Use the Proportional Font" in the Fonts section of the General Preferences dialog box.

Styles for quoted text
Many messages contain text from earlier correspondence. You can format that text with a special style and size to set it apart from the current message's contents.

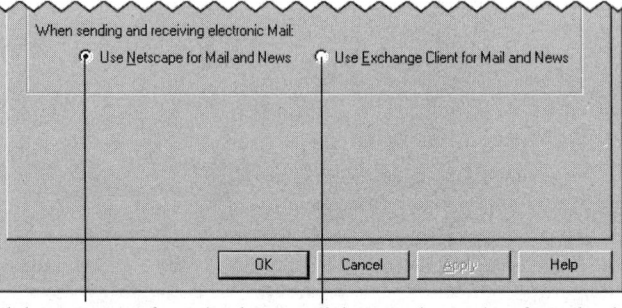

Click Plain, Bold, Italic or Bold Italic to format quoted text with the corresponding style.

Click Plain to keep the quoted text at the same size as regular text. Choose Bigger or Smaller to change the size of quoted text.

Mail program
If you already use Microsoft's Exchange Client for e-mail with Windows 95, you can continue to do so, while using Netscape just for browsing. When you check for mail or news, the Exchange Client window will appear.

Click Use Netscape for Mail and News to use Netscape for all mail and news operations. This is the default option.

Click Use Exchange Client for Mail and News to use Microsoft's software for Mail and News. (Windows 95, only.)

Mail and News Prefs

Composition

Click the Composition tab in the Mail and News Preferences dialog box to choose a bit format for your messages, whether or not to e-mail or save a copy of them, and if Netscape should automatically quote the original message when you compose its reply.

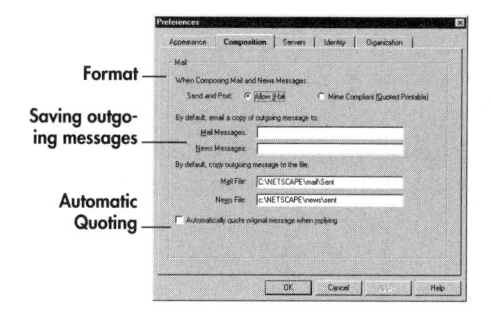

Format

Saving outgoing messages

Automatic Quoting

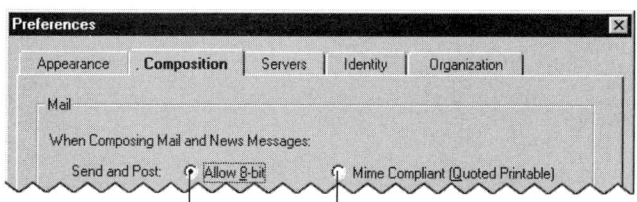

Click Allow 8-bit for widest compatibility with e-mail servers in the US and Europe.

Click Mime Compliant to make Netscape interpret messages from MIME mail readers correctly.

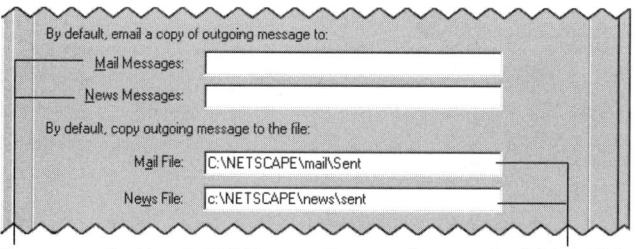

Type an e-mail address in Mail Messages or News Messages to send a copy of all outgoing messages to that address.

Enter a path on your hard disk in Mail File or News File to save a copy of all outgoing messages to your hard disk.

Mark the Automatically quote original message when replying checkbox to have Netscape automatically quote the original message in the Message Composition window when you select Reply or Reply to All in the Message menu.

Format
Most e-mail servers in the US and Europe use 8 bit messages. If you are receiving messages from a MIME mail reader, you can change the setting to see the characters correctly.

Saving outgoing messages
Incoming mail messages are automatically saved to your hard disk. Outgoing e-mail and news messages are not. Use these options to save these messages automatically.

Automatic Quoting
When you reply to an e-mail message or news posting, it's often a good idea to remind the recipient what they were talking about by quoting their original message. You can have Netscape quote messages all the time (using this option) or just sometimes *(see page 112)*.

235

Chapter 21

Servers

Click the Servers tab in the Mail and News Preferences dialog box to enter information about the server name, your name, where mail should be stored, how large messages can be, whether they should be left on the server and if Netscape should check for mail automatically.

Mail Server Data

Miscellaneous Mail

Miscellaneous News

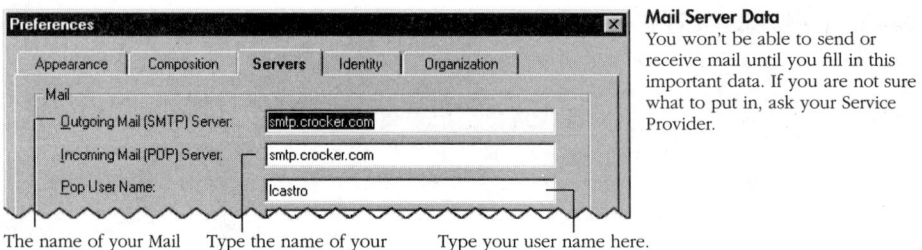

Mail Server Data
You won't be able to send or receive mail until you fill in this important data. If you are not sure what to put in, ask your Service Provider.

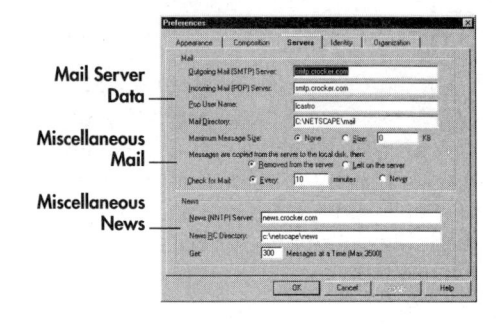

The name of your Mail Server goes here.

Type the name of your Outgoing Mail Server here.

Type your user name here. This is the part of your e-mail address before the @ symbol.

Miscellaneous Mail
Choose where to store mail messages on your hard disk, their maximum size, whether or not to remove them from the server, and if Netscape should check for mail automatically.

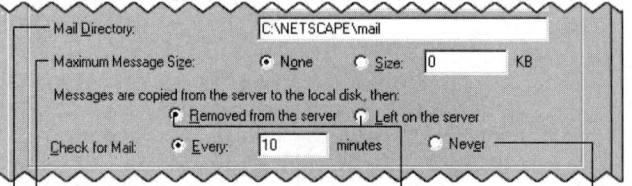

Enter the path to the directory on your hard disk where mail messages should be stored.

You can limit Mail messages to a certain size by typing a number for Size. Otherwise, click None.

Netscape automatically copies incoming mail to your hard disk. Choose whether to leave a copy on the server as well.

Have Netscape check for mail automatically by clicking Every and entering a number of minutes. Otherwise, click Never.

Miscellaneous News
In this area, you enter the name of your news server (ask your Service Provider), the directory where your newsgroup settings (News RC) should be stored, and how many messages you want to retrieve at a time.

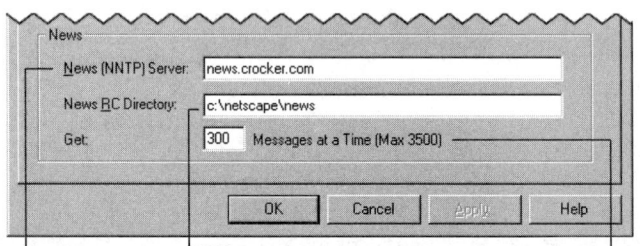

Enter the name of your news server here. Ask your Service Provider if you're not sure.

Enter the path to the directory on your hard disk where the News RC file should be stored. The News RC file contains information about which newsgroups you've subscribed to, among other things.

Choose how many news messages should be loaded from a newsgroup at once. The default is 100.

Mail and News Prefs

Identity

Click the Identity tab in the Mail and News Preferences box to enter information about yourself, including your name, e-mail address, the e-mail address where you want to receive replies, and the name of your organization. You can also specify a signature file that will be appended to every outgoing message.

Personal information

Signature File

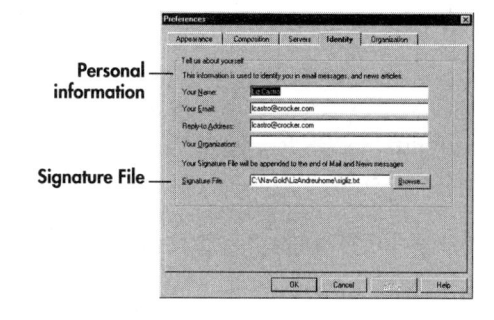

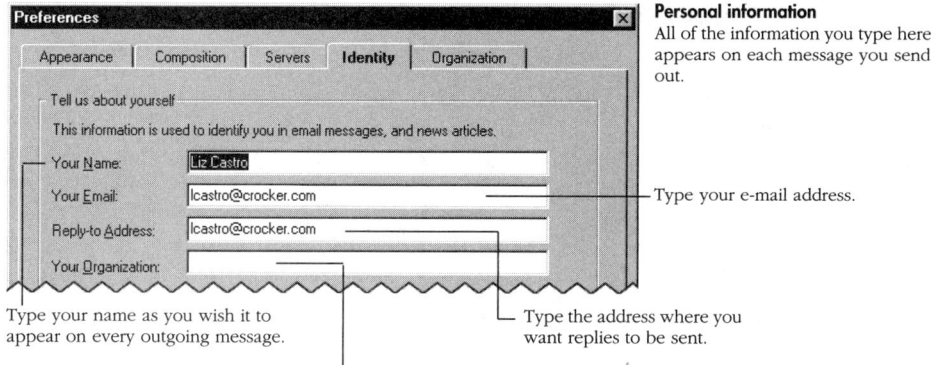

Personal information
All of the information you type here appears on each message you send out.

Type your name as you wish it to appear on every outgoing message.

Type your e-mail address.

Type the address where you want replies to be sent.

Type the name of your organization. If you don't type anything here, Netscape will use the name of your Service Provider automatically in all outgoing correspondence.

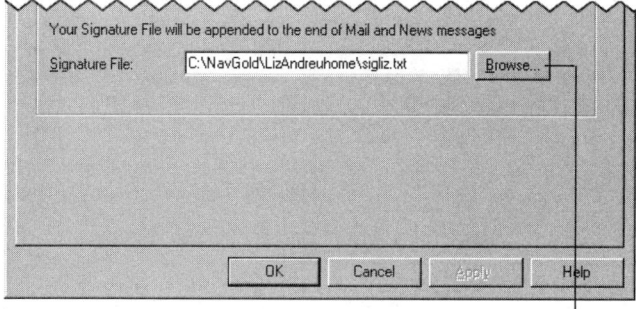

Signature File
You can create a text file and then have Netscape automatically add it the end of each message you send. Most signatures include the writer's name, e-mail address, sometimes their snail-mail address, and a cute quote. The only requirement is that it be saved in Text Only format.

Click Browse to locate your signature file (any text file) on the hard disk. For more information on signatures, consult *Creating a signature file* on page 119.

237

Chapter 21

Organization

Click the Organization tab in the Mail and News preferences dialog box to set certain defaults for the Mail and News windows. You can have Netscape remember your password, and automatically thread and sort messages as desired.

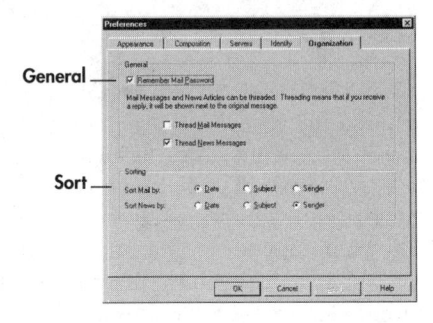

General ──

Sort ──

General
You'll need to let Netscape remember your password if you want it to check your mail automatically every few minutes. Threading your messages shows replies under the original message, slightly indented.

Click Remember Mail Password so that Netscape doesn't ask you to enter the password each time you check your mail. You must check this box if you want Netscape to check your mail automatically.

You can choose to thread mail or news messages by default. For more information, consult *Threading messages* on page 96.

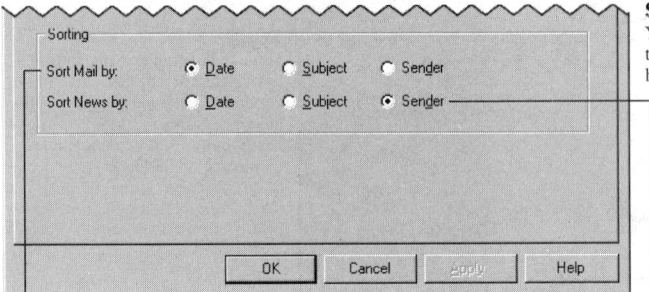

Sort
You can choose default settings for the order in which Netscape sorts both Mail and News messages.

Click Date to order mail messages by date, Subject to order them by subject, and yes, Sender to order them by Sender, by default, each time you open the Mail window.

Click Date to order news postings by date, Subject to order them by subject, and yes, Sender to order them by Sender, by default, each time you open the News window.

For more information on sorting mail and news messages, consult *Putting your messages in order* on page 93.

238

Network Preferences

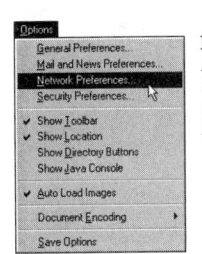

Figure 22.1 *Choose Network Preferences in the Options menu to view the Network Preferneces dialog box.*

The settings in the Network Preferences dialog box control how Netscape works over a network. To access the Network Preferences dialog box, choose Network Preferences in the Options menu.

The Network Preferences dialog box has three tabs. Click a tab's title to make it active and access its settings. Each tab is described in detail on the following pages.

Once you've made the desired changes to the settings, click OK to save the changes. Click Cancel to close the dialog box without saving changes. Click Help to access the Netscape Help file.

Chapter 22

Cache

Click the Cache tab in the Network Preferences dialog box to change the settings for the Disk and Memory caches, to change the directory and to decide how often Netscape should compare a page saved in Cache with the actual page on the server.

Memory and Disk Caches

Disk Cache Directory

Verify Document

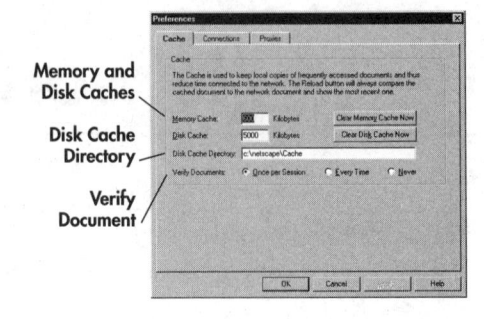

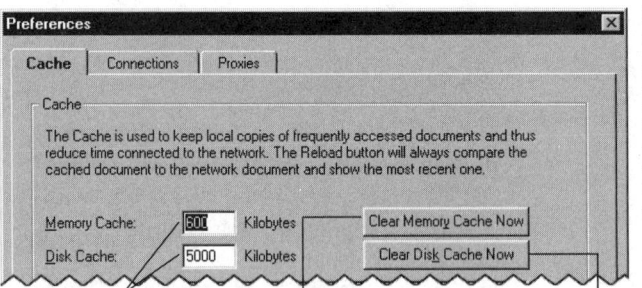

Memory and Disk Caches
Netscape saves as many of the pages and images that you browse in its Memory and Disk Caches. Once a page or image is stored in a cache, it takes much less time to display. Netscape organizes the Cache when you exit the program. If it seems to take too long, try reducing the size of the Disk Cache.

Type a number in the text boxes to set the size of the Memory (RAM) or Disk (storage) caches. The defaults are shown here.

Click the Clear Memory Cache Now to make the specified amount of RAM available to other programs. The Memory Cache is automatically erased each time you close Netscape.

Click Clear Disk Cache Now to erase all the pages and images in the disk cache and make more space available on your hard disk.

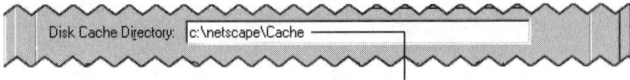

Disk Cache Directory
You can choose where to store the disk cache on your hard disk.

Type the path to the directory where you want the disk cache to store the pages and images that you browse.

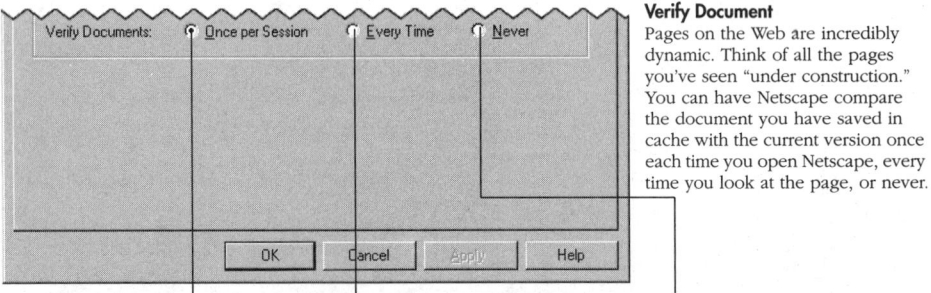

Verify Document
Pages on the Web are incredibly dynamic. Think of all the pages you've seen "under construction." You can have Netscape compare the document you have saved in cache with the current version once each time you open Netscape, every time you look at the page, or never.

Click Once per Session to have Netscape compare the cached version with the real page on the server only the first time you access the page during a session with Netscape.

Click Every Time to make Netscape compare the cached version with the server each time you browse the page. If you select this option, it doesn't make sense to have a big cache.

Click Never to have Netscape always use the cached version without checking for changes.

240

Network Preferences

Connections

Click the Connections tab in the Network preferences dialog box to define the number of connections that Netscape can make at one time, and to set the size of the network buffer.

Number of Connections

Network Buffer Size

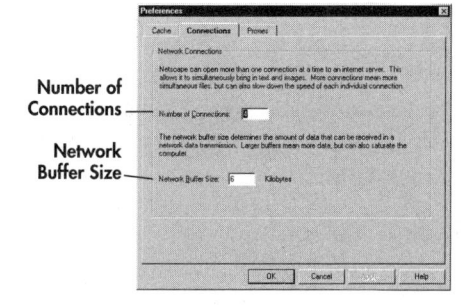

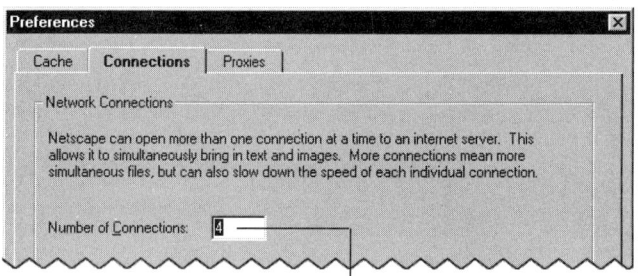

Number of Connections
The text and images on a page are distinct files on the server. Netscape can open more than one connection to the server in order to load the page more quickly, although the speed of each individual connection may deteriorate as a result.

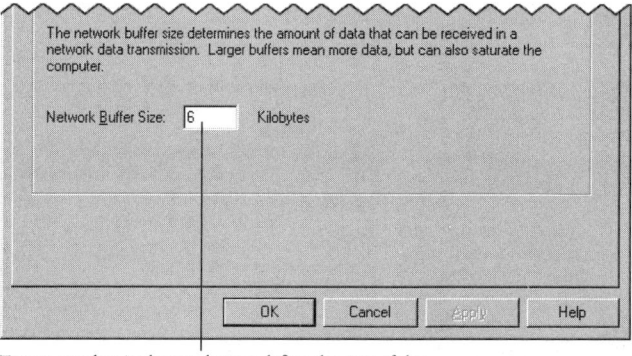

Type a number in the text box to determine how many connections Netscape should make at a time. The default is 4.

Network Buffer Size
The size of the network buffer determines the amount of data that can be received at a time. A larger number means more information can be received, but may saturate the computer.

Type a number in the text box to define the size of the network buffer. The default for Windows is 32K.

241

Chapter 22

Proxies

Click the Proxies tab in the Network preferences dialog box to change how Netscape interacts with proxy software. In situations where a firewall protects internal computer networks from external access, Netscape needs proxy software to get by the firewall to remote servers without compromising security.

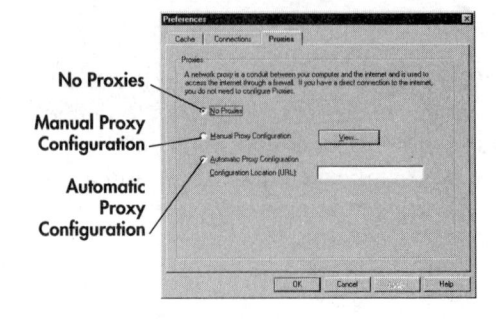

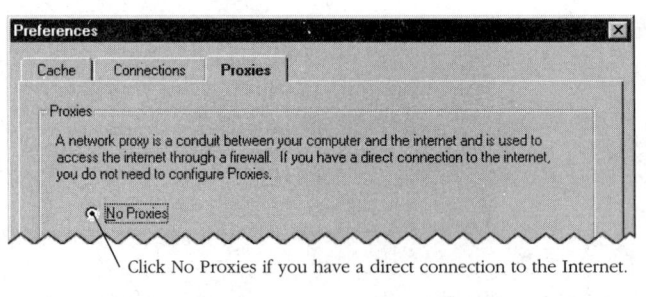

No Proxies →

Manual Proxy Configuration →

Automatic Proxy Configuration →

Click No Proxies if you have a direct connection to the Internet.

No Proxies
If your computer is not on a network and/or if you have a direct Internet connection, you don't have to worry about proxies at all, and should choose No Proxies.

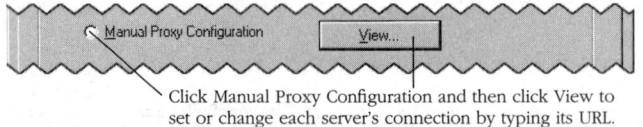

Click Manual Proxy Configuration and then click View to set or change each server's connection by typing its URL.

Manual Proxy Configuration
You can customize your own proxy configuration.

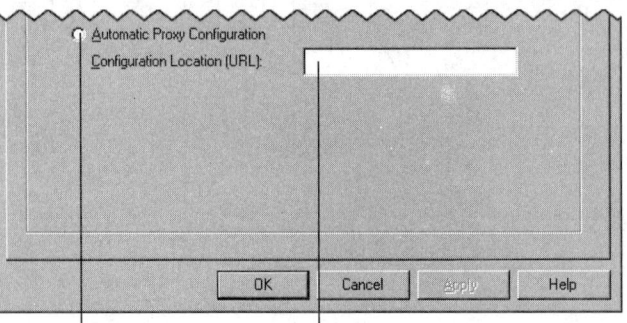

Automatic Proxy Configuration
You can also set Netscape up to take advantage of an already constructed configuration file.

Choose Automatic Proxy Configuration if you have already set up a configuration file for connecting to different servers.

Type the configuration file's URL in the text box so that Netscape can find it.

242

Security Preferences

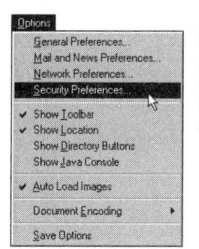

Figure 23.1 *Choose Security Preferences in the Options menu to view the Security Preferences dialog box.*

The settings in the Security Preferences dialog box help you protect your network, computer or data. To access the dialog box, choose Security Preferences in the Options menu **(Figure 23.1)**.

The Security Preferences dialog box is divided into two sections called *tabs*. Click a tab's name to make it active and access its settings. Each tab is described in detail on the following pages.

Once you've made the desired changes to the security settings, click OK. Click Cancel to close the dialog box without saving the changes. Click Help to access the Netscape Help file.

Chapter 23

General

Click the General tab in the Security preferences dialog box to disable Java and to determine when Netscape should alert you about the security status of certain areas or documents.

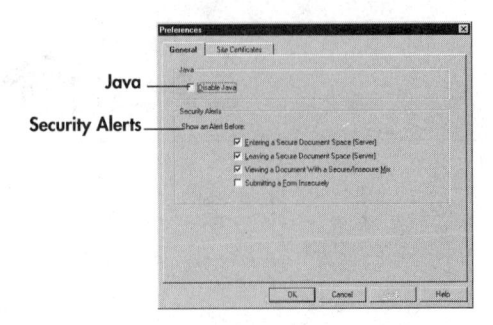

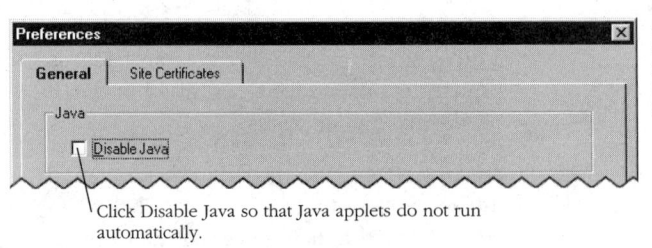

Java
Security Alerts

Click Disable Java so that Java applets do not run automatically.

Java
Since Java applets are applications running on your hard disk, they could conceivably be a security risk (i.e., if the program were malicious).

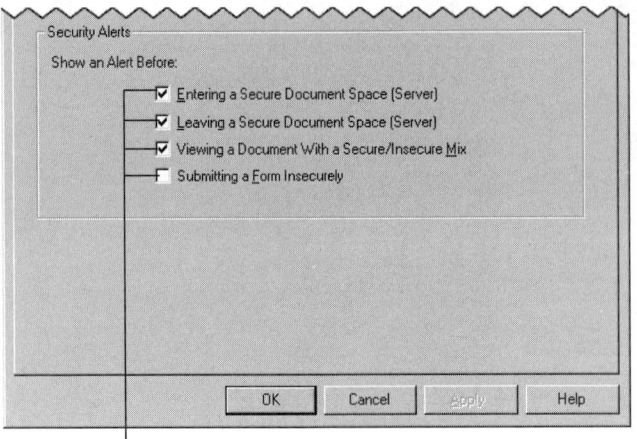

Security Alerts
You can have Netscape alert you of possible security problems. The individual alert boxes contain a "Show this Alert Next Time" button which, when unchecked, gives the same result as checking one of the options in this dialog box.

Check the situation in which you wish Netscape to alert you.

Security Preferences

Site Certificates

Choose the Site Certificates tab in the Security preferences dialog box to change settings regarding site certificates. A site certificate indicates who the site is, so that if you send information to them, you can be sure that they are who they say they are.

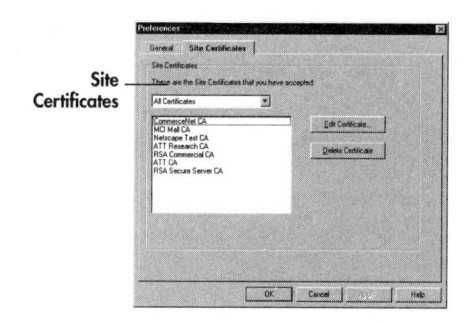

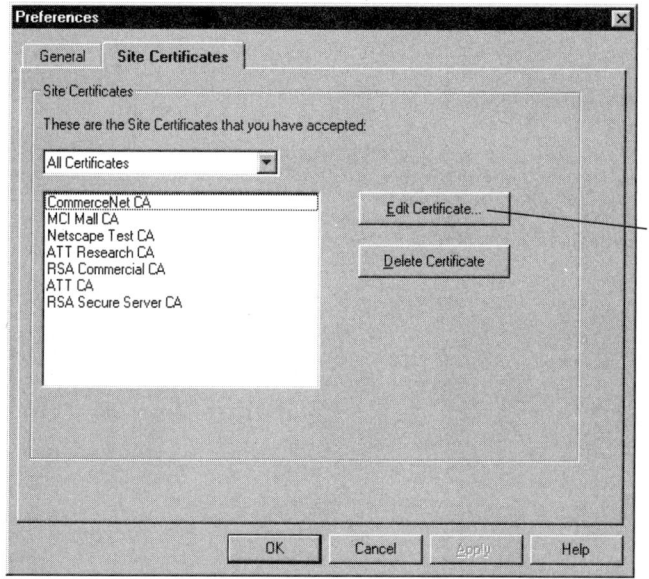

Site Certificates

Site Certificates
You may receive various site certificates from companies that want to be able to securely identify themselves to you.

Click Edit Certificate to see the information in a site certificate and change its options.

Index

A
About Netscape, command *66*
About Plug-ins, command *66*
accessing
    FTP site *40*
    Gopher site *41*
Add Bookmark, command *72*
Add Bookmark for this Link, command *72*
Add Folder, command *87*
Add from Newest Messages, command *144*
Add from Oldest Messages, command *144*
Add List, command *124*
Add Newsgroup, command *137*
Add to Address Book, command *123*
Add User, command *122*
adding
    alternative text *181*
    basic character formatting *166*
    bookmarks *82*
        choosing folder *70*
    horizontal lines *190*
    HTML tags manually *206*
    images *180*
    JavaScript *210*
    nonbreaking spaces *205*
    space around images *186*
Address, button *147*
Address, command *171*
Address Book, command *121*
Address Book, window *121*
    adding addresses *122*
    opening *121*
address books *121–130*
    importing *129*
    opening as Web page *130*
    saving *128*
    using as home page *14*
addresses
    adding *122*
    adding from message *123*
    changing and deleting *126*
    finding *58*, *127*
    of organizations *59*
    saving address book *128*
    using *125*
advertising pages *218*
aliases, creating for bookmarks *74*
Align Left, button *176*
Align Right, button *176*
aligning
    images *189*
    text *176*
Altavista, search service *57*

alternative text, adding *181*
Always Use My Colors, Overriding Document,
    option *21*
anonymous FTP *40*
Appearance tab, in Editor Preferences *231*
Appearance tab, in General Preferences *14*, *21*,
    26, *222*
Appearance tab, in Mail and News Preferences
    99, *234*
Apps tab, in General Preferences *226*
Ascending, command *93*
ASCII images, and signature files *119*
Attach, button *116*, *117*
Attach File, command *116*, *117*
attaching
    files *116*
    URLs *117*
Auto Load Images, command *29*
automatic image download, and alternative text
    181
Automatically quote original message, option *111*

B
Back, button *23*
    and frames *37*
Back, command *23*
Back in Frame, command *37*
Blank, command *153*
Blank Page, option *14*
Blink, command *166*
blinking formatting *166*
Block Quote, option *177*
block quotes
    creating *177*
    in browser *16*
Bold, command *166*
bold formatting *166*
bookmark folders
    creating *75*
    deleting *76*
    editing *76*
bookmark icon *70*
bookmarks *67–82*
    adding from other file *82*
    adding from Web site *72*
    adding manually *73*
    adding separators *77*
    adding to specific folder *70*
    bright marks and ? marks *69*
    checking what's new *69*
    creating aliases of *74*
    creating folders for *75*
    creating from History window *25*
    definition *67*

Index

deleting 76
dragging links to create 72
editing 76
file type 79
file, using as home page 14
folders with bookmark icon 70
importing 82
menu icon 71
opening as Web page 81
opening different file 80
organizing 75
saving 79
separators 77
sharing 80
sorting 78
surfing with 68
title of 72
Bookmarks, command 67
Bookmarks menu 68
adding separators 77
choosing folder for 71
sorting 78
Bookmarks window
navigating with 68
opening 67
boolean operators 53, 56
borders, around images 188
Break below Image(s), command 185
browser 13–16
appearance 15
choosing fonts for 16
Directory buttons 15
jumping to newsgroups 138
Location field 15
opening and closing 13
resizing 15
saving appearance 15
Bullet List, button 174
By Date, command 93
By Message Number, command 93
By Sender, command 93
By Subject, command 93

C

Cache tab, in Network Preferences 240
canceling a subscription 139
Center, button 176
changing
addresses and lists 126
horizontal lines 191
links 202
size of images 187
Character Properties, command 169, 170
Character Properties, toolbar 162
character styles 166–170
applying several at once 169
basic 166
clearing 170
text color 168
text size 167

Character submenu 166
Character tab, in Text Properties 169, 170
checking mail 84, 101
periodically 102
checking what's new (bookmarks) 69
Clear all character styles, command 170
Clear All Settings, command 170
Clear All Styles, button 170
Clear Style Settings, command 170
clearing character styles 170
Close, command 13
colors
and images 183
for page 192
Colors tab, in General Preferences 21, 224
composing new messages 105
Composition tab, in Mail and News Preferences 111, 235
Compress this Folder, command 92
compressing folders 92
Connections tab, in Network Preferences 241
conserving disk space 92
Copy, command 49, 90
copying
images from other pages 158
links 194
messages 90
parts of page 49
Create Link using selected, command 201
creating
block quotes 177
borders around images 188
links 193–202
links manually 196
lists in Web page 173
mailing lists 124
pages with Page Wizard 156
signature files 119
targets for links 198
Current Page Link, icon 195
custom quoting 113

D

Decrease Font Size, icon 167
Decrease Indent, button 175
Default Color, command 168
Default Publishing Location, command 217
Deferred Delivery, command 108, 149
Deja News, search service 60
Delete, command 76, 126
Delete Folder, command 91
Delete Message, command 91
deleting
addresses and lists 126
links 202
messages and folders 91
Description Text, command 171
Description Title, command 171
diamond, green 95, 141
Directory buttons 15

Index

disk space, conserving *92*
display text, definition *193*
Document, command *160*, *192*
downloading
    files *42*
    images *48*

E

Edit, button *154*
Edit Document, command *154*, *158*
Edit Document Source, command *208*
editing
    basic character formatting *166*
    existing pages *158*
    HTML *208*
        specifying program for *209*
    messages *110*
    saved files/pages *159*
    text size *167*
Editor Preferences *229–232*
    Appearance tab *231*
    General tab *209*, *230*
    Publish tab *216*, *232*
Editor Preferences, command *209*, *216*
Editor window *153–164*
    numbers in lists *174*
    opening blank *153*
    toolbars and palettes *163*
e-mail. *See* mail, messages
Empty Trash Folder, command *92*
emptying Trash folder *92*
Excite, search service *57*

F

FAQs
    for newsgroups *133*
    Netscape's *64*
File/Edit Tools, toolbar *162*
files
    attaching to messages *116*
    attaching to news posting *147*
    downloading *42*
    transferring *39–44*
    uploading *43*
    uploading multiple *44*
Find, button *62*
Find, command *62*
Find, command in Address Book *127*
Find Next, command *62*
finding
    addresses *127*
    boolean operators *53*, *56*
    by keyword *56–57*
    by subject *54–55*
    in open page *62*
    info about Netscape software *66*
    Netscape documentation *64*
    newsgroup articles *60*
    organizations *59*

people *58*
shareware *61*
stuff on Web *53–66*
technical support *65*
tips *53*
First Flagged, command *104*
First Unread, command *104*
Fixed width, command *166*
fixed width fonts *16*, *99 See also* fonts
fixed width formatting *166*
Flag Message, command *94*
flagged messages *88*
flagging messages *94*
folders
    changing name *86*
    compressing *92*
    creating for mail *86*
    deleting *91*
    importing *87*
    mail *85*
Font Color, icon *168*
Font Size, command *167*
Font Size, pop-up menu *167*
fonts
    and HTML *165*
    and quoted material in messages *111*
    choosing for browser *16*
    in messages *99*
Fonts tab, in General Preferences *16*, *223*
footer in printed page *52*
formats
    and address books *128*
    images *48*, *179*
Formatted, command *171*
formatting
    aligning text *176*
    applying paragraph styles *172*
    basic character *166*
    block quotes *177*
    clearing character styles *170*
    colored text *168*
    indenting a paragraph *175*
    lists *173*
    many character styles at once *169*
    many paragraph features at once *178*
    paragraph styles *171*
    text size *167*
    Web pages *165–178*
Forward, button *23*, *114*
    and frames *37*
Forward, command *23*, *114*
Forward in Frame, command *37*
Forward Quoted, command *115*
forwarding messages *114–115*
frames *33–37*, *207*
    description *33*
    going back and forward *37*
    links *34*
    mailing *118*
    opening in new window *35*

249

Index

printing 51
resizing 36
scrolling around 36
framesets, definition 33
Frequently Asked Questions, command 64
Frequently Asked Questions See FAQs
From, message part 106
From Template, command 154
From Wizard, command 156
FTP 13
    accessing site 40
    downloading files 42
    surfing to 22
    uploading files 43
    uploading multiple files 44

G

General Preferences 221–228
    Appearance tab 222
    Apps tab 226
    Colors tab 21, 224
    Fonts tab 223
    Helpers tab 227
    Images tab 225
    Language tab 228
General tab, in Editor Preferences 209, 230
General tab, in Security Preferences 244
Get Mail, button 101
Get More Messages, command 144
Get New Mail, command 101
GIF, format 179
Go menu
    going back and forward 23
    going further back/ahead 24
    going home 26
Go to Bookmark, command 68
Go to Bookmarks, command 67
Gopher 13
    accessing site 41
    surfing to 22
Graphics Interchange Format See GIF
greater than sign, and quoted messages 113
green diamond 95, 141

H

Handbook, command 64
header in printed page 52
Heading (1, 2, ...), command 171
helper applications 30
    doing without 32
    setting up 31
Helpers tab, in General Preferences 31, 32, 227
hiding toolbars and palettes 164
History, command 25
History window 25
    vs. Go menu 24
Home, button 26
Home, command 26
home pages 14, 26

Netscape's 63
real, definition 19
Horizontal Line, button 191
Horizontal Line, command 190, 191
Horizontal Line Properties, command 191
horizontal lines See lines
How to Get Support, command 65
HTML
    adding manually 206
    and copying and pasting 49
    and Web pages 18
    description 203
    editing manually 208
    saving with Web page 46
    specifying program for editing 209
    standard vs. nonstandard 204
HTML Tag, command 206
HyperText Markup Language See HTML

I

Identity tab, in Mail and News Preferences 120, 237
Image, command 180–189
images
    adding space around 186
    adding to Web pages 179–192
    aligning 189
    and alternative text 181
    and size, resolution and number of colors 183
    automatic download 29
    background 192
    borders 188
    changing display size 187
    formats 48, 179
    inserting 180
    links to 201
    loading 29
    low resolution for speedier viewing 182
    replaced with icons 29
    saving 48
    stopping text wrap 185
    viewing 29
    viewing offline 50
    wrapping text around 184
Images tab, in General Preferences 225
Immediate delivery, command 108
Import, command 82, 129
importing
    address books 129
    bookmarks 82
Inbox folder 85
Include Original Text, command 112
Increase Font Size, icon 167
Increase Indent, button 175
Indent one level, command 175
indenting a paragraph 175
Insert Bookmark, command 73
Insert Folder, command 75
Insert Horizontal Line, button 190

250

Index

Insert new Link, command *197, 199*
Insert Separator, command *77*
Internet Directory, command *57, 63*
Internet Search, command *57, 63*
Internet White Pages, command *57, 63*
Italic, command *166*
italic formatting *166*

J

JavaScript (Client), command *210*
JavaScript (Server), command *210*
JavaScript, adding *210*
JPEG compression *179*

K

keywords, adding to Web page *160*

L

Language tab, in General Preferences *228*
letter icon *84, 101*
lines
    adding *190*
    changing *191*
    printing options *52*
Link, button *195*
Link, command *196, 197, 199, 201, 202*
Link Properties, command *200, 202*
links
    adding bookmark for *72*
    and frames *34*
    and URLs *193*
    changing appearance of *21*
    changing or deleting *202*
    copying from other source *194*
    creating *193–202*
    creating manually *196*
    creating targets for *198*
    creating to a target *199–200*
    display text *193*
    dragging to create bookmarks *72*
    following *20*
    new vs. visited *20*
    opening in new window *20*
    to images *201*
    to newsgroups in mail messages *150*
    underlined *21*
List Item, command *171, 173*
lists
    changing and deleting *126*
    creating *124, 173*
    numbers in Editor window *174*
    using *125*
Load Images, button *29*
Load Images, command *29*
Load this Image, command *29*
loading
    images *29*
    stopping *28*

Location field *15*
    and newsgroups *138*
    pop-up menu *22*
    surfing with *22*
low resolution images, using *182*
Lycos, search service *57*

M

mail
    adding addresses *122*
    address book *121–130*
    and advertising your Web page *218*
    attaching files to *116*
    attaching URLs to *117*
    changing appearance of messages *99*
    checking *84*
    checking for periodically *102*
    composing messages offline *108*
    composing new messages *105*
    creating folders *86*
    custom quoting *113*
    deleted *85*
    deleting messages and folders *91*
    editing messages *110*
    flagging messages *94*
    folders *85*
        changing name *86*
        creating *86*
        deleting *91*
    forwarding messages *114–115*
    getting new *101*
    importing from other folder *87*
    jumping to newsgroups *138*
    letter icon *84*
    mailing frames *118*
    mailing Web pages *118*
    marking read/unread *95*
    new *85*
    password *84*
        and automatic checking *102*
    quoting individual messages *112*
    quoting messages *111*
    reading *103*
    replying to *107*
    saving address *121*
    selecting messages *88–89*
    sending from News window *150*
    showing additional information *103*
    signature files *119, 120*
    sorting messages *93*
    threading messages *96*
    viewing parts of message *106*
Mail and News Preferences *233–238*
    Appearance tab *234*
    Composition tab *111, 235*
    Identity tab *120, 237*
    Organization tab *238*
    Servers tab *144, 236*
Mail Bcc, message part *106*
Mail Cc, message part *106*

Index

Mail Document, command *118*
Mail Frame, command *118*
Mail New Message, command *125*
Mail To, message part *106*, *148*
Mail window *83—99*
    changing order/size of columns *98*
    getting mail *101*
    jumping to Newsgroups *138*
    navigating in *104*
    opening *84*
    parts of *83*
    resizing panes *97*
mailing lists
    changing and deleting *126*
    creating *124*
    using *125*
Make Alias, command *74*
Make Link, button *199*, *200*, *201*, *202*
margins, printing options *52*
Mark as Read, command *95*, *141*
Mark as Unread, command *95*, *141*
Mark Group, button *142*
Mark Newsgroup Read, command *142*
Mark Thread, button *141*
Mark Thread as Read, command *141*
marking read/unread *95*
menu icon *71*
messages *95*
    adding address from *123*
    additional information *103*
    appearance *111*
    attaching files to *116*
    attaching URLs *117*
    changing appearance *99*
    checking for new *102*
    composing new *105*
    composing offline
        mail *108*
        news *149*
    copying *90*
    creating signature files *119*
    custom quoting *113*
    deleting *91*
    editing *110*
    flagging *94*
    forwarding *114—115*
    getting more (news) *144*
    hiding read *143*
    mailing Web pages *118*
    marking as read *141*
    moving *90*
    posting *146*
    printing *51*
    quoting every *111*
    quoting individual *112*
    reading (mail) *103*
    recovering deleted *91*
    replying to
        mail *107*
        news *148*

    selecting *88—89*
    sending from Outbox *109*
    showing newsgroups with new *140*
    sorting *93*
    threading *96*
    using signature files *120*
    viewing parts *106*
messages. *See also* mail, news
Microsoft Word, and editing HTML *208*
minus sign, and newsgroups *135*
Move, command *90*
movies, viewing *30*

N

names of newsgroups *133*
navigating, in Mail and News windows *104*
navigational buttons *201*
NCSA Mosaic *218*
Netscape
    documentation *64*
    extensions *204*
    logo inserted in pages *157*
    pages *63*
    software, information about *66*
Netscape Galleria, command *63*
Netscape Mail, command *84*
netscape.navigator (Netscape's newsgroup about
    Navigator) *134*
Netscape's Home, command in Directory menu *63*
Network Preferences *239—242*
    Cache tab *240*
    Connections tab *241*
    Proxies tab *242*
New Bookmarks Folder *70*
    adding new bookmarks to *72*
New Document, button *153*, *155*, *157*
New Document, command *153*, *154*, *156*
New Folder, command *86*
New Mail Message, command *105*, *150*
New News Message, command *146*, *149*
New Web Browser, command *13*, *22*
    and frames *35*
New Window with this Link, command
    and frames *35*
news *131—150*
    additional information *103*
    and Outbox folder *149*
    canceling subscriptions *139*
    changing appearance of messages *99*
    composing postings offline *149*
    getting more messages *144*
    hiding read messages *143*
    listing all newsgroups *135*
    listing new newsgroups *136*
    marking as read
        messages *141*
        newsgroups *142*
        threads *141*
    names of newsgroups *133*
    news hosts *134*

Index

newsgroup FAQs *133*
posting messages *146*
reading postings *145*
replying to postings *148*
showing active newsgroups *140*
showing subscribed newsgroups *140*
subscribing to newsgroups *139*
threading messages *96*
using News window *132*
viewing from other windows *138*
viewing newsgroup by name *137*
news hosts *134*
News window *131–144*
    opening and closing *132*
    parts of *131*
    sending mail *150*
    using *132*
newsgroups
    and advertising your Web page *218*
    canceling a subscription *139*
    FAQs *133*
    finding articles in *60*
    getting more messages *144*
    hiding read messages *143*
    listing all *135*
    listing new *136*
    marking as read *142*
    marking messages as read *141*
    marking threads as read *141*
    names *133*
    showing active *140*
    showing subscribed *140*
    subscribing *139*
    viewing by name *137*
    viewing from other windows *138*
Newsgroups, command *147*
Newsgroups, message part *106*, *146*, *148*
    not appearing *147*
Next Flagged, command *104*
Next Message, command *104*
Next Unread, command *104*
Nonbreaking Space, command *205*
nonbreaking spaces *205*
Numbered List, button *174*

O

offline
    composing messages
        mail *108*
        news *149*
    reading Web pages *50*
    sending deferred messages *109*
Open, command *80*
Open File, command *50*, *81*, *130*, *159*
Open File in Browser, command *212*
Open File in Editor, command *159*
Open Link in New Window, command *20*
Open Location, command *22*
Open News Host, command *134*
Open Text, search service *56–57*

opening
    address books as Web page *130*
    bookmarks files *80*
    browsers *13*
    Editor window
        blank *153*
        with Page Wizard *156*
        with template *154*
    Mail window *84*
    News window *132*
Organization tab, in Mail and News Preferences *84*, *238*
organizations, finding *59*
organizing bookmarks *75*
Outbox folder *85*
    and deferred mail messages *108*
    and deferred postings *149*
    and moving and copying *90*
    editing messages in *110*
    removing items from *108*, *110*
    sending messages in *109*

P

Page Wizard, creating pages with *156*
palettes, in Editor window *163*
    hiding and showing *164*
panes, resizing *97*
Paragraph, submenu *172*
Paragraph/List properties, command *178*
Paragraph Properties, toolbar *162*
paragraph styles *171–178*
    applying *172*
    eliminating *178*
    pop-up menu *172*
    using *171*
Paragraph tab, in Text Properties *173*, *176*, *177*, *178*
parts, of messages *106*
password for mail
    and automatic checking *102*
    saving *84*
Paste, command *49*
Paste as Quotation, command *113*
Plain Text, format *46*
plus sign, and newsgroups *135*
Post and Send Reply, command *148*
Post Reply, command *148*
postings
    composing offline *149*
    finding *60*
    printing *51*
    reading *145*
Previous Flagged, command *104*
Previous Message, command *104*
Previous Unread, command *104*
Print, button *51*
Print, command *51*
Print Preview, command *51*
printing *51–52*
    options *52*

Index

Properties, command 76, 126
proportional fonts 99
Proxies tab, in Network Preferences 242
Publish, command 214
Publish tab, in Editor Preferences 216, 232
publishing pages 211–218
    advertising 218
    setting default location 216
    viewing 217

Q

question marks, and bookmarks 69
Quote, button 112
quoting
    custom 113
    every message 111
    individual messages 112

R

Re: All, button 107
Re: Mail, button 107
read/unread messages 95, 141
reading
    mail 103
    postings 145
red checkmark (flag) 94
Refresh, command 27
refreshing a page 27
Registration Information, command 66
Release Notes, command 66
Reload, button 27
Reload, command 27
reloading a page 27
    after stopping 28
Remember Mail Password, option 84
Remove Link, command 202
Remove Links, command 202
Remove News Host, command 134
Remove one indent level, button 174
Remove one indent level, command 175
Reply, command 107
Reply To, message part 106
Reply to All, command 107
replying
    to mail 107
    to postings 148
resizing
    frames 36
    panes in windows 97
resolution, and images 183

S

Save, command 161
Save As, command
    address books 128
    bookmarks 79
    browsed pages 46
    created pages 161
Save this Image as, command 48

Save this Link as, command 47
saving
    address books 128
    addresses 121
    bookmarks 79
    browsed pages 46
        without jumping 47
    created pages 161
    images 48
    mail password 84
search services
    Altavista 57
    Deja News 60
    Excite 57
    Lycos 57
    shareware.com 61
    WhoWhere? 58–59
    Yahoo! 54–55
secnews.netscape.com 134
Security Preferences 243–245
    General tab 244
    Site Certificates tab 245
Select All Messages, command 89
Select Flagged Messages, command 88
Select Thread, command 89
selecting messages 88–89
Send, button 105, 146
Send, command 105
Send Later, button 108
Send Later, command 108, 146
Send Mail in Outbox, command 109
Send Now, command 146
Send Reply, command 148
sending
    mail from News window 150
    mail messages 105
    messages in Outbox 109
    news messages 146
Sent folder 85
separators
    adding 77
    and sorting 78
    deleting 76
servers, definition 19
Servers tab, in Mail and News Preferences 102, 144, 236
Set to Bookmark Menu Folder, command 71
Set to New Bookmarks Folder, command 70
shareware, finding 61
shareware.com, search service 61
Show Active Newsgroups, command 140
Show All, command 106
Show All Headers, command 103, 145
Show All Messages, command 143
Show All Newsgroups, command 135
Show Character Format Toolbar, command 164
Show File/Edit Toolbar, command 164
Show New Newsgroups, command 136
Show Only Unread Messages, command 103, 143
Show Paragraph Format Toolbar, command 164

Index

Show Subscribed Newsgroups, command *140*
showing, toolbars and palettes *164*
signature files
    creating *119*
    using *120*
Site Certificates tab, in Security Preferences *245*
size, of images *187*
slow pages, aborting load *28*
Software, command *66*
Sort Bookmarks, command *78*
Sort submenu *93*, *96*
sorting
    bookmarks *78*
    messages *93*
sounds on pages *30*
Source, format *46*
space, adding around images *186*
spaces, adding nonbreaking *205*
Stop Loading, command *28*
stopping
    loading *28*
    text wrap *185*
Strikethrough, command *166*
strikethrough formatting *166*
subscribing to newsgroups *139*
Subscript, command *166*
Superscript, command *166*
superscripts and subscripts *166*
surfing *17–37*
    following links *20*
    frames *33–37*
    going back and forward *23*
    going back and forward in frames *37*
    going further back/ahead *24*
    going home *26*
    multimedia *30*
    reloading a page *27*
    stopping a page from loading *28*
    to FTP site *40*
    to Gopher site *41*
    to your home page *26*
    viewing images *29*
    with bookmarks *68*
    with History window *25*
    with Location field *22*
    with URL *22*

T

tables *207*
Target (Named Anchor), command *198*
target icon *198*
targeted windows, and frames *35*
targets
    creating *198*
    creating links to *199–200*
technical support *65*
templates, using *154*
testing your page *212*
Text, command *169*, *170*, *173*, *176–178*
Text, format *46*

text color, changing *168*
Text Color, command *168*
text files, displaying vs. downloading *42*
Text Properties
    Character tab *169*, *170*
    Paragraph tab *173*, *176–178*
text size, changing *167*
Thread Messages, command *96*
threads *96*
    marking as read *141*
    selecting *89*
titles, adding to Web page *160*
To: Mail, button *105*
To: News, button *146*
toolbars
    browser *15*
    Editor window *162*
        hiding and showing *164*
        repositioning *163*
transferring files *39–44*
    downloading *42*
    uploading *43*
    uploading multiple *44*
    via e-mail *116*
Trash folder *85*
    and deleted messages *91*
    compressing *92*
    emptying *92*
    recovering deleted messages *91*

U

Underlined, option in General Preferences *21*
Uniform Resource Locators *See* URLs
uploading
    individual files *43*
    multiple files *44*
URLs
    adding bookmarks for *73*
    and History window *25*
    and links *20*, *193*
    and Location field *15*
    attaching to message *117*
    attaching to news posting *147*
    definition *193*
    saving in bookmarks *72*
    surfing to *22*
    upper and lower case letters *73*

V

variable width fonts. *See* proportional fonts
View menu *106*
viewing
    images *29*
        offline *50*
    movies and other multimedia *30*
    parts of message *106*
    published pages *217*

255

Index

W

Web Browser *See also* browser *13*
Web pages
    adding bookmarks for *72*, *73*
    adding keywords *160*
    adding title *160*
    advanced techniques *203*
    and address books *130*
    background color/image *192*
    colors on *192*
    copying and pasting *49*
    creating from scratch *153*
    creating from template *154*
    creating with Page Wizard *156*
    definition *18*
    editing existing *158*
    editing saved *159*
    finding *53–66*
    formatting *165–178*
    from bookmarks file *81*
    images *179–192*
    inserting images *180*
    mailing *118*
    Netscape's own *63*
    printing *51*
    publishing *211–218*
    saving *46*, *161*
    saving links to *47*
    testing *212*
    text color *168*
    text size *167*
    viewing offline *50*
Web sites *19*
What's Cool!, command *63*
What's New!, command *63*
What's New?, command *69*
WhoWhere?, search service *58–59*
wrapping text around images *184*
    stopping *185*

Y

Yahoo!
    and advertising your page *218*
    search service *54–55*
yellow checkmark (newsgroups) *139*